# Thinking about Stories



*Thinking About Stories* is a fun and thought-provoking introduction to philosophical questions about narrative fiction in its many forms, from highbrow literature to pulp fiction to the latest shows on Netflix.

Written by philosophers Samuel Lebens and Tatjana von Solodkoff, it engages with fundamental questions about fiction, such as: What is it? What does it give us? Does a story need a narrator? And why do sad stories make us cry if we know they aren't real? The format of the book emulates a lively, verbal exchange: each chapter has only one author while the other appears spontaneously in dialogues in the text along the way, raising questions and voicing criticisms, and inviting responses from their co-author. This unique format allows readers to feel like they are a part of the conversation about the philosophical foundations of some of the fictions in their own lives.

Key Features

- Draws on a wide range of types of narrative fiction, from *Harry Potter* to *Breakfast of Champions* to *Parks and Recreation.*
- Explores how fiction, despite its detachment from truth, is often best able to teach us important things about the world in which we live.
- Concludes by asking in the final chapter whether we all might be fictions.
- Includes bibliographies and suggested reading lists in each chapter.

**Samuel Lebens** is an Associate Professor of Philosophy at the University of Haifa. He works on a wide variety of philosophical topics, including metaphysics, epistemology, the philosophy of literature, and the philosophy of religion. Recent books include *The Principles of Judaism* (Oxford UP, 2020) and *Philosophy of Religion: The Basics* (Routledge, 2022).

**Tatjana von Solodkoff** is an Assistant Professor of Philosophy at University College Dublin in Ireland. Tatjana thinks and writes about fiction, ontology, the methods of metaphysics, and death.

# Thinking about Stories

## An Introduction to Philosophy of Fiction

Samuel Lebens and
Tatjana von Solodkoff

Routledge
Taylor & Francis Group
NEW YORK AND LONDON

Designed cover image: © jamesteohart / Getty Images

First published 2024
by Routledge
605 Third Avenue, New York, NY 10158

and by Routledge
4 Park Square, Milton Park, Abingdon, Oxon, OX14 4RN

Routledge is an imprint of the Taylor & Francis Group, an informa business



ISBN: 978-0-367-64755-1 (hbk)
ISBN: 978-0-367-64751-3 (pbk)
ISBN: 978-1-003-12610-2 (ebk)

DOI: 10.4324/9781003126102

Typeset in Bembo
by Deanta Global Publishing Services, Chennai, India

# Contents

# Introduction

We are (in alphabetical order) Samuel Lebens and Tatjana von Solodkoff. We're both academic philosophers who love reading, watching, listening to, and otherwise engaging with works of fiction. Together, we've written this book as a friendly introduction to the philosophy of fiction.

Each chapter has one lead author (other than this introduction, which we've written together). But the other author doesn't disappear entirely. Instead, they will be raising questions and voicing criticisms for the lead author to respond to along the way. This format, we hope, will give readers the sense of a live exchange between two philosophers. We hope that you, the reader, will imagine yourself joining in the conversation, as we think about fiction together.

Why are we thinking about fiction? Well, novels, movies, video games, poems, comic strips, paintings, songs, plays, and musicals are all valued parts of our culture as human beings. They can all count as works of fiction. People devote hours of their lives and large sums of money to engage with these pastimes. Philosophy literally means the love of wisdom. It involves scrutinizing each and every element of our lives in the attempt to make sense of the world in which we live. When we start to scrutinize our engagement with fiction, it turns out that there are lots of puzzles to explore.

In this book, we will focus on narrative fiction – that is, works of fiction that tell a story, typically by presenting or describing a sequence of connected events. The video game *Final Fantasy* classifies as a narrative fiction, a game that clearly has a story, while Leonardo da Vinci's *Mona Lisa* doesn't. Though the *Mona Lisa* is subject to many theories around its creation, and whether its bemused-looking subject is fictional, the painting itself does not show us a step-by-step unfolding of events. So, it certainly doesn't count as a narrative fiction.

Can a narrative be counted as a fiction if all of the events it described actually happened, or is it somehow crucial that a fiction be disconnected, in some important way, from fact? This brings us to the central question of Chapter 1, "What Is Fiction?". Until then, let's just say that works of fiction typically contain imagined characters and imagined events, but that the creators of these works don't intend to deceive their audiences about the fact that they're merely imagined. That's part of what distinguishes fiction from lying!

DOI: 10.4324/9781003126102-1

In Chapter 2, "What Is a Work of Fiction?" Sam will bring the philosophy of fiction into conversation with the philosophy of literature and art more generally. What is a piece of music? Is it the sound waves in the air, the notes on the written score, or the ideas in the head of a composer? What, for example, is the difference between a piece of music, and a *performance* of that piece of music?

Similar questions can be asked about pretty much every artistic medium and form, including fiction. Is Melville's novel *Moby Dick* a string of words in the English language? If so, what happens if you're reading a translation of it, in a *different* language? Are you reading the same novel? And what's the difference between a novel and its copies in print? Exploring these questions will help us get a grip over the place that narrative fictions occupy in the broader context of artistic creations, and help us pinpoint what exactly it is that we are valuing when we appreciate a piece of narrative fiction.

In Chapter 3, "What Are Fictional Characters?", Tatjana will discuss different views on what kind of things Eleven, Gandalf, and Celie, the heroine of *The Color Purple*, are. Are they flesh-and-blood people living in another world, a world that is equally real to our world but which we can't reach, either by plane, phone, or teleportation? Or are they rather not people at all but *things*? Not physical things such as candles and stones, but more like numbers and ideas, which don't have a particular location, but nonetheless exist in some sense. In Chapter 4, Tatjana continues this discussion by asking, "Do Fictional Characters Really Exist?".

Surely, we all agree that imagination plays an important role when it comes to reading fiction. We imagine that Harry fights Voldemort, and we imagine Hermione burying her nose in magic textbooks. In Chapter 5, "Imagination and Fiction", Tatjana asks what kind of imagining we engage in when we engage with works of fiction. We'll also think about the role that imagination plays when it comes to *watching* fiction. After all, we actually *see* Harry fight Voldemort in the movie *Harry Potter and the Deathly Hallows – Part 2*. Is there much left to be imagined?

After all this talk about fiction, by the time we reach Chapter 6 ('Interpreting Fiction'), we'll be ready to read a story. What Sam does, in Chapter 6, is to take the opening of a particular novel, *Breakfast of Champions* by Kurt Vonnegut, and see what happens. Within just a few sentences of the book, Sam claims to have learnt a number of things that are true about the story, and a number of things that are false. The question that then occupies the rest of the chapter is what it means for something to be true or false, in a fiction – given that the whole fiction is pretty much false to begin with – and how it is that a reader is able to discover what's true, and what's false, about the stories she reads.

The kinds of fictions that we focus on in this book are narrative fictions; fictions that tell a story. Where there's a narration, there is (you might think) always someone doing the narration, and that's the narrator. Or so a rather simple argument would have it. But how plausible is the idea that even stories that don't mention a narrator have an implicit storyteller? And when we see moving images while we're watching a movie, are we supposed to imagine that a narrator is showing us these images or are we to imagine that we are directly seeing Superman and Veronica Mars? These questions are the topic of Tatjana's Chapter 7, "Does Every Story Have a Fictional Narrator?"

Having discussed our imaginative engagement with fiction over the course of many chapters, the book then turns to a discussion of our emotional engagement with fiction. In Chapter 8, "Why Are You Crying?", Sam rehearses a debate about the rationality of crying about fictional characters. After all, if you assume that Anna Karenina isn't real, why are you crying? And are you really crying for Anna Karenina? Just asking these questions raises further questions of their own. For example, does it make sense to call an emotion *rational* or *irrational* in the first place? But whoever it is we're crying for, and whether it's rational or not, there's no doubt that we're crying. In fact, people seem to love a story that will make them cry.

Indeed, drama, horror, and tragic fiction are extremely popular genres. People pour into theatres or bookshops to watch *Leaving Las Vegas* or buy their copy of *My Sister's Keeper*, knowing very well that they are setting themselves up for sadness, frustration, and ultimate heartbreak. After all, none of these tragic stories even have a happy ending. In Chapter 9, "The Paradox of Tragedy", Tatjana takes a look at the reasons people may have for engaging with tragic fiction, wondering whether it's for pleasure or for a different reason altogether.

Chapter 10 is dedicated to a phenomenon called *imaginative resistance*. In "The Puzzle of Imaginative Struggles", Tatjana wonders why we sometimes cannot, or even *refuse* to imagine things to be the way a fictional work describes them to be. The silent movie *Birth of a Nation* celebrates the Ku Klux Klan as a heroic organization, asking us to imagine that white people are superior to people of colour. But many of us, when asked to imagine immoral propositions, find that we resist the request, even if we're only asked to imagine it for the sake of engaging with fiction. What exactly explains this resistance? Does the question reveal something special about engaging with fiction that differs from merely imagining things to be true?

In Chapter 11, Sam draws from much of what we will have learnt from the previous chapters, in order to ask, "What Can We Learn from Fiction?" Even though fictions can be set in other worlds, or in distant times and places, the various discussions we will have had throughout the course of this book will help us to understand the mechanisms by which even the most fantastical of fictions can help us learn things about the world in which we live: historical, scientific, and mathematical facts, as well as facts about ourselves, the human condition, and the demands of ethics and justice.

In the final chapter, Chapter 12, Sam will share with us his eccentric view that we are all characters in a fiction. He will argue for two claims. His first claim is that if you believe in the existence of God, you'll have to accept that, in a significant sense, you are a character in a story that God is telling. This might not bother you much if you don't happen to believe in God. But his second claim is that, even if God doesn't exist, it's still highly likely that we're all fictional characters in some story or other. Will the philosophy of fiction that we'll have learnt in the eleven previous chapters help Tatjana and our readers to resist these peculiar conclusions, or motivate readers to adopt this view too?

Our hope is that the journey upon which we're about to embark will enrich people's engagement with fiction and inspire people to think philosophically about the world in which we live, and the hobbies – such as reading or binge-watching Netflix – with which we fill up much of our time. Moreover, because we'll be touching on all sorts of philosophical topics, along the way, we hope that our discussion about fiction will also serve as an interesting and informative introduction to various areas of contemporary philosophy to boot.

At the end of each chapter we'll include a bibliography, listing all of the articles and books we have quoted in that chapter ('Works Cited'), as well as a list of suggested further readings ('Further Reading') in case you want to delve further into the issues raised.

And now, if you're sitting comfortably, let's begin …

Chapter 1

# What Is Fiction?

*Sam*

Before diving into any other philosophical question about fiction, there's one thing we have to get straight. What *is* fiction? The question is surprisingly difficult to answer. When we think about what fiction *is*, we're tempted to contrast it with *non*-fiction. Non-fiction is supposed to be concerned with fact. So, fiction, you might think, is *opposed* to fact.

But it can't be that simple. It's not the case that any old *untruth* counts as fiction, is it? When somebody *lies* to you, it's not the same thing as them telling you a story. And, when somebody tells you a fictional story, even though the story isn't describing real historical events, they're not *lying* to you. We needn't condemn J. K. Rowling as a liar, even though there's no such thing as wizards.

Moreover, what if it turns out that a fictional story was, by complete accident, an accurate description of events? What would you say if, just before the rise of Darwinism, somebody wrote a fantasy novel about the evolution of species. They weren't writing a science book. It was intended as fiction. It just turned out to be, by complete and utter fluke, a stunningly accurate description of the *actual* origin of species. Does that mean that it was never *really* fiction, just because it was (accidentally) factual all along? Or did it start off as fiction before *becoming* non-fiction? The relationships between truth, lies, fact, fable, fiction, and non-fiction are more complicated than they seem.

We also have to consider the dazzling array of things that we might categorize as works of fiction: short stories, novels, plays, and films. And what about poems or pictures? What about computer games? What about jokes? What's in and what's out … and why?

*Tatjana:* What about songs? "25 Minutes Too Late" or "Jesse's Girl" are probably songs about events and people that are just made up, no? So, they should count as fictions too, right?

*Sam:* Yep. That's a fair point, although it forces us to ask whether the song is the fiction, or just the lyrics, and if it's just the lyrics, is that not simply a poem? Having said that, I'm inclined to think that the

DOI: 10.4324/9781003126102-2

> tune and the words are inseparable in a good song, and I'm quite happy to say that the songs, rather than just the lyrics, of Bob Dylan were worthy of his Nobel Prize.

In short, we've already found ourselves in pretty deep water, and we've only just begun!

In order to navigate our way through this territory, I'm going to present a number of different accounts of what fiction is, before I offer my own opinion. I'm going to focus on accounts that philosophers have developed in the past fifty years or so. I'm going to start with John Searle (Searle, 1975).

## Fiction According to Searle

To grasp Searle's definition, we first have to recognize that we use language to do all sorts of things. We ask questions with language. We issue orders in a language. Somebody declares parliament open using language, and thereby creates a new state of affairs. Before the declaration, the parliament was closed. The declaration causes it to be open. Likewise, the officiant at a wedding will declare a couple married; and so it shall be. In addition to all of these uses to which language is put, another thing we do with language – perhaps the most central thing – is to make assertions.

Making an assertion is a linguistic practice. It's also a *social* practice. Like all such practices, it operates according to certain *rules*. Searle offers the following account of the social rules that govern assertion (I paraphrase):

1. When a person makes an assertion, they commit themselves to defending the truth of what they say.
2. A person shouldn't make an assertion, unless they can provide evidence or reasons for thinking it to be true.
3. A person shouldn't make an assertion if it's so obviously true as to be not worthwhile asserting.
4. A person should only assert what they sincerely believe.

If you make an assertion, you'll be held accountable to these rules. So be prepared! If you make an assertion, you may be asked to defend your position. If you can't, you'll lose a certain amount of social standing. If you too often state the obvious, you'll find it difficult to make many friends. Worse still, if you're regularly found out to have been lying, you risk becoming a social outcast; or you'll get eaten by wolves.

Sometimes, my wife and I would confront our son, when he was about five or six years old, with assertions he'd made, such as "I will tidy my room". We would ask him why he hadn't yet lived up to his assertion.

*Tatjana:* It sounds like he's not just asserting something. He's promising something. When you say, "I will tidy my room" – that's a promise. But he never had the intention, so he was dishonest. He said something that everyone takes to be a promise, but he never meant it. Isn't that what's going on?

*Sam:* Yes, probably. Although, grammatically, it does looks like an assertion about the future: "I will tidy my room!" But I take your point. Practically, he wasn't asserting a matter of fact, he was making a promise.

And yet, come to think of it, there's going to be a fine line here. According to Searle, to make an assertion is (in part) to commit yourself to the truth of something. To make an assertion about what you're going to do in the future, and to make a promise about what you're going to do in the future, might be strange cases in which to assert and to promise amount to the same thing, since to commit to the truth of what's been said is simply to commit to doing something! Either way, whatever it is was that our son was doing exactly, he certainly didn't get the relevant rules. I say this because he didn't get why it's not okay to say, "I lied" and thereby exonerate himself!

In order to explain himself, he'd look at us with innocent eyes, and explain: "I lied". He didn't seem to recognize that he was confessing to having done something wrong. He was simply explaining that he didn't intend to be held to his words, and he seemed a little bit frustrated that we didn't seem to understand why that was okay. In short: he didn't (yet) get the rules.

With these rules in hand, Searle turns to the opening paragraph of Iris Murdoch's novel *The Red and the Green*:

> Ten more glorious days without horses! So thought Second Lieutenant Andrew Chase-White … as he pottered contentedly in a garden on the outskirts of Dublin on a sunny Sunday afternoon in April nineteen-sixteen.
>
> (Murdoch, 1965, p. 3)

The language of this quote looks like the sort of language a person might use to make an assertion; an assertion about what a certain Second Lieutenant was thinking, on a sunny afternoon in Dublin. But note: when you read the novel, you don't hold Murdoch accountable. It would be quite out of place for you to write to Ms. Murdoch (were she still alive), requesting that she provide some evidence for what she's said. If you were to search the records and discover that Dublin was overcast every Sunday in April 1916, this wouldn't give you grounds for rebuking her. This is because you don't take her to *believe* that what she's said is (literally) true. And since the rules of assertion simply don't apply, it's safe to conclude that she's not making an assertion.

So far, perhaps Searle is guilty of breaking one of his own rules. In telling us that Murdoch isn't making an assertion, he seems to be stating the obvious! But Searle's suggestion is that fiction and assertion are intimately *related*, even though they're clearly not the same thing. In fact, as far as Searle is concerned, there *could* be no fiction if there were no such thing as assertion-making. According to Searle, *to create fiction is to pretend to make an assertion.*

Pretending to be something, or pretending to *do* something, can be deceptive. Searle offers the example of dressing up as Nixon so as to fool the secret service and gain entrance to the White House. I don't advise this as a tactic for would-be intruders. Searle was writing when Nixon was still president (and still alive).

The point is this: if Searle *had* dressed up as Nixon, his pretence would have been *deceptive.*

*Tatjana:* But isn't this only because he had the intention to fool the secret service. If Searle had dressed up as Nixon for Halloween, he wouldn't be deceiving anyone, would he? It sounds to me like pretence isn't so much the issue, but intention is.

*Sam:* Well, according to Searle, it *is* intention that matters. But it's the intention to pretend without deceiving that generates fiction.

It's actually more complicated than that. He thinks that the intention in question has to be something like, *a reasonable intention not to deceive.*

What we can reasonably presume to be deceptive clothing in the White House, might not be at all deceptive at a Halloween party, where people are expecting fancy dress. So, for Searle, context will matter, because context will decide whether it was reasonable to expect that your behaviour would deceive. I'll come back to this point later on.

Murdoch, by contrast, *isn't* deceiving anyone. Telling a fictitious story is not the same as telling a lie. Searle would therefore have us distinguish between deceptive and non-deceptive pretence. To create fiction is to pretend, *non-deceptively*, to make assertions. So here's our first definition of fiction:

**Searle's Account**

Fiction is created when language is used with the intention to pretend, non-deceptively, to make assertions.

For Searle, whether or not a text, or a speech, or anything else, should count as fiction, depends upon the *intentions of the author*. Pretending is an *intentional action*. Part of what that means is that you can't pretend by accident. It also means that whether or not you're pretending depends upon you and your *intention*.

Earlier on, I asked you to imagine a novel, written just before Darwin developed the theory of evolution. That novel was, by complete fluke, an accurate account of the origin of species. Was that novel non-fiction by accident? Did it start off as fiction and only then *become* non-fiction? Searle has a clear answer for us. If the author was only *pretending* to make an assertion, and if the author *intended* to do so non-deceptively, then it was fiction. It doesn't matter that it happened to be true. And it always *will* be fiction, whatever other people come to think about it. As Searle puts it:

> There is no textual property … that will identify a text as a work of fiction. What makes it a work of fiction is, so to speak, the … stance that the author takes toward it, and that stance is a matter of the complex … intentions that the author has when he writes or otherwise composes it.
>
> (Searle 1975, p. 325)

To use technical jargon, Searle's account of fiction is *intentionalist*.

*Tatjana:* Do I understand this correctly: an account of fiction is intentionalist if and only if it holds that whether a work counts as fiction wholly depends on whether its creator intended to produce fiction?

*Sam:* Yes, that's right. Although it can be a little more sophisticated. Some intentionalists, like Searle, will say that what makes a work into a work of fiction will be a *reasonable* intention to produce fiction. But that just raises a thorny question as to what makes an intention reasonable!

This is controversial, as Searle freely admits. It conflicts with an influential school of literary criticism. According to this school, the intentions of the author are completely irrelevant. All that's relevant to literary criticism, according to some, is the *text*, and your encounter with it. Roland Barthes called this "the death of the author" (Barthes, 1977). But according to Searle, the author is very much alive. It is the author's intentions, and nothing else, that determines whether something is a work of fiction or not. We might say that, for Searle, it's the reader who's dead!

But that would be unfair. The audience *does* play a role for Searle. What makes it the case that some acts of pretence are deceptive and that others are not? For Searle, the answer to *that* question has a lot to do with social conventions, and social conventions are sustained, in large part, by the actions of all of us; authors and readers alike.

Conventions make it the case that if a text is sold with a certain sort of cover in a certain section of the bookshop, or website, then we know to treat it as fiction and therefore we won't be deceived by it. With a different cover, in a different section of the bookshop, the same text would, so to speak, be trying to pass itself off as non-fiction. And so, whether or not the author's pretence is deceptive will depend upon how her actions relate to our expectations and our social practices; where in the book shop did the author intend it to be placed; what sort of cover did it have?

But this leads us to a problem with Searle's account. Let me share an anecdote. I was once a counsellor at a summer camp for adults with learning disabilities. One of my campers was in his sixties. One night, I was putting him to bed, and he asked me where babies came from. I was a little bit flummoxed by the question. I sort of assumed that he knew already. Nevertheless, I did my best to describe the secret of the birds and the bees to him.

After I had finished, he said, "Yes. But sometimes men have babies too." I tried to explain that that wasn't right. But he insisted. Finally, it became clear that he had seen the movie *Junior.* It had left him with the firm conviction that Arnold Schwarzenegger, then Governor of California, had once given birth to a baby. He'd seen it in a movie. He had been deceived.

*Tatjana:* But why should we say he had been deceived? If he had been deceived, he would have to have been deceived by someone. The obvious candidate would be the movie makers. But "deceive" is an intentional verb, as you say yourself. It's something a person does intentionally. But the moviemakers never intentionally let anyone to believe that Arnold had a baby. Isn't the man just confused about what fiction is? Isn't he just confused about how to engage with fiction?

*Sam:* He certainly was confused about what fiction is. But a number of people are. It's not unknown for actors in soap operas to receive fan mail, or even abuse on the streets, from people who don't seem to understand that they are not actually the character they portray! This is relevant to Searle, because he *doesn't* only refer to intention, he refers to *reasonable expectations* and *reasonable* intentions. If you can predict that some people will be deceived by your actions, and the makers of *Junior* really could have done that, then they can't straightforwardly be said to have had a *reasonable expectation* not to deceive.

Surely the makers of *Junior* could have realized that *some* of the people who would likely watch their film (perhaps children, and people with certain sorts of learning disabilities) wouldn't have the capacity to distinguish between fact and fiction. If they *knew* that, then what clears them of the accusation that their actions were deceptive? Do we have clear guidelines here? If not, then Searle's "definition" of fiction is only as clear as our very hazy and culturally relative notion of *deceptiveness*. You might point out that the makers of *Junior* didn't harbour a *serious* intention to deceive. But as Gregory Currie rightly points out:

> [T]he boundary between nonserious and serious intention to deceive is vague, perhaps very vague. But the distinction between fiction and nonfiction is, intuitively, a rather sharp one.
>
> (Currie, 1985, p. 389)

*Robinson Crusoe* is a novel by Daniel Defoe. But when he published it, he credited it to a certain "Robinson Crusoe". This led some to believe that it wasn't a novel at all, but a true to life autobiography. Given the social mores and conventions of his time, Defoe could have and should have expected that marketing his work as he did, he would end up deceiving people. Accordingly, his act of writing and publishing the book doesn't count as a non-deceptive pretence of assertion. Will Searle have to concede that *Robinson Crusoe* isn't a work of fiction, but a pack of lies? That doesn't seem right. Everyone knows that *Robinson Crusoe* is a novel (or at least they do now). *Robinson Crusoe* appears to be a counter-example to Searle's definition: a clear case of a work of fiction that Searle's account can't handle.

Another counter-example – or rather, a whole set of counter-examples: what about non-linguistic fiction? As far as Searle is concerned, fiction is basically a sort of language game; a way of *using* language. But must a fiction *always* use language? Can a *picture* not be a work of fiction? Can a mime? Can a dance? Perhaps we can stretch Searle's account by adopting a very liberal approach as to what counts as language. Perhaps there are visual languages, and body languages. But is it really plausible that a mime or a painting could have been intended as a pretend *assertion*? It seems like quite a stretch to me.

And a final counter-example: plays. Searle spends some time thinking about the difference between standard prose-fiction and plays (Searle 1975, pp. 328–329). One way of construing his conclusion is this: a novel or a short story is a self-contained work of fiction. The text itself is the mark of an author's attempt to pretend to make an assertion without deceiving anybody. The text of a *play*, by contrast, is quite different. The playwright isn't pretending to *assert* anything. Instead, the playwright writes a set of instructions for *actors*, set-designers, stage crew, and directors. Those instructions tell the actors what *they* should pretend to assert and when. In a sense, then, for Searle, the text of a play *isn't* a work of fiction, but an instruction manual for the *production* of fiction. The fiction only emerges, for Searle, when somebody pretends to make an assertion, and that only happens when the actors act it out.

*Tatjana:* Maybe that isn't too implausible. A film script is also a manual that tells the actresses and other crew members what to say and what to do. It's definitely a manual on how to produce a work of fiction. Is it also a work of fiction itself? Maybe. If the script is, then so is the play. If it isn't, then the play isn't either. Only a performance of the play, created with the help of the script, would count as fiction.

*Sam:* I think Searle himself didn't see a problem here either. There's not much I can do to persuade you, if you simply don't share my intuitions. But here's something I can say: I grant you that a performance of a play, and a film, are fictional, of course. And, I grant you that the screenplay and the theatrical script *do* provide performers and crew with instructions. But try reading a play, or a screenplay. I often do, and I enjoy it. And because I do, it's really odd for me to say that I'm not reading and enjoying a work of fiction; that when we read *Hamlet* at school we weren't reading a work of fiction but *only* a set of instructions for the creation of fiction. But if you're not convinced, there's not much more I can say!!

Searle's account of fiction was a good start. But it has left us with worries and consequences that we might hope to escape. The status of a work of fiction, as Searle construes things, seems to be too closely dependent upon the author's intentions – even though I'm willing to concede that author's intentions matter; they can't be *all* that matter; otherwise, an author couldn't *fail* to write a work of fiction. If *only* the intention of an author mattered, and in belching, an author intended to pretend to make an assertion without deceiving anyone, then his belch would be a work of fiction! Perhaps you could say that the intention needs to be *reasonable*, just as the intention has to include a reasonable expectation of not *deceiving* people, but defining reasonability might be harder than defining fiction. Troubles abound.

Moreover, as we've seen, Searle's account will struggle to deal with mime and other wordless fiction, and he has to treat plays and novels as fictional in different ways. But that seems wrong. Plays and novels differ in all sorts of ways, but surely not by being *fictional* in different ways.

## Fiction According to Gregory Currie

Gregory Currie (1985, 1990) rejects Searle's account. It isn't essential, as an author writes her story, that she *pretends* to assert something (she *can*, if she *wants* to, pretend that she's asserting the things that she's writing, but that's wholly up to her). By contrast, it *is* essential that her text (in conversation with various conventions) issues instructions for her *readers* to pretend. If her text fails to do *that*, then she hasn't created a fiction with which we can engage.

Likewise, it isn't essential for the playwright to pretend anything as she writes her play (she might *choose* to act out each and every line, playing each role as she writes it; but again, that's wholly up to her). By contrast, it *is* essential that she issues instructions for her readers (be they actors or the general public) to pretend. And thus, despite the various differences between plays and novels, they can both be counted as fictional in exactly the same way, on Currie's account, because they are both construed as *an invitation to pretend that certain things are true*.

Some problems are going to arise with Currie's account. Authors don't always want you to pretend that *everything* written in their story is true. Some stories are deliberately written so as to have unreliable narrators. And even when the author *does* want us to pretend that *everything* that's written in the text is true, they often (if not always) want us to pretend *more* than that. They want us to *import* into the story some propositions that aren't mentioned in the text at all. They want us to pretend that things never mentioned in the text of the story are true. As Currie puts it:

> If Holmes leaves London and arrives in Edinburgh without his mode of transport being described we are clearly called upon to make-believe that he travelled there by some conventional means of transport available in the late nineteenth century, presumably by railway. We are not to make-believe that he travelled by a teleportation device of his own invention, for it is surely false "in the fiction" that he used such a device.
>
> (Currie 1985, p. 390)

But Currie wisely counsels us not to let these complications interfere with our definition of fiction. We can afford to be a little bit vague at this point about what *exactly* a fiction asks us to pretend, so long as we come back to the question later, when we address the different question: what is truth, and what is falsehood, in a fiction; and how do we work out what's supposed to be true and false, in a fiction? These are issues that we'll come back to in Chapter 6.

Currie's account contains one more detail. A problem we raised with Searle was that he places too much weight upon the author's intention. And it would seem, for all I've said, as if Currie does the same thing. So long as the author *intends* to invite you to pretend something, she has created a work of fiction. Can it really be that easy?

A related problem was Searle's inability to allow that *Robinson Crusoe* is a work of fiction. If it was produced with the wrong *intention*, if it wasn't sufficiently free of an intention to deceive, or if it wasn't sufficiently free of an *expectation* that it would deceive, then Searle will have to count it out. So too will Currie, if he's not careful. The text of *Robinson Crusoe*, if it really was passed off by its author as non-fiction, was an invitation, not to *pretend*, but to *believe*. And yet Currie makes a suggestion that can save him.

Currie's solution to the *Robinson Crusoe* problem is to distinguish between "core" works of fiction and "secondary" works of fiction (Currie 1985, p. 388). A core work of fiction becomes a work of fiction due to the author's *intention*: she intends and invites her readers to play along. A *secondary* form of fiction, by contrast, is a text that a culture has decided, for one reason or another, to *treat* as an invitation to make-believe. *Robinson Crusoe* may have started off life as a string of deceptive assertions; but it *became* a work of fiction.

In one fell-swoop, Currie has allowed that an author's intention isn't *necessary* for the production of fiction, even if it can be *sufficient*. It might be necessary for *core* works of fiction, but not for *secondary* works.

But even this seems too permissive. Can the author's intention alone *ever* suffice? Remember that belch? If an author belches with the intention to invite you to pretend that, once upon a time there was a superhero from Krypton, does that make her burp a work of fiction? Surely not. The invitation has to come along with a reasonable expectation that her audience will understand her invitation, but even then, we should worry, as we worried when discussing Searle, that it won't be easy to define a "reasonable expectation".

So this is Currie's definition of fiction:

**Currie's Account**

A work of fiction is a text written, or sentences uttered, as an invitation, issued with a reasonable expectation that an audience will understand it as an invitation, to make-believe that certain things are true, in recognition of the author (or storyteller)'s intention. Or (at least) it is a text that a group of readers have decided to treat in this way.

*Tatjana:* What do you mean by "make-believe"? Is it the same as "pretend"?

*Sam:* That's a great question, but I'm going to leave off answering it. In fact, I'm going to leave it up to you, in Chapter 5, to tell me what sorts of imaginings, or pretendings, or make-believings are most distinctive of fiction. So, let me just say that, for our purposes right now, we can treat pretending and make-believing as the same thing!

So, in addition to our worries about "reasonable expectations", where does this account go wrong (if, indeed, it goes wrong at all)?

Well, along with Searle's account, it still rejects the possibility of non-linguistic fiction, like mime, or a cartoon-strip without any words. But perhaps this could be fixed. Currie's key idea seems to be that fiction is an invitation to pretend that certain things are true; it seems to be less central to his suggestion that the invitation really has to involve *words*.

*Tatjana:* So I guess pictures, dance moves, maybe even gestures, in any case, visuals, are another way to issue this invitation. Are there other ways too, I wonder? Maybe not. It seems that invitations to pretend depend on human communication. But the main ways we communicate with each other are with words, signs, and body language. Would you agree?

*Sam:* Yes, I would. And actually, I think the open-endedness here (i.e. the fact that new ways of inviting people to pretend can evolve over time) is an attractive feature of the account.

We certainly seem to be making progress. We're no longer putting *all* of the power in the hands of the author and her intentions. We're no longer excluding *Robinson Crusoe* and we're no longer excluding non-verbal fiction.

*Tatjana:* Can you remind me why we are not excluding *Robinson Crusoe* on Currie's account but we did on Searle's? Is this the explanation? Defoe was deceiving people into thinking that they were reading a diary, while in fact he made it all up. Why was his work deceptive? Because it was reasonable of him to expect that his readers would interpret his work as a report of facts.

Searle's account is all about the author's intentions. To create fiction, an author has to pretend, without the intention to deceive, that things are as she describes them to be. But this would mean that *Robinson Crusoe* isn't a fiction, since Defoe didn't pretend without intention to deceive. He didn't do what is required on Searle's account to make a work a work of fiction. But for Currie, it's enough if readers decide to treat a work as fiction for this work to be fiction. It's fiction for this particular group. Thus, *Robinson Crusoe* is fiction for us because we decided to treat it like this.

*Sam:* Absolutely. That's exactly right.

But are we now *including* too much?

How many readers, or consumers of a fiction, does it take to transform something that wasn't originally fiction into a fiction? Can anything whatsoever be treated as an invitation to pretend that something is true, and thereby become a fiction? If I decide to treat your shopping list as an instruction to pretend something, does that make your shopping list a work of fiction?

Perhaps we should make a distinction between a *work* of fiction and fiction. *Anna Karenina* is a *work* of fiction. When I tell a joke, I'm spinning a yarn. It seems fair to call it fiction, or fictional, but surely not a *work* of fiction. Likewise, a computer game invites us to pretend that certain things are true, but it might be so open ended and so up to us how we're to take things, that it deserves to be called fictitious without perhaps qualifying as a *work* of fiction.

*Tatjana:* As someone with experience at creating visual novels, which are basically text-based games, I'm not sure I agree. The creator of a video game needs to create a complete story: the story that will have been told if the player finishes the game as intended, whether this story is entirely language-based or entirely visual, or anything in between.

In fact, the creator of the video game will have to tell several alternative stories. They may not always be verbally poetic. They might contain lines such as, "If the player grabs a flower, the flower will explode." Adventure games, quests, point-n-click games, etc., all have an important storyline. The question may be: what *is* the work of fiction here. Is it whatever each player plays? Or is it the complete game? Or …?

*Sam:* Come to think of it, I think you're probably right. It's hard to find good examples here, but I still think we can make a distinction between fiction and *works* of fiction. But it's not all that easy to find uncontroversial examples of a fiction that fails to be a work of fiction! Maybe the games of which you talk are a fiction that fail to be a single work of fiction, but are many works! Perhaps you can think of a better example of a fiction that isn't one or more works of fiction. Perhaps jokes are better examples. I don't know.

If Currie's idea is that we can be very liberal as to what we *treat* as a fiction, I'm all in favour. I'm a liberal guy. But if his idea is that we can make something into a *work* of fiction, in some absolute and objective sense, simply by *deciding* that it's a work of fiction, then that seems to be far too permissive.

Perhaps he's less permissive than that. Perhaps he's saying that a particular *culture* has to make the decision, in order to transform a non-fictional text into a work of fiction. But how many people within the culture have to decide? Come to think of it, how many people comprise a culture to begin with? What are we actually saying? I'm losing the thread here. What's my name again?

Perhaps we shouldn't care too much about what makes something into a *work* of fiction. Perhaps it's enough to achieve some clarity on what we mean by *fiction*, even if it's less than clear what makes some fictions into *works* of fiction, and what prevents other fictions, like a joke, from counting as a *work* of fiction. If that's our real interest, then perhaps we can avoid certain worries that needn't detain us here (the idea of defining fiction without trying to define a *work* of fiction is a road suggested by Currie, 2014, and Davies, 2015, pp. 49–54).

Searle's suggestion is that a fiction is a string of intentionally non-deceptive pretend assertions. Currie's suggestion is that a fiction is something that was intended as, or, at least, that we came to treat as, an *invitation* to pretend that certain things are true. Perhaps we can leave the more complicated question of what constitutes a *work* of fiction to one side.

In terms of telling us what fiction is, Currie does a better job than Searle. His view can easily be extended so as to account for non-verbal fiction; he treats plays and novels as fictitious in the same way; he recognizes that the author's intention (when sufficiently reasonable) *can* make something a fiction, but that a text *can* be treated as a fiction with or without the author's intention. Perhaps he makes the creation of *works of fiction* too easy, but we're clearly making progress, even if some details need working out. And thus, we have a promising suggestion on the table, until …

## Enter Stacie Friend

Stacie Friend is a philosopher who has sought to undermine any definition of fiction in terms of *pretence*, or in terms of *invitations* to imagine. She therefore opposes Searle *and* Currie. Her point is that non-fictions often contain the very things that Searle and Currie would point to as the signatures of fiction. She writes:

> Many, and probably most, works ordinarily classified as non-fiction invite imagining… For instance, any text may prompt visual or other imagery. And non-fiction narratives aim to get us to imagine "the world of the story": that is to form a mental representation of the situation described in more detail than the text provides.
>
> (Friend, 2011, p. 164)

A good piece of long-form journalism certainly hopes to engage our imagination without saying anything false. Sometimes a work of non-fiction quite explicitly *invites* you to imagine something. Friend brings the following example from Simon Schama's *A History of Britain*:

> Take a look at [Disraeli's] Buckinghamshire country house, Hughenden Manor, with its stupendous over-decoration (unerringly like Osborne House); imagine its terraces full of peacocks …
>
> (Schama, 2003, p. 259)

Is Schama's history book a work of *fiction*? He explicitly invites us to *imagine* something! Currie anticipates this worry. To escape it, he adds a little qualification to his account. He claims that *in addition* to prescribing that we imagine certain things, a fictive utterance can be no more than *accidentally* true (Currie, 1990, p. 46). Schama's work isn't true by accident. The pre-Darwinian fiction that we imagined earlier in this chapter, by contrast, was true, but only by *accident*. Currie's idea is that fiction prescribes imagination, *without* prescribing belief. Schama's book, by contrast, prescribes *both*. But this qualification doesn't satisfy Friend.

First of all, note: there are plenty of fictions that *do* contain, alongside prescriptions to imagine, prescriptions also to *believe*. George Orwell's *Animal Farm* is a prescription to believe all sorts of claims about totalitarianism. Believe it or not, I learnt a lot about the Parisian sewer system by reading *Les Misérables*. Victor Hugo didn't merely invite me to pretend. He invited me to believe (at least *some* of what he wrote). He'd done his research on Parisian sewers after all.

This needn't worry Currie too much because he can define a fiction as a patchwork of prescriptions *only* to imagine alongside prescriptions both to imagine and to believe. So long as we're not invited to believe it *all*, and so long as we *are* invited to *imagine* it all, we're still talking about a fiction.

But now, note that there are plenty of works of non-fiction that *do* contain prescriptions to imagine something *without* asking us to believe everything that we're supposed to imagine. In actual fact, this book (the one that you're reading) is a counter-example of its own. This book is a work of non-fiction. It asks you to believe all sorts of things. It also hopes to engage your imagination. But there are some things we ask you to imagine, *without* asking you to believe. For example, I asked you to imagine that somebody wrote a novel about the evolution of species before Darwin developed his scientific account. I asked you to *imagine* it, without asking you to *believe* it. Surely, that can't be enough to make this book, or any part of it, a work of fiction.

Perhaps you can imagine how Currie would respond. We shouldn't confuse the notion of a *work* of fiction with the notion of *fiction*. Remember? Let somebody else define *works* of fiction. Whatever the status of this book, the idea that somebody wrote that pre-Darwinian novel, that *idea* is a fiction, even if this *book*, which *contains* that idea, is a work of non-fiction.

A chemist isn't worried by the fact that the water that comes out of our taps is a mixture of $H_2O$ and other molecules. That doesn't undermine the theory that pure water is $H_2O$. Likewise, Currie assures us, we shouldn't worry if a work of fiction is a mixture of fictive and non-fictive utterances. But that's not good enough. At some point, a chemist is going to say that there's not enough $H_2O$ in that liquid to justify calling it water. At some point they're going to tell us not to drink it. They're going to tell us that it contains too many toxins, for example. And, we hope, there's a science to all of this. But Currie can provide no such formula. It's also bizarre to think that when a novelist includes facts in her novel, she's somehow diluting its fictionality. As Kendal Walton notes:

> It will not do to regard asserted sentences in a historical novel as, in general, interpolations of nonfiction woven into an otherwise fictional fabric. Tolstoy does not stop work on his fiction when he writes that Napoleon invaded Russia, even if in writing this he was claiming that Napoleon [in the real world beyond the fiction] actually did invade Russia.
>
> (Walton, 1990, p. 79)

Kathleen Stock suggests a fix (Stock, 2011, p. 154). Perhaps we can classify a work of fiction as a work that has at least *one* proposition which it asks us to imagine and *not* to believe. There's a formula for you! The idea would be that anything that engages the imagination throughout, and which isn't *purely* non-fiction, should count as fiction. But that's obviously not going to work! We've already seen that the book that you're reading right now – this very book – is a work of non-fiction containing some fictive elements. Accordingly, Stock continues to run the risk of miscategorizing *this* book as a work of fiction. But Stock would insist that the fictive elements of a book like this aren't *connected* in the right way to the rest of the book, so as to render the whole book a work of fiction.

My idea about a pre-Darwinian book is just an isolated thought experiment in a work of nonfiction. To transform this book into a fiction, that thought experiment would have to be connected to the whole book in the right way. But it remains unclear just what it would mean for a fictive element to be connected in the *right* way, and what it would mean for it to be connected in the wrong way, to the rest of the book, so as to render a whole book a work of fiction. Stock requires just one such element, connected in the right way. But we're not sure, exactly, what that means.

According to David Davies (2015), what matters, when confronted with a fiction that contains all sorts of non-fictive elements, isn't that the factual content be accidental (which was Currie's suggestion), or that the fictive elements somehow outweigh the non-fictive elements, or that the fictive elements be connected in the right way to the rest of the work, but that the truths in question aren't included (at least not primarily) *because* they're true. On this account, what's distinctive of fiction is that when there are non-fictive elements, they're not included primarily because they're true, but because they will serve the purposes of the narrative.

I imagine that Friend wouldn't be moved by this variation on Currie's theme. Are all non-fictive elements of a work of fiction there to move the story along?

I'm led to recall the sewers in *Les Misérables*. It's far from clear that the overabundance of details about the Parisian sewer system really did all that much to move the narrative along, or that its inclusion was motivated by such a desire. Much the same, I think, could be said about the non-fictive elements of *Moby Dick*. Some authors seem to enjoy showing off their knowledge about all sorts of facts.

These considerations lead Friend to conclude that *prescriptions to imagine* are a red herring. They cannot help us to distinguish between fiction and non-fiction, be it at the level of a whole work or at the level of a single utterance. And, she urges, it's a wrong-turn to try to define *fiction* without (at the same time) defining *works of fiction*. So, what is Friend's alternative?

## Fiction According to Friend

Friend's final word on the matter can be summed up as follows: Fiction is that stuff that we call *fiction*. Non-fiction, by contrast, is that stuff that we call *non-fiction*. Admittedly, it's a slightly unfair characterization of her view. She obviously has a serious point to make, and my summary makes it sound as if she's asserting a tautology. She isn't. So, let me explain.

Friend starts out with a definition of "*genre*". A genre, she tells us, is a way of classifying a work. And this classification then "plays a role in a work's correct interpretation and evaluation" (Friend, 2012, p. 181).

That sounds like a good definition. Knowing the genre of a work *does* help us to know how we're supposed to relate to it. For example, some people derided the *Die Hard* movie franchise for being unrealistic. And yet the same critics don't generally deride Tolkien's work for being unrealistic, despite all of its elves and trolls. Why? Because Tolkien's work belongs to a genre that allows for elves and trolls, whereas the *Die Hard* franchise aimed for a gritty realism, and yet it expected us to believe that an everyday cop could accurately jump "a car off a highway railing so as to cause it to strike a helicopter fifty feet in the air" (Hazlett & Mag Uidhir, 2011, p. 41).

When I was a kid, a film was shown on TV called *Alive*. This was in the days before streaming content online and on demand. This was in the days where all you could watch on TV was what the small number of stations happened to be broadcasting when you tuned in. *Alive* was based on a true story about a plane crash over the Andes, and how the survivors managed to stay alive, including by resorting to cannibalism; a traumatic film to watch.

That night, a friend of mine and his brother had tuned into the wrong station. Based on what they'd seen in the newspaper, they thought they were tuning in to watch a comedy. They weren't. *Alive* is anything but a comedy. They had made a mistake. Unaware of their error, they tried really hard to watch it as a comedy, because that's what they'd been told to expect. While other people watching the movie would have been absorbed by the compelling drama, these two kids were having a completely different experience. They sat there, in front of their screen, completely confused, searching for any sort of dark humour that they could somehow read into it, before recognizing the mistake they had made. Since they had a different genre in mind to other viewers, they had a different experience.

To cut to the chase: Friend's view is that *fiction* is just a genre – albeit a genre with many sub-genres, such as science-fiction, fantasy, romance, magical realism, and more. Likewise, according to Friend, *non-fiction* is also a genre – albeit a genre with many sub-genres, such as biography, history, self-help, journalism, and more.

*Tatjana:* What do Searle and Currie think fiction is if not, like Friend, a genre?

*Sam:* Well, I suppose that for them you can have genres of fiction, but fiction itself isn't a genre. Rather, fiction is either a pretend assertion, or it is an invitation to pretend. Only once we're in the world of fiction can we start distinguishing different genres of it. Also, I suppose, Searle and Currie wouldn't call non-fiction a genre either. They would allow that there can be genres *of* non-fiction, but not that non-fiction itself is a genre.

To appreciate Friend's suggestion, we need to explain what a *family resemblance* is. The notion is owed to Ludwig Wittgenstein. Some meaningful phrases, he argued, don't admit of precise definitions. His key example was the word "game". Intuitively, we all know what the word means. But it's really hard to come up with a set of properties had by every game and only by games.

Perhaps all games have rules, but so does driving, and driving isn't a game (even if some drivers treat it as one). Many games have multiple players, or winners and losers, but not *every* game does. Wittgenstein suggests that there are a *cluster* of properties that help us to identify games, much as there is a cluster of properties that might make all of the members of a family look alike.

People tell me that my kids look like me. They certainly look like one another. But I don't think that there's a single distinctive feature that we *all* share, or a single feature that *only* we share. Instead, there's a cluster of properties, which generates a somewhat fuzzy but certainly tangible, *family resemblance*.

As a philosopher, I always want to find hard and fast definitions to get my teeth into. But, we should remember: a genre is a way of classifying *artefacts*, *human creations*, and *human activities*. All of these things are based upon convention more than they are based upon laws of nature. If fuzzy definitions should ever be allowed, then here would seem like a fitting place to use them. Accordingly, it seems fair to think that genres should be defined in terms of *clusters* of properties rather than in terms of strict definitions; in terms of a family resemblance that threads its way through the category rather than a set of one-size-fits-all entry requirements.

How do we know whether to consider a work a comedy or a drama? Friend suggests that there's not going to be some clearly defined list of properties shared by all and only the comedies. Rather, we're going to sort works of art and literature into categories in conversation with a looser "cluster of non-essential criteria" (Friend, 2012, p. 195). Some of these criteria focus on features internal to the work – for example, comedies tend to have certain formats, or features, such as a tendency to make us laugh. But also, the criteria will include "facts about the work's origins, in particular the category in which the artist intended the work to be appreciated, or in which the artist's contemporaries would have placed it", or how it's been marketed or sold (ibid., p. 187).

Kendall Walton (1970, p. 357) adds that part of how we classify a work into a genre depends upon which category would render the work most pleasing. *Alive* (to the best of my memory) isn't a great movie. But it certainly makes more sense (and is, to that extent more satisfying, artistically) when categorized as a drama, than as a comedy.

How then do we identify a work as a work of *fiction*? Well, it might start with the words, "Once Upon a Time" – that's often a clue. It might start with a disclaimer: "No identification with actual persons (living or deceased), places, buildings, and products, is intended or should be inferred." Alternatively, you might identify a work as a fiction because you found it in a certain section of the bookshop (or website). It might be because you know the author as a writer of fiction. But then, once you've placed a work in this genre, the *fiction* genre, however provisionally you've done it, your expectations of that work will change.

How so? A genre will be associated with certain standard characteristics. So, for example, if we take a text (or a film or any other work) to be a work of *fiction*, "we will expect it to engage us imaginatively through narrative; to deploy certain literary devices; to include invented elements … to make claims that are not assertions by the author; and so on" (Friend, 2012, p. 189). This doesn't mean that a work of non-fiction can't have such features. It can, but we won't *expect* them in the same way. Moreover, standard features are *standard* but not *definitive*, so a work that belongs to a genre can fail to have any one of the features you might be expecting. This allows for phenomena like genre-bending.

*Tatjana:* This seems interesting given that Friend thinks fiction is a genre. Maybe historical novels or dramatized documentaries that contain lots of fictional elements, such as *Manhunt: Unabomber*, can be viewed as genre-combining.

They combine standards for the genre of fiction and standards for the genre of history book/documentary, all at the same time. What do you think?

*Sam:* Yes, I think that Friend's account is well placed to deal with these sorts of fuzzy cases that bend conventions, or combine fiction and non-fiction. An example that often comes up is *Dutch*, by Edmund Morris – a biography of Ronald Reagan, by a serious biographer, but who chose to document the key events of Reagan's life in the voice of a fictional narrator (and the book included other fictional elements too). It defied most of the conventions available at the time (and today) for distinguishing between a work of fiction and a work of non-fiction. On Friend's account that sort of challenging phenomenon is to be expected.

Sometimes these deviations please us, and sometimes they are a source of disappointment; generating criticism.

To be fair, Friend is actually open to the notion that there may be *some* features that a fiction *has* to have if it wants to qualify as a fiction (some features that *all* fictions have, even if some non-fictions happen to have them too). But she's also open to the possibility that there are no necessary conditions here.

*Tatjana:* Does this mean that we must accept that there are fuzzy cases? Works that are neither clearly fiction nor non-fiction? Maybe *Manhunt* is such an example. But don't we need to know whether a work is either fiction or non-fiction? Isn't it the case that they *must* be one or the other?

*Sam:* I suppose Friend would just accept that there really *can* be fuzzy cases. And works like *Manhunt* and *Dutch* give us reason to think that she might be right, I suppose.

To qualify as a member of a particular genre, a given work will certainly have to have *some* of that genre's standard features, but there needn't be *one* standard feature shared by all of the members of the genre. Again, we're talking about a family resemblance.

Sure, it's hard to imagine that we'd ever want to categorize something as a fiction if it didn't invite us to *imagine* anything; but then again, writers and artists are always pushing boundaries, so perhaps we shouldn't rule it out. Before *Tristram Shandy* it would have been hard to imagine a fiction that didn't have the sort of narrative coherence that *Tristram Shandy* lacks. Who could have imagined a fiction with the characteristics of *Ulysses* before James Joyce? Indeed, genres can change over time because of the ways that rules are tested and pushed. For these reasons, Friend would caution against dogmatism. Indeed, Friend asks us to:

> Compare the situation with painting. Flatness is a standard but not necessary condition for [something being a] painting, given the existence of collagist paintings and the like. One might be inclined to think, though, that at least the use of paint is necessary for something to count as a painting. But digital paintings are now an accepted genre, and there are other works that use materials such as fabric to achieve painterly effects; these are often called "paintings without paint". If there can be paintings without paint, presumably there can be fictions without invention [or without the invitation to imagine that things are true]. That said, there can be no doubt that the inclusion of made-up content is a particularly significant standard feature of fiction.
>
> (Friend, 2012, p. 191)

Fiction is fiction not because of some magic ingredient, had by fiction and only by fiction. Instead, we categorize some works as fiction, and some works as non-fiction, and some works, perhaps, as occupying a genre-bending grey area. We do this in conversation with an evolving set of practices, in a given cultural context, that shapes our engagement with text. And that's why I started out by characterizing Friend's account as, "fiction is that stuff that we call *fiction*!"

*Tatjana:* But who are these "we"? You and Me? Literary critics? Creators of written and visual works? Bookstore folks? Europeans? Who?

*Sam:* That's a great question, and I don't think that Friend's account supplies a ready-made answer to it. On the other hand, her account is contextualist. This means that whether a work counts as a work of fiction depends upon the context. The question could conceivably receive a different answer depending upon who's being asked! Fiction is the stuff that "we" call fiction, where the "we" in question can change from context to context.

Until this point, we'd been struggling to see how a patchwork of imaginary and factual elements can come together to give rise to a work of *fiction* in a novel, whereas a patchwork of imaginary and factual elements in a history book come together to give rise to a work of *non-fiction*. For Friend, by contrast:

> [The] right way to distinguish between fiction and non-fiction focuses attention, not on how the parts of a work add up to the whole but instead [on] how the whole work is embedded in a larger context, and specifically in certain practices of reading, writing, criticizing, and so on.
>
> (Friend, 2012, p. 187)

To use the technical jargon, Friend's account is *non-reductionist*: it doesn't try to define fiction in terms of some more basic magical ingredient that makes fiction fiction. Her account is also *contextualist*: it claims that whether a text (or for that matter, a picture, or a dance) is a work of fiction depends upon the wider context in which it's situated. In short:

**Friend's Account**

Fiction is a genre. A work of fiction is anything that, in a given cultural context, has a sufficient number of the standard features associated, in that culture, with fiction, for us to categorize it as fiction.

*Tatjana:* Just to make sure I understand you correctly: An account of something – fiction, nature, pillows – is *non-reductionist* precisely when it refuses to define the term in question by reducing fiction, nature, or a pillow to a fixed set of properties that a thing must have to count as fiction, nature, or a pillow. Conversely, a reductive account does just that. I guess I feel a greater sense of satisfaction if I have a reductionist account for a kind of thing. I would love to have the list of magical ingredients that combined make something a fiction, nature, knowledge, or a pillow.

*Sam:* Yes, that's exactly what I mean by calling a theory of an account non-reductive. Moreover, a reductive account won't try to define fiction in terms of being fictional, or pillows in terms of being pillow-like. That's why I share your preference, wherever possible, for reductive accounts.

## Fiction According to Kendall Walton

I understand what pushes Friend towards her non-reductive, family resemblance account of fiction. But I prefer clean-cut definitions whenever possible. The notion of family resemblance should, I think, be a last resort.

Also, I think Friend was wrong to say that: "If there can be painting without paint, presumably there can be fictions without invention." Just because "false-teeth" has the word "teeth" in it, it doesn't mean that false-teeth are teeth. Just because "fool's gold" has the word "gold" in it, it doesn't mean that fool's gold is gold. Likewise, just because we might call something a "painting without paint", it doesn't mean that it's *really* a painting.

Just as I'm not keen to give up on the requirement that real paintings have to use paint, I'm not eager to give up on the requirement that fiction has to have *something* to do with imagination and pretence. But the problem is this: as we've seen, *non*-fiction can contain imagination and pretence too, so what is the magic ingredient that takes imagination and pretence and makes a *fiction* out of them?

As far as Kendall Walton (1990) is concerned, there's no need for an extra magic ingredient. A work of fiction is a prop in a game of make believe. Nothing more. He describes how children might use tree stumps in an impromptu game of make-believe in which the stumps are supposed to be bears. Accordingly, those tree stumps are props in a game of make-believe. They are fictionally bears. Similarly, a community of readers can use a text, say the text of *Animal Farm,* as a prop in a game of make-believe, in which the text is treated as a real record of events, or as the report of a real person, etc.

Walton rejects intentionalism. Sure, an author can write a text, intending for it to be used as a prop in a game of make-believe. Perhaps, in our society, that's a crucial feature of a fiction because, in our society, we might think it important to respect the wishes of authors, and only to treat a text as a prop in a game of make-believe if that's what the author wanted us to do. But even if this were true, which it probably isn't, it wouldn't have to be true of every society. As Walton declares:

> In our society the function of a text or picture, how it is to be used, may be determined partly by its maker's intentions. But another society might give less weight to this consideration or none at all …
>
> (Walton, 1990, p. 88)

Indeed, if a computer with no intentionality of its own, spewed out a text of a certain form, there's no reason why a community couldn't decide to treat it as a prop in a game of make believe, just as those children chose to treat those tree stumps as a prop in their game of make believe.

*Tatjana:* That's tricky. Those tree stumps don't really have the function to serve as props in a game of make-believe; or not the right sort of function to make them into works of fiction at any rate.

According to Walton, representation (or fiction) requires that it be the prop's *social* function to be used in this way. It takes a society to bestow that sort of function upon something.

*Sam:* Yes. That's right. Technically, the tree stumps don't have the social function of being props unless a *society* bestows that function upon them. A book doesn't have the function of being a prop in a game unless a *society* bestows that function upon it. But you could ask, how many people in the society have to agree? Why can't the kids themselves, playing in the forest, count as a society, such that, for them, the tree stumps do have that social function?

Just as the playwright creates a script to aid the make-believe of the actors, who – in turn – aid the make-believe of their audience, a novelist creates a novel to aid the make-believe of its readers. The playwright and the author don't have to pretend to assert anything. They don't have to intend to issue any sort of invitation. They don't have to ensure that there's at least one untruth in what they write, properly integrated into the whole. They just need to make something that would serve as a good prop, in exactly the same way that the painter, the sculptor, and the doll manufacturer don't have to pretend that they're painting, or sculpting, or manufacturing something real; nor do they have to intend to issue any sort of invitation. They merely have to "produce props for others to use in their imaginative activities" (Walton, 1990, p. 83).

Despite his utter rejection of intentionalism, if Walton's account reminds you of Currie, then you're doing well. Currie was keen to acknowledge that his account of fiction *was* inspired by Walton. But there are two key differences (in addition to Walton's utter rejection of intentionalism).

*Tatjana:* I'm not sure I would call it an utter rejection of intentionalism. It's not like he thinks that the author's intentions never play any role.

*Sam:* Okay. It might play a role in some situations, but it doesn't have to. The intention of an author is neither necessary nor sufficient for making something a fiction, unless some society says that it is. In fact, the intention of the author is only relevant to the extent that a given society says so. That's all I meant by "utter" rejection. But I take your point. In our society, for example, whether the author intended to write a work of fiction is highly relevant.

Walton's account is contextualist, whereas Currie's isn't; and – as I'll later explain – Walton's account is *revisionary*, whereas Currie's isn't supposed to be. Let me first explain how Walton's account is contextualist.

According to Walton, there is no objective fact of the matter as to whether a given text (or object) is a work of fiction. Instead, in contexts in which various games of make-believe are played, we can assess whether the relevant social conventions bestow that function on a text (or object), or not. If the context gives the text the appropriate function, then, relative to that context, the text is a work of fiction. If it doesn't give the text the appropriate function, then, relative to that context, the very same text will *not* be a work of fiction. This is the same with tree stumps and whether we should think of them as fictional bears.

*Tatjana:* Walton does not think that it's the function of the stumps to serve in games of make-believe, so he doesn't think they are representations, and they are not works of fiction, even though they can be used as props in games of make-believe.

*Sam:* That's right. I'm not being fair to his official position. Just because the kids use the tree stumps as props, it doesn't mean that those stumps have that as their social function, until a society bestows that function upon them in a more lasting way than we would find with a single game of kids in the forest. But still, as I've said in an earlier text box, it's a little bit vague at what point a group of people is large enough, and established enough to give an object a lasting function. If the kids could constitute a society, then they'd have the power to make those tree stumps into works of fiction!

In some contexts, a tree stump is treated as a fictional bear. In other contexts, the very same stump isn't treated as a bear at all. This is what makes Walton's account contextualist.

Currie, by contrast, will claim that irrespective of any context, if the author, in writing a text, had the intent to invite people to make-believe, then that text is objectively and absolutely a fiction; irrespective of context. Likewise, Currie seems to think that if a culture, at any point in time, has decided to treat a text as an invitation to make-believe, then that text is objectively and absolutely a fiction, from that point onwards; irrespective of context.

The other difference is that Walton's account is revisionary. What this means is that Walton isn't trying to capture what we normally mean, in our everyday talk, by the fiction-non-fiction distinction. Instead, he wants to *revise* the way we speak. He might agree with Friend that the rough and ready ways in which we tend to classify some texts as fiction and some texts as non-fiction are just that: rough and ready. Walton wants to make things more precise than they are in our everyday conversations and thus, for him:

> Any work with the function of serving as a prop in games of make-believe, however minor or peripheral or instrumental this function might be, qualifies as "fiction"; only what lacks this function entirely will be called nonfiction.
>
> (Walton, 1990, p. 72)

Walton is, of course, welcome to use the word "fiction" in any way that he wants. He can just stipulate that, for his purposes, when he uses the word "fiction", he's referring to props in games of make believe. For all we have a right to complain, he can use the word to refer only to potted plants, if he wants to. Provided we abide by certain moral constraints on what should and shouldn't be said, we're all entitled to use words however we want to. Of course, this response is a little facetious. Walton's point is that his use of the word "fiction", even if it deviates slightly from the ways it's used outside of the philosophy seminar room, is related closely enough to the original concept to be relevant to the study of fiction but boasts an added clarity.

*Tatjana:* What is the added clarity?

*Sam:* Well, for one thing, we saw how Searle and Currie's definitions ended up being fuzzy, relying on somewhat vague notions like, "reasonable expectations" and "serious intentions". Friend's definition relied upon family resemblances, which are also fuzzy. Walton's definition provides us with a much sharper distinction. That's a form of clarity.

This leaves us with two questions:

1 How far does Walton's revisionary account end up deviating from what we might call our native conception of fiction?
2 Is it really true that the only way to add precision to our concept of "fiction" is to revise it?

The answer to the first question, I think, is: quite far! Walton considers a so-called *true-crime* novel by Norman Mailer, called *The Executioner's Song*. Even though it's called a *novel*, it's very controversial to insist that it's a *fiction*. The book was marketed as a "true life novel", whatever exactly that was supposed to mean. It was written on the basis of extensive research and hours of interviews. It aims to be as faithful as it can be to the facts of the actual story that it's about. And yet, for Walton, it's clearly a fiction, since "There can be no doubt that a central purpose of Mailer's *Executioner's Song* is to serve as a prop in games of make-believe" (Walton, 1990, p. 93). It's written in such a way as to encourage you to imagine, with your mind's eye, the story unfold.

Admittedly, it won the Pulitzer Prize for Fiction, so Walton isn't alone in categorizing it as a fiction, but there's a sense in which the journalistic integrity of *The Executioner's Song* is compromised by calling it a fiction. Moreover, beyond this one novel, and beyond the phenomenon of true-crime stories, there's a whole school of writing called "new journalism" which aims for the factual accuracy of traditional journalism but seeks to present its journalistic, non-fictional stories, in literary ways; freely borrowing techniques from long-form fictional prose. Walton is unapologetic that his definition of fiction swallows up *The Executioner's Song*. In that respect, he's no different from the judges of the Pulitzer Prize. But Walton's definition will extend to pretty much all of new journalism – and so it will include pretty much every feature-length article in, for example, *The New Yorker*.

*Tatjana:* I wonder whether this only seems problematic for us because we have a bias that fiction contains lots of stuff that is made up. Well, maybe it's not a bias. Maybe this simply is how we ordinarily use the word "fiction". But the thing is, if the way we ordinarily use the word leads to several false classifications or borderline cases, maybe it's time to clarify the concept and revise our usage. And Walton should be fine with it turning out that almost every article in a magazine like *The New Yorker* turns out to be fiction, since he makes the case that make-believe is all pervasive throughout our lives.

*Sam:* Yes. I think that's precisely what Walton would say.

Technically, we have no right to complain. Afterall, Walton is totally open about the fact that his "definition" of fiction is revisionary. He's not telling us what people outside the philosophy seminar room tend to mean by "fiction". Instead, he's trying to *revise* and *refine* the rough and ready notion with which we started and to come up with something sharper.

That being said, I think it's important for us to note just how far his revisionary definition takes us from the ordinary, everyday concept. I'm happy to accept, along with Walton's definition of fiction, that a picture can be a work of fiction.

*Tatjana:* Do you mean something like a painting? It's only a work of fiction if it is its function to serve as a prop in games of make-believe. Botticelli's *Birth of the Venus* is a fiction. It functions as a prop in games of make-believe in which we imagine that a woman, Venus, is emerging from the sea on a shell.

*Sam:* Yes. And, given this analysis of the painting as a prop in a game of make-believe, Walton's definition accommodates the painting well.

Not all fiction requires words or text, but what about a doll, and those tree stumps in the children's game, and what about new journalism – are all of those things works of fiction?

*Tatjana:* Walton would say: yes, or no, depending on the individual text and whether it's a function of the text, or object, to be used as a prop in make-believe games.

*Sam:* I know that he would. I just think it odd to say, of a doll, in a pretty normal context, that it, itself, is a work of fiction. I know that Walton doesn't mind. He's definition is supposed to be revisionary. I'm just pointing out the extent to which it is!

Despite the fact that we use them as props in games of make-believe, I'm inclined to say that none of them are works of fiction. At least, not in any ordinary, or everyday sense of the word. Accordingly, it seems that Walton's revision is more radical than we may have hoped.

Perhaps this is just the price we have to pay if we want a sharp definition. We have to impose precision where, in the real world, beyond the philosophy seminar room, we make do with fuzziness. In other words, to do rigorous philosophy of fiction, we may have to make do with a slightly revisionary definition of fiction; imposing precision upon the messiness of the underlying phenomenon. But that leads us to our second question, is it really true that the only way to achieve any precision in drawing the fiction-non-fiction distinction is to revise it?

I'm not sure that my optimism will pay off, but I haven't yet given up hope of finding a non-reversionary, and wholly reductive definition, without appeal even to family resemblance. For that reason, the search goes on!

*Tatjana:* I'll admit that overall I am a big fan of Walton's project in his seminal book *Mimesis as Make-Believe*. It has completely changed how I think about works of art more generally. Are there issues with his views? Of course! But his *way* of thinking about fiction and representational art was and still is inspiring.

*Sam:* I totally agree. *Mimesis as Make-Believe* is, to my mind, one of the greatest contributions that any philosopher has really made to the field.

## Fiction According to Me

Richard Wollheim argued that viewing a representational painting requires something that he called *seeing in* (Wollheim, 1987, e.g. p. 46). For example, you might *see* a bemused woman *in* the painting called *The Mona Lisa*. If you manage to look at a painting and to *see* something *in* it, according to Wollheim, it's because you're simultaneously aware of the paint on the canvas *and* of the object that's being pictured by the painting; the object that you *see in* the painting.

This visual experience of being simultaneously aware of the work of art *and* of the object that the work of art depicts, Wollheim describes as a "twofold" visual experience (ibid.). My interest isn't to defend Wollheim's account of the visual experience of looking at paintings and pictures. Instead, I want to suggest that a notion similar to twofoldedness can probably help us arrive at a working definition of fiction.

Peter Lamarque (2014) appeals to a Wollheim-like twofoldedness in *his* account of fiction. He says that fiction is *opaque* rather than *transparent*. When you appreciate a painting, it's not like looking through a clear window onto a scene that lies beyond. Rather, you're aware of the painting *and* of what it pictures. Lamarque thinks that something very similar is going on when we read a work of fiction. We don't just pay attention to the story. Instead, we pay attention to the story and to how it's being told. To use his language, we "foreground" the formal features of the narrative. "To appreciate the novel, *attention* to its structure is all important" (ibid., p. 54).

Lamarque (ibid., p. 3) appeals to the following analogy: to read a work of fiction is to see a story, but not through a transparent window. Instead, to read a story, and to appreciate how it's being told, and how it's been crafted, is like looking at the story through a stained-glass window.

Lamarque's Wollheim-like twofoldedness is not the sort of twofoldedness I want to appeal to. Indeed, I agree with Peter Kivy. In criticizing Lamarque, Kivy recognizes that *some* readers pay attention to the form of the narrative. He calls them structural readers. But Kivy contends that structural readers account for only a "miniscule percentage of, for example, the forty million – *forty million!* – said to have read Harper Lee's *To Kill a Mockingbird*" (Kivy, 2019, p. 65).

Most readers love to get *lost* in a story; to be *swept away*. Opacity cannot be the *central* feature of our account of fiction. Structural readers are not the ones who put a novel on the *New York Times* best-seller list. It is *ordinary readers* who do that. Are ordinary readers ""improper" readers?" Kivy asks, before answering, "No, no, and no!" (ibid.).

Moreover, like Walton's revisionary account, Lamarque won't be able to exclude new journalism from the realm of fiction. When I listen to *This American Life*, I'm presented with beautifully told true stories. I pay attention both to the form and to the content. That doesn't make it fiction. It's just beautiful journalism. Opacity is neither necessary nor sufficient for the creation of fiction.

But even once we've put opacity to one side, I do think there's a certain sort of twofoldedness that *might* help us to define fiction. Sadly (or perhaps happily), I don't have the space here to provide a fully worked-out definition, or to argue for it systematically. Instead, I'm going to provide a *sketch*. It seems to me that this sketch is on the right lines, but I wouldn't want to bet my house on it. Enough with these preliminaries! What is my "sketchy" account of fiction?

First of all: to engage with a fiction is to engage with a fictional world. What do I mean by a "fictional world"? A fictional world, for our purposes here, can be thought of as a set of propositions. A proposition is the meaning of a sentence. For example: the English sentence "snow is white" and the German sentence "Schnee ist weiß" both mean the same thing; so they express *the same proposition*. Propositions are the meanings of sentences. A fiction will always invite you to pretend that certain propositions are true. That much I take from Currie.

Or, if you prefer Walton's account, you can say that a fiction always functions as a prop in a game of make-believe that requires you to pretend that certain propositions are true. So, when I talk about a "fictional world", I just mean a set of propositions that the fiction invites (or otherwise requires) us to make-believe, or to pretend.

*Tatjana:* I'm not so sure about this explanation. The reason for this is because I think that fictional worlds are complete but the descriptions of them given to us in fictional works are not. Now, a fictional world may be viewed as a complete set of propositions, containing, for any proposition, *p*, either *p* or its negation, but the fictional work will not prescribe us to imagine all of them. A work of fiction will not specify enough details to pick out one specific fictional world. Instead, it will point towards a set of fictional worlds, depending upon how we fill in the gaps.

*Sam:* Yes. That's right. A possible world has to describe some way that the entire world could be. To do that, it can't leave anything out. It has to be a complete set of propositions, that is to say, for any proposition whatsoever, a possible world has to include either that proposition or its negation. But, by "fictional world" in this context, I just mean the incomplete set of propositions that we're invited to make-believe for the purposes of a given fiction. It's not really a world. As we'll see when we get to Chapter 6, and just as you say, the text of a fiction will actually pick out a whole range of worlds. But we don't need to raise that complication here. So, for our purposes, think of a fictional world, either as the set of worlds picked out by a fiction, or as something less complete than a full possible world.

But this detail isn't enough. It's a necessary ingredient of fiction, to demand some sort of make-believe, but it isn't sufficient.

What makes fiction *distinctive*, I think, is that it asks you to be aware of (at least) two worlds at once: to engage with a fiction is to be aware of at least one fictional world *and the actual world*, simultaneously; hence my appeal to twofoldedness. In fact, when we talk about interpreting fiction (in Chapter 6), we'll see vividly the ways in which readers of fiction *have* to be keyed into the actual world *and* to the world of the fiction; all at once.

The technical jargon that we'll introduce in Chapter 6 will allow us to say that the consumption of a fiction (even for an ordinary reader) always involves (1) a fictional world, (2) the actual world, and (3) a comparison class (which is a set of propositions that are part of the fictional world, but which are also true of the actual world). Before Chapter 6, it would be hard for me to say much more than that, and hence my definition remains nothing more than a sketch. But the basic idea is that fiction is always asking us to compare a fictional world with the actual world, or the world of the fiction with the way our world really is (if you want to be convinced of that claim, turn to Chapter 6).

Simon Schama's history of Britain asks you to imagine something, but his book, including the things he asks you to imagine, is exclusively about the actual world, as is *The Executioner's Song*. Consequently, these are works of nonfiction. *This* book – the book that you're reading right now – asks you to entertain all sorts of possibilities that are far from actual, and, perhaps at those moments, this book will require a sort of twofolded attention from its readers, as you're invited to think about all the funny, unreal examples that the book provides, and to compare them with reality. But that's not going to be enough to make this book a work of fiction. A work of fiction requires twofolded attention from beginning to end.

A work of fiction requires twofolded attention from beginning to end, because a work of fiction, as a whole, has a twofolded sort of *aboutness*. A work of fiction is always about at least one fictional world, in addition to, and at the same time, as being about the actual world (in virtue of the existence of the *comparison class*, and the role that it plays in our consuming fiction – which we'll explore in Chapter 6). That sort of twofoldedness, I think, would be a good place to start, in giving a non-revisionary, and perfectly reductive account of the nature of fiction.

What about a work of fiction that's *accidentally* true, like the pre-Darwinian novel we've imagined about evolution? Well, without wanting to succumb to any extreme form of intentionalism, it seems fair to say that that book wasn't written *about* the actual world. It was, instead, written about a fictional world *and* the actual world; but the author didn't know that *his* fictional world *was* the actual world.

*Tatjana:* Is this because we can write about *x*, even if *x* is not there? Because it's not obvious to me that the pre-Darwinian novel describes a fictional world. But here is one thing I think could be said about it, which relates to what I wrote earlier in a comment.

There are several worlds that are compatible with the novel as a description of one of these worlds. It's compatible with our real world, but it's also compatible with many others. There is no clear intention that the author wanted to write about the real world, as opposed to one of the many other worlds that are compatible with the author's description.

So, because of the lack of intention to write about the *real* world, we should say that he was writing about a fictional world (after all, there are many more fictional worlds compatible with the description but there is only one real one).

*Sam:* Yes. I think that's absolutely right. But, it's also crucial to note, that even though he didn't intend to write about the real world, he did intend us to compare whichever fictional world or worlds he may have had in mind, with the real world.

It's certainly a strange case, but it seems to me fair to say that it still contains, in a somewhat tortured fashion, the twofolded aboutness that's distinctive of fiction.

So, that's what *I'd* say a fiction is: a work of fiction is any work that exhibits this type of twofolded aboutness, requiring (from beginning to end) twofolded attention – attention to the world of the fiction and attention to the real world. But like I said, I wouldn't bet my house on it.

## Works Cited

Barthes, R. (1977) The Death of the Author. In R. Barthes, *Image, Music, Text* (trans. S. Heath). London: Fontana, pp. 142–148.

Currie, G. (1985) What is Fiction? *The Journal of Aesthetics and Art Criticism*, 43(4): 385–392.

Currie, G. (1990) *The Nature of Fiction*. New York: Cambridge University Press.

Currie, G. (2014) Standing in the Last Ditch: On the Communicative Intentions of Fiction Makers. *Journal of Aesthetics and Art Criticism*, 72: 351–363.

Davies, D. (2015) Fictive Utterance and the Fictionality of Narratives and Works. *British Journal of Aesthetics*, 55: 39–55.

Friend, S. (2011) Fictive Utterance and Imagining II. *Proceedings of the Aristotelian Society, Supplementary Volume*, 85: 163–180.

Friend, S. (2012) Fiction as a Genre. *Proceedings of the Aristotelian Society*, 112: 179–209.

Hazlett, A. & Mag Uidhir, C. (2011) Unrealistic Fictions. *American Philosophical Quarterly*, 48(1): 33–46.

Kivy, P. (2019) *Once Upon a Time: Essays in the Philosophy of Literature*. New York: Rowman & Littlefield.

Lamarque, P. (2014) *The Opacity of Narrative*. New York: Rowman & Littlefield.

Murdoch, I. (1965) *The Red and The Green*. London: Chatto & Windus.

Schama, S. (2003) *A History of Britain, Volume 3: The Fate of the Empire* 1776–2000. London: BBC Books.
Searle, J. (1975) The Logical Status of Fictional Discourse. *New Literary History*, 6(2): 319–332.
Stock, K. (2011) Fictive Utterance and Imagining. *Proceedings of Aristotelian Society Supplementary Volume*, 85: 145–161.
Walton, K. (1970) Categories of Art. *Philosophical Review*, 79: 334–367.
Walton, K. (1990) *Mimesis as Make-Believe: On the Foundations of the Representational Arts*. Cambridge, MA: Harvard University Press.
Wollheim, R. (1987) *Painting as an Art*. Princeton, NJ: Princeton University Press.

## Further Reading

Abell, C. (2020) *Fiction: A Philosophical Analysis*. Oxford: Oxford University Press.
Davies, D. (2022) Definition of Fiction: State of the Art. *British Journal of Aesthetics*, 62(2): 241–255.
Deutsch, H. (2000) Making Up Stories. In A. Everett & T. Hofweber (eds), *Empty Names, Fiction, and the Puzzle of Non-Existence*. Chicago: University of Chicago Press, pp. 149–181.
Garcia-Carpintero, M. (2019) On the Nature of Fiction-Making: Austin or Grice? *British Journal of Aesthetics*, 59: 203–210.
Garcia-Carpintero, M. (2021) Documentaries and the Fiction/Nonfiction Divide. *Studies in Documentary Film*, 15: 163–174.
Matravers, D. (2014) *Fiction and Narrative*. Oxford: Oxford University Press.
Stock, K. (2017) *Only Imagine: Fiction, Interpretation, and Imagination*. Oxford: Oxford University Press.

Chapter 2

# What Is a Work of Fiction?

*Sam*

In Chapter 1, we spoke about what fiction is. The way to distinguish between fiction and *non*-fiction. In this chapter we'll be asking a different question. We'll be asking what is a *work* of fiction? And by that, I mean something like this: what sort of *object* is a work of fiction?

You might have a copy of *Animal Farm* on your bookshelf. But that papery inky object isn't the work of fiction itself. If you put it through a paper shredder you wouldn't be destroying the actual work of fiction.

Perhaps that's because your copy of the book is just that: it's a *copy*. What happens if you could get your hands on George Orwell's original manuscript? Is *that* the actual work of fiction?

Well, no. I imagine that if the manuscript still exists it would be pretty much priceless. But let's imagine that you get your hands on it, and recklessly pass it through the shredder too. You still wouldn't have destroyed the work of fiction. The work of fiction would still exist.

It seems as if an English work of fiction can continue to exist so long as there remains some copy of it somewhere in the universe (be it in paper or digital form) and somebody still knows how to read English, or – at least – so long as somebody can remember it word for word to allow for its future reproduction.

*Tatjana:* Why does the language of the copy of the novel matter? What if the only copies of the novel were written in Indonesian? It seems to me that if that were the case, we'd still be happy to say that the work still exists. Also, some books come in several editions. The third edition of a novel will differ in some ways from the manuscript, I assume. If third editions of a novel were all that were left, would we have to say that the work of fiction (e.g. *To Kill a Mockingbird*) has been destroyed? I don't think that's what we should say.

DOI: 10.4324/9781003126102-3

*Sam:* These are great questions. I can only really circle back to them later on, in this chapter, when I will have something to say about translations.

*In the meantime, I can say this much:* sometimes, as readers, we're not just interested in the storyline, or what the fiction says, but we're also interested in the use of language. To that extent, a translation can only approximate what the original author did because part of what the author did was to use a particular language in a particular way.

So, to the extent that Orwell's creation was in English, if the only surviving copy is a translation, we'd have no way of using the translation to arrive reliably at exactly the same use of English that Orwell constructed.

Have you ever tried using google translate to translate from one language to another, and then back again? Back-translation very rarely gets you exactly what you started with – even if you're using sensitive human translators.

So yes, there's a sense in which the novel has been lost if all that remains of it is a translation. But, of course, there's another sense in which the fact that the translation remains is significant. It leads me to want to say that the novel is still clinging on to its existence!

The fact that I can't answer this question clearly, and the fact that I also can't answer clearly your question about saving just one edition of a book that had multiple editions, will eventually push me to the somewhat surprising conclusion of this chapter.

If you're dead set on reducing the work of fiction to a *physical* thing – perhaps you're an adherent of the view known as physicalism, according to which the only things that exist are physical – you could say that *Animal Farm* is not any single physical copy of the work, but is something like the set of all past, present, and future copies (be they in paper, digital, or even neurological format, in the brain of someone who remembers it word for word).

*Tatjana:* We could talk about collections of all of these items, couldn't we? Collections can be concrete.

*Sam:* Yes. I'd be happy to accept that collections, or sets of items, can be classified as concrete. Philosophers are keen on drawing a distinction between abstract things and concrete things, but it turns out to be a very difficult distinction to draw.

But a collection of concrete items, I'd be willing to say, is also a concrete item. But just because I'd accept that it's *concrete* doesn't mean that it's *physical.* A collection of physical items, might be something concrete. But the collection itself, it seems to me, shouldn't be thought of as physical. Having said that, some philosophers disagree. Penelope Maddy (1992), for example, thinks that collections of physical items are, in and of themselves, physical items.

But if readers are getting a little lost, I will come back later on in this chapter, to the distinction between the concrete and abstract – so don't worry about it too much now!

Now, this still won't be good enough for a die-hard physicalist, unless you're also willing to say that the set itself is a physical thing (which is a somewhat weird thing to think). Perhaps this physical set-thing is an object that's spread out through space and time, partly located in every place that some copy of the book is located. This theory is going to result in some pretty wacky consequences. For example:

- Your so-called copy of *Animal Farm* isn't actually a *copy* of the work at all. It is, rather, a *part* of Orwell's work of fiction (a non-essential part that can be destroyed without destroying the entire work, but a part nonetheless).
- The shape and size of *Animal Farm* keeps changing over time, as copies get produced, destroyed, and moved about.
- *Animal Farm*, over the course of time, has had, and continues to have, papery bits, electronic bits, and neurological bits, and lots of gaps between all of its different bits (such as the gap between my copy of the book, and your copy of the book).
- George Orwell gets credit for creating the work of fiction, but in actual fact he only created one little bit of it (namely the original manuscript). The physical item that he created – the only part of the work that he's primarily responsible for having created – can now be destroyed without doing any significant damage to the work as a whole. Countless typesetters and printers are actually responsible for the creation of larger parts of the work than Orwell ever created.

*Tatjana:* But this seems indeed right to me. It would be a shame if all manuscripts were destroyed, but once a manuscript has been published, there's not much for it to do anymore. If our computers (and the computers of our editors) all died shortly after this book is published, and our manuscript were to be destroyed forever, does it matter? We would sigh a sigh of relief that no significant damage has been done to our work indeed because it has already been published.

*Sam:* I agree with you. The thing that I think is counter-intuitive about this bullet-point isn't that the manuscript can be destroyed without destroying the work. It can be. But what's weird, is the thought that all of those printers are responsible for the creation of a larger *part* of the work than Orwell was.

All of this seems wrong. Consequently, most people are going to say that a work of fiction isn't a physical object. (Many physicalists will agree, so long as their physicalism isn't too extreme. Moderate physicalists will allow that non-physical things exist, so long as those non-physical things are, in turn, somehow dependent upon physical things/events.) Nor is it any sort of collection or fusion of physical objects. So, what is it? Platonism offers us our first suggestion.

## Platonism

Platonism in the philosophy of art seeks to identify works of art with abstract structures – not with concrete physical objects, or events, but with something more like *a property*; something that can be held in common between multiple physical objects, or multiple events.

If, for example, you're a Platonist about works of *music*, then you're going to say that Beethoven's Ninth Symphony is identical to the sonic structure embodied by its performances. No particular performance, or recording, or musical score (even the original score, or the first ever performance) can claim to be *the actual work of music*. The work of music is, rather, what all of those things share: the sonic structure that they encode.

Another example: the Platonist about the visual arts will say that the *Mona Lisa* is identical to the precise pictorial and tactile form embodied by the relevant piece of canvas in the Louvre.

*Tatjana:* If it were just a matter of abstract form as opposed to concrete matter, could I not paint the *Mona Lisa* myself at home with a very good colour-by-numbers blueprint?

*Sam:* Yeah! I think that's one of the wacky consequences of Platonism about artworks. You'd be unlikely to create an *exact* replica via colour-by-numbers. You don't just need to get the right colours in the right places. You also need to get the texture right. An exact replica would have to take into account the amount of paint, its thickness, and the exact effect of each brush stroke. But yes, if you could make an exact copy, the Platonist will have a hard time denying that you have created your very own *Mona Lisa*. Not a copy – but an instance of the very same work of art.

The canvas itself isn't the work of art. Neither is the paint that sits on its surface. Again, the work of art is something like the visual and tactile structure that the paint on the canvas captures.

Platonism about works of fiction is going to say that *Animal Farm* isn't identical to any physical copy of the book, or any collection of them. Rather, the work of fiction is going to be what all of those copies have in common. As a first stab we'll say that *Animal Farm* is the ordered set of English sentences that one can find in any accurate copy (I'll come back to this, because you don't have to read *Animal Farm* in English. You might read a translation of it, but for the time being, let's put that complication to one side).

**Platonism**

A work of fiction is a set of sentences in an order.

## Problems with Platonism

One could raise a host of problems with the Platonic answer to our question. I'll concentrate on three.

- Problem #1: Amie Thomasson (1999, p. 8) points out that one of *Animal Farm*'s essential properties is that it's a work of anti-Stalinist satire. If it lost that property, then it wouldn't be the same work. Platonism can't accommodate this fact.

If *Animal Farm* is just a linguistic structure – just an abstract ordered set of sentences of English – then I guess that *Animal Farm* has existed forever, or at least for as long as the English language has, or at least for as long as the youngest word that the novel contains has existed.

*Tatjana:* Is this because sentences – under one meaning of the word – are also abstract? A copy of *Animal Farm* contains many concrete sentences, but whatever abstract thing *Animal Farm* is, if it is abstract, the sentences it's composed of are abstract, too.
*Sam:* Exactly.

As soon as the words existed, then so did the sentences, even if nobody had ever spoken them. They were waiting to be spoken; latent in the potential of the English language.

But if this is true, then *Animal Farm* exists, not just independently of George Orwell, but independently of Stalin too. And, if the work can exist in a world that never gave rise to Stalin, then it cannot *essentially* be an anti-Stalinist satire. In other words, the Platonist account cannot accommodate the fact that works of fiction seem to possess certain essential properties merely as a consequence of their historical provenance.

*Tatjana:* But is it so obvious that being an anti-Stalinist satire is an *essential* property of the novel? What if Stalin had never existed and Orwell had written *Animal Farm* – the exact same words – sure, the significance of the novel would be different, but do we have to say that Orwell, in these circumstances, would have created an entirely different work?
*Sam:* I think Amy Thomasson would say that, yes, it would be an entirely different work. Just as you've missed the whole point of the work if you don't get that it's an anti-Stalinist novel, it's also the case that had Orwell written the same words in a world with no Stalin, it wouldn't have had the same point and, thus, wouldn't be the same work! But I entirely accept that different people's intuitions pull in different directions in response to questions like this. The fact that these questions evoke very different intuitions – yours that it would be the same work, and Thomasson's that it would be a different work – is part of what will motivate my ultimate conclusion in this chapter.

- Problem #2: The second problem is similar to the first. If *Animal Farm* is just an ordered set of English sentences, then George Orwell didn't create it. It turns out that a Platonist will have to deny that writers actually create works of fiction; or that artists create works of art. The best that the Platonist can do is to affirm that writers can *discover* works of fiction. Orwell *discovered Animal Farm*. Good for him!
- Problem #3: The third problem concerns plagiarism and forgery. If it turns out that George Orwell had copied *Animal Farm* from someone else, this

shocking fact couldn't be counted as a defect in the work itself, since the work itself is just a set of sentences – a set that, on this hypothesis, Orwell happened to copy from someone else.

*Tatjana:* Do you mean by this that the author of the novel is essential and not acknowledged in this version of Platonism?

*Sam:* Yes. I think that's part of it. But there's something more too. Some philosophers think that forgery is a defect in a work of art. According to the Platonist, a forgery, like your home-made *Mona Lisa*, is no different to the original. That thought makes it impossible to locate forgery as a defect in the work of art itself. Imagine that I wrote a book that contained whole paragraphs pilfered from someone else. Doesn't that make the book, as a whole, less good than it would have been, had passages not been plagiarized? And yet, for the Platonist, my book has existed in Plato's heaven for just as long as the book from which I copied. Accordingly, the book itself – the book I wrote – can't be somehow impaired by my act of plagiarism, since my book existed before my act of plagiarism did!

None of these objections, I think, are devastating to the Platonist, so long as they're willing to bite certain bullets

Nicholas Wolterstorf (1991) has argued that the Platonist can escape the first worry. It's true that *Animal Farm* isn't essentially an anti-Stalinist satire, in and of itself. But, we can still say that it's an anti-Stalinist satire, even essentially so, as long as we're talking about the work *relative to Orwell's discovery of it.*

*Tatjana:* I'm not sure I get this. Could you explain in somewhat more detail, please?

*Sam:* I can try. You could paraphrase his point like this: "Look, if your problem with Platonism is that you can't say things like *Animal Farm* is essentially anti-Stalinist, then don't worry. You can still say something very similar. What you can say is this: sure, in other possible worlds, somebody could have written the very same book, and it wouldn't have been anti-Stalin, but, if you want to understand what the book and its discovery meant in this world, then you're talking about something that can't be understood at all without reference to Stalin. And, perhaps that's all we really mean when we say that *Animal Farm* is essentially anti-Stalin. We mean, that its discovery and manifestation in this world, as history unfolded, is impossible to disassociate from Stalin."

The second worry is that authors are demoted from being creators to becoming mere discoverers. But maybe that's not so bad. First of all, it sometimes takes a very creative mind to be able to discover something; such as the creative mind that allowed Einstein to discover general relativity. So, it's not as if we're denying that authors are, in some important sense, *creative*.

Moreover, the artist does create *something* tangible. She creates a token of the abstract structure in question (or a set of instructions for creating them (as in a script for a play, or a score for a musical performance, or a mould for sculptures)). It is through this physical creation that the rest of us get access to the hitherto undiscovered Platonic object.

Orwell created the first ever manuscript of *Animal Farm* and thereby gave the world access to the valuable ordered set of sentences he'd discovered. But does this really do justice to Orwell's creativity? Was his creativity exhausted in the mere creation of a *manuscript*? Was his creativity nothing more than the creativity of a scientist who discovered something awaiting discovery? Or did he rather create something *new*? Something from *nothing*?

Niels Bohr, the Nobel Prize winning physicist, is reported to have said that if history had occurred without him, any scientific principle that he had happened to discover would simply have been discovered by somebody else; since they were out there waiting to be discovered. But had history occurred without *Shakespeare*, Bohr reputedly claimed, nobody would ever have written his Sonnets. The scientist discovers what's out there to be discovered. The author, by contrast, creates something wholly new.

I guess the Platonist simply has to say that Bohr was wrong. And perhaps he was. Scientific theories very often manifest the idiosyncrasies of the scientist. Moreover, perhaps the relationship between science and reality is too crudely captured by Bohr's picture, according to which crystal-clear laws of nature are out there waiting to be discovered, such that the identity and personality of the scientist has no tangible impact upon the science. Science is more human than that; more bound up with the language and the conceptual schemes that humans use to capture and explain the data.

Perhaps the only salient difference between scientific and artistic discovery is that there are so many *more* works of fiction to discover than there are actual and accurate laws of nature. Shakespeare might have numerous doppelgangers in various parallel universes, each one writing each Sonnet with one word (or letter) difference. In other words, the chances of any two people finding the exact same work of fiction is infinitesimally small, whereas we do sometimes find scientists stumbling upon the exact same theories independently of one another.

*Tatjana:* Authors sometimes talk about discovered qualities of their characters. But it seems like metaphorical talk to me.

What they seem to mean is that during the writing process, it occurred to them that a person with this set of characteristics may also have this surprising quality. You never hear authors talk about discovering a story, but if one did talk this way, I would most naturally interpret it as metaphorical talk as well.

Having said that, Michelangelo apparently once said about his sculptures: "The sculpture is already complete within the marble block, before I start my work. It is already there, I just have to chisel away the superfluous material."

*Sam:* I agree with you. I would tend to take this type of talk metaphorically too (although I'm not sure what to say about Michelangelo and his sculptures). Artists discover something that they've created had properties they didn't realize it would have, which then caused them to take the work in a slightly different direction. But still, it's creativity rather than discovery that seems to be the operative notion (most of the time). The Platonist, of course, has to resist this. She has to take "discovery" talk literally and "creativity" talk metaphorically!

The final worry had to do with forgery and plagiarism. But once again, the Platonist can bite the bullet and accept that our normal ways of talking are a little bit inaccurate. Just as *Animal Farm* isn't essentially satirical, but merely satirical relative to Orwell's discovery of it; and just as Orwell didn't create *Animal Farm* so much as *discover* it, the Platonist will find a new way of talking about plagiarism and forgery.

Alfred Lessing (1995) suggests that forgery and plagiarism are only *moral* defects. They're not an artistic impairment. They don't make a work of art any less good as a work of art. If George Orwell really had copied *Animal Farm* from someone else, that fact wouldn't constitute any sort of literary impairment in the work of fiction. It would merely constitute a dark episode in the biography of George Orwell.

*Tatjana:* But if works are just sets of sentences, and authors just discover them, when does something count as plagiarism at all? After all, both authors can claim that they made exactly the same discovery. It's something that can happen in science. It's difficult to prove that something is plagiarism rather than just coincidence in science, I imagine.

My point is that describing fiction-making as discovering makes it difficult to assign blame to the alleged forger, simply because the forger can rather easily claim that they discovered the set of sentences at the same time. But this is decisively not what we think when we read a novel that is (near) identical to another one.

*Sam:* But I think that that's the point. What you're articulating here is both the third objection to Platonism, and Lessing's response. The third objection is that Platonism isn't able to locate plagiarism as a defect in the work of art itself. After all, and as you say, "if works are just sets of sentence and authors just discover them" then the work itself can't be accused of containing plagiarism.

According to the opponents of Platonism this is an absurd consequence because we do tend to think that plagiarism is an artistic fault. A work that is largely plagiarized is less good a work for being largely plagiarized. But Lessing's response is just to say, no! It's not the work that's guilty of containing plagiarism – it's the author who's guilty of passing something off as his own discovery when he or she actually copied it (or much of it) from someone else. The defect is not in the work, but in the artist.

Of course, the artist can claim that any likeness to other works is just coincidence. And if that can be demonstrated to our satisfaction then we rescind the accusation. Although, if the coincidence looks too fluky, we're unlikely to believe them.

If you're uncomfortable with any of these responses to these three worries, then you might want to gun for an alternative theory.

## Performance Theory

David Davies argues that a work of fiction is actually, believe it or not, an historical event (Davies, 2004). Of course, there is no historical event in which certain animals got together to overthrow their farmers only to be subjugated under the tyranny of the pigs. But there *is* an historical event in which a certain George Orwell sat down (presumably over multiple sittings) to write certain words in a certain order.

According to Davies, *that* historical event – which he calls a "generative performance" – is the thing we're talking about when we talk about *Animal Farm* as a work of fiction.

Think about it. What is it that you appreciate when you behold a work of art or literature, if not the creator's creative *activity* – her brushwork, her appreciation of light, or her way with words? What you're appreciating when you appreciate a work of art is a *generative performance* of some creator or other.

But what, exactly, is an *event*? Well, there are various philosophical theories about that. But, events are things that happen in *time*. So, you might think, one of the things that makes an event what it is – is the precise time, or stretch of time, over which it occurred. An event is something like a localized slice of the time-line. But, if that's the case, and if *Animal Farm* just is the event of Orwell's writing (or typing), then he couldn't have written it one day earlier or one day later without it being a different event (given its different location on the time-line) and therefore a completely different work. That seems wrong.

To avoid this problem, Davies postulates a special class of event, which he calls "doings" or "happenings" (Davies, 2004, pp. 116, 167–178). There has been some complicated debate among philosophers as to exactly what Davies meant by this distinction (see, for example, Dilworth, 2005). I happen to think that Davies' basic point, or something like it, can be explained after a brief detour through something called counterpart theory.

When you think about *me*, you think about a particular person in the actual universe. The guy who's writing these words. But you're not bound to think about how I *actually* am. You can also think about the sort of person I *could* have been, and also, the things that I *couldn't* have been.

One way of thinking about what we're doing when we're talking about all the things I might have been, is to imagine that there are lots of alternate universes out there. When you ask whether I could have been a dentist, for example, you're asking whether there's any universe out there, among all of those alternative universes, in which I have a counterpart who actually *is* a dentist. And, I suppose, what it would take to be a counterpart of *me*, is to be a lot like me, and for there to be nobody else in the universe in question who's as like me.

So, in some universes I have no counterpart, because nothing in them is enough like me. In other universes – such as the world of Sams (where everyone is just like me) – I have no counterpart because there is no single winning candidate among the people there for being the *most* like me.

If I could have been a dentist, it means that there is some universe somewhere where I do have a counterpart who's a dentist.

When you say that I couldn't have been a fish, you mean that there is no universe in which there's something that really qualifies as being a fish that's also sufficiently like me to count as being my counterpart.

David Lewis, a philosopher we'll repeatedly meet in this book, believes in the existence of all of these possible worlds and all of these counterparts. As far as he's concerned each of those possible worlds is a concrete universe, and each of those counterparts are real people (Lewis, 1986). But, even if you just take it as a figure of speech, it can be a useful way of describing what we're doing when we're thinking about how things might (and might not) have been; that there are multiple possible worlds, and that we have counterparts in them.

You'll notice that our definition of a counterpart is a little bit fuzzy. To be your counterpart, something needs to be the single most similar being to you, in its universe. But, even if it *is* the single most similar being to you, it also needs to be *sufficiently* similar in and of itself. But what does that mean? How similar is sufficiently similar? There's no clear answer. David Lewis argues that this fuzziness is a good thing.

In some conversations we want to be really strict and only accept very similar beings as counterparts. For example, we might be having a serious conversation about what careers you'd like to consider pursuing. In those conversations, to think about counterparts who are much taller or shorter than you are might be a wasteful distraction since there are some jobs for which you, as you actually are in the actual world, are simply too short or too tall (for example). Accordingly, in that conversation, you'll want to be pretty strict about how similar a counterpart needs to be to you.

But, we can have more imaginative conversations where we dream about what we'd do if we were basketball players in the NBA, and in those conversations, it might be worthwhile considering counterparts who are much taller than you actually are. And thus, in that conversation, you'd do well to be more liberal as to what counts as sufficiently similar.

We can even go wild and imagine what your life would be like if only you had been a dolphin – or indeed, to contradict what we said moments ago, a *fish*. In those sorts of conversations, we go extremely liberal in terms of the beings that we're willing to count as your counterparts. The fuzziness here simply tracks the fact that what we're willing to count as a counterpart varies from conversation to conversation.

Now … back to Davies and his distinction between (1) events and (2) happenings/doings. An event is something that couldn't have happened sooner or later, because its exact position in time is written into its identity. A *doing* or a *happening*, by contrast, and as I understand Davies, is just the very same slice of space-time that we'd normally call an event, but, by calling it a "doing" or a "happening", we're saying that we're willing to be a little more fast and loose as to what we'd accept as a counterpart.

Davies discusses the sinking of the *Titanic* (Davies, 2004, p. 171). Construed as an *event*, it couldn't have happened any sooner or any later than it actually did. If you have a very similar event in a different possible world, which happens sooner or later, in its own world's history than the sinking of the *Titanic* happened in our world's history, then you're thinking of a *different* event. That's how events work. Events only allow for counterparts in other possible histories that occur at exactly the same time.

But, Davies continues, if you think of the sinking of the *Titanic* as a *happening* (or as a *doing*, which means the same thing), rather than as an *event*, then you're thinking of something like the sinking of a ship *called* the *Titanic* by an iceberg on that ship's maiden voyage across the Atlantic. This happening would have been the same happening had it happened a little earlier or little later than it actually did, so long as "other general features of early-twentieth-century history are held constant" (ibid.).

Likewise, Davies will say, George Orwell's writing of *Animal Farm* should be thought of, not as an event, but as a *doing*. Thought of that way, we become a little more liberal than we do when we think about *events*. This means that it would be identified as the very same *doing*, and therefore as the very same work of literature, even had it happened slightly earlier, or slightly later, in the history of the world.

Some *doings* will allow for more liberal, and some doings will allow for less liberal, construals of the counterpart relation. Let me explain. My childhood drawing of a daffodil would be much the same work of art set into a very different history. Had Margaret Thatcher been elected dictator for life of the United Kingdom when I was drawing it, it wouldn't have made much difference to my drawing. I probably wouldn't have noticed! Andy Warhol's *Brillo Pads*, by contrast, couldn't really be understood for the work of art that it is had it occurred at a very different juncture in the history of art.

But that's fine, depending on the work of art in question, and depending upon our interests, we can be more or less strict as to what we would count as a counterpart, and thus, we can be more or less strict as to what exactly we mean by a *doing*, in a given context.

**Performance Theory**

A work of fiction is a historical *doing* in which a person (or a group of people) set down, upon a manuscript or script, or simply utter for the first time, a set of sentences in an order (or some people perform some other meaningful activity).

## Problems with Performance Theory

What should we make of this theory? On the one hand, it gets a lot right. It allows that George Orwell really was the creator of *Animal Farm*. He is the person who performed the action in question.

It allows that *Animal Farm* is essentially an anti-Stalinist satire, since any *doing* that generates the same words in a different world history that knew no Stalinism would doubtful count as a counterpart of the doing in question.

The copy of *Animal Farm* on your bookshelf is not the work itself. The book is a "product" of a "process". The process (i.e. the writing of the book) is the work of art itself. This means we can explain what forgery is. A forgery is the product of a certain sort of deceitful process.

In these ways, performance theory has answered all of the questions with which Platonism struggles.

Moreover, as Davies would urge, the theory gets right what it is that we really value when we value a work of fiction. We value what it is that the author *did*.

The process is the work of art. The product (i.e. the book, or the canvas with painting on it) is just what the work has left behind. The product is valuable only to the extent that it gives us access to the process – like a window onto the past.

But is that right? Are we only ever interested, when we're actually appreciating the work as a work of art, in the historical process that gave birth to it? Imagine that I know nothing about art history, cannot appreciate a deft brush stroke, nor have any knowledge of the sorts of processes that gave rise to the painting before me. Perhaps all I'm appreciating is the form of the thing; the pretty Platonic pictorial-structure; just as the musical ignoramus may only be appreciating the sonic structure of a musical work, rather than its achievement, or its place in musical history. Uncouth as I am, I'm still appreciating a work of art, am I not?

So too, the reader of *Animal Farm* may have little appreciation for who George Orwell was and what he achieved. She may simply be engrossed in the *story*. But can't we say that, in all her naivety, she's still enjoying, engaging with, and appreciating the work of fiction, even if she doesn't care to know anything about its author or the events that gave rise to the words on the page? We'd hope that she'd recognize its message about totalitarianism, but she might be pretty ignorant about the particular Russian history to which it originally applied.

These reflections might lead you to think that, for all its strengths, Davies has still misidentified the sort of thing that a work of fiction actually is.

*Tatjana:* I wonder whether I can appreciate the process even if I know nothing about who the author is, how they wrote it, and in which context. I have a rough idea of what the writing process is, is this not sufficient? I know some writing has been going on. I might not be able to fully appreciate the work without knowing more details about the process, but what I am clumsily appreciating is still the work of fiction (the process of writing it).

On the other hand, there are several actions we perform relative to a work that just don't fit well when we think of the work as a process. We criticize, cite, admire, translate, categorize … It just doesn't seem plausible that we are only talking about a process. But it could be the process plus the abstract end result?

*Sam:* Davies, I'm pretty sure, would insist that what you're really criticizing, and admiring, and even categorizing, is the performance of the writer. But, I think your examples of citing and translating are going to put more pressure on him. I also think your suggested amendment is a good one. Someone could say that the work of art is something like the process plus the product; some combination of the two. In fact, that's the general spirit of the next suggestion we're going to explore.

One benefit of your suggestion is that it explains the difference between the real *Mona Lisa* and your home-made identical copy. Both of them give me a window onto what it was that Leonardo Da Vinci did (even if one window is, so to speak, more direct). But only one of the paintings is the actual product of that performance.

Let's look at one more alternative theory.

## Impure Platonism

Philosophers are keen on distinguishing between concrete beings and abstract beings (if, indeed, you believe that abstract things actually exist). What exactly do we mean by "concrete" and what do we mean by "abstract"? For our purposes, we won't go far wrong if we define these terms as follows:

- **Concrete:** An entity is concrete if it is located somewhere in space and/or if it can enter into causal relations (and what that means is that it can be part of the cause of some effect, or it can be affected by some cause, or other). A single concrete entity is called a *concretum*. In the plural, they can be described as *concreta*.
- **Abstract:** An entity is abstract if and only if it isn't concrete. A single abstract entity is called an *abstractum*. In the plural, they can be described as *abstracta*.

If you think that *Animal Farm* is some sort of strange physical object built up out of all of its copies (past, present, and future), or if you think that *Animal Farm* is some sort of historical event (a doing of George Orwell), then you're thinking that *Animal Farm* is a concretum. If, with the Platonists, you think that *Animal Farm* is some sort of abstract structure, something like an ordered set of sentences, then you're thinking that *Animal Farm* is an abstractum.

Each of the theories we've discussed has faced various problems. Perhaps what we need to do is to rethink the divide between the concrete and the abstract and somehow open up a third category between the two. This is what Amie Thomasson has argued, and this is how she put the point (Thomasson, 1999, p. 90):

> [W]orks of literature and music seem to fall between the cracks of traditional category systems: accommodating them will require acknowledging intervening categories for temporally determined, dependent abstracta: abstract artifacts created by human intentional activities.

What she means is that a work of fiction has certain features that make it seem concrete – for example, it doesn't exist before its author wrote it; and so it was caused to come into being – that's the sort of thing that makes a being concrete. On the other hand, we want to say that works of fiction are not located in space, and that they can't be causally interacted with once they've come to exist – at least, not in quite the way that concrete entities tend to allow for. Sure, you could erase all of the copies of *Animal Farm*, and once all memory of the exact set of sentences had been forgotten, there's a sense in which you would have causally brought about its destruction. You can't do that to normal abstract beings. Nothing could ever obliterate the number 7. But, on the other hand, you can't bump into *Animal Farm*, and you can only have an effect over it by manipulating its *copies*; the work itself is somehow beyond the material world. That makes it sound abstract. In short, our two categories – concrete and abstract – might have to become three in the following way:

- **Concreta:** An entity is concrete if it is located somewhere in space and time and/or if it can enter directly into causal relations.
- **Impure abstracta:** An entity is an impure abstractum if and only if: (a) it isn't located in space, (b) its existence *does* have a beginning in time, and (b) its existence depends upon the existence of certain concreta. The only way to causally manipulate an impure abstractum would be to do so indirectly, via the concreta upon which it depends for its existence.
- **Abstracta:** An entity is abstract if and only if it is neither a concretum nor an impure abstractum.

One way to flesh out the impure abstracta theory, inspired by the work of Jerrold Levinson (1990), looks like this. For any collection of objects, we can talk about the set which contains them. Think, for example, of all red objects. You've just (mentally) gathered together the set of red objects. All of the members of that set are going to be concrete objects. You can't be red if you're not concrete. On the other hand, the set itself – unless you adopt that strange theory from earlier on, in this chapter, according to which a set is located in space and time, spread out wherever its members are – isn't something that's concrete. The set itself isn't located anywhere, nor can it be directly interacted with. The set itself is an impure-abstractum.

Why? Well, it's not concrete, but it *does* depend for its existence upon concreta. If there was nothing red, it wouldn't exist. And it can't be said to have existed before there were red things. Maybe a work of literature is something like that. Maybe it's a set, but some of its members are concrete, and that makes it an impure abstractum.

Okay, so *Animal Farm* is a set. But what's *in* this set? Well, we should put the ordered set of English sentences that make up the story in the set. That means that one of the members of this set, is itself a set. Failure to include that set – the set of English sentences that make up the story – in the actual make-up of the work of fiction is what made us suspicious of the performance theory. We don't just admire Orwell's *performance*. We admire the story itself!

But, then again we should also put Orwell's historical doing into the set. That's what's going to tether this work of art to the concrete realm of real history. The English sentences existed before Stalin, and would have existed even without Stalin. But Orwell's performance of writing was a direct response to Stalin. By putting that performance (that *doing*) into the set itself, alongside the ordered English sentences, we do justice to the fact that *Animal Farm* couldn't have existed without being a response to Stalin.

So, there we have it: *Animal Farm* is a set. It has two members: (1) an ordered set of English sentences, and (2) George Orwell's literary doing, in which he used those sentences in that order to tell a story. Since the second member of this set is a concrete event, the set itself is an impure abstractum.

**Impure Platonism**

A work of fiction is an impure abstractum. When the fiction is literary rather than, say, pictorial, it will be a set with two members: (1) a set of sentences in an order, and (2) an historical *doing* in which an author (or some authors) use those sentences, in that order, to tell a story.

## Problems with Impure Platonism

Christy Mag Uidhir (2013, ch. 4) tells us that he's responsible for there being two doghouses in his backyard. He created them. It seems to follow that, in addition to building the doghouses, he also brought "the set of dog houses in his backyard" into existence. Before him, there were no doghouses in his backyard. Therefore there was no "set of doghouses in his backyard" to speak of.

Moreover, Mag Uidhir is responsible for that set having a prime number of members. Had he built one more, it would have had three members. Three isn't prime. Had he built one less, it would have had only one member, and – depending on how strict your definition of a prime number – one isn't prime either.

But, of course, it doesn't follow that Mag Uidhir made the number two a prime number! That would be a ridiculous claim.

*Tatjana:* I agree that would be a ridiculous claim! But I don't quite see why this should follow from the claim that he brought the set of dog houses in his backyard into existence. Could you please explain this a bit more?

*Sam:* It's good that you agree that it's a ridiculous claim. And it isn't supposed to follow from the fact that he brought the set into existence.

But, according to Mag Uidhir, as I hope to explain, impure Platonism seems to treat certain properties as if they were created by artists, when they clearly weren't. He's going to say that impure Platonism is committed to claims that are equally ridiculous as is the claim that Mag Udhir made the number 2 prime, simply by causing a set to exist with two members.

If you think that that's ridiculous, and Mag Uidhir wants you to think that that's ridiculous, then you're ultimately – he hopes – going to have to conclude that impure Platonism is ridiculous too!

Mag Uidhir thinks that impure Platonism is bound to make an analogously ridiculous claim about the power of artists.

Take a sonata by Beethoven. Impure Platonism is going to regard it as a set that contains, as its members, (1) a particular sonic structure, and (2) Beethoven's historical act (his *doing*) of indicating that sonic structure, and writing it down. This set was brought into existence by Beethoven, just as the set of doghouses in Mag Uidhir's yard was brought into existence by Mag Uidhir.

Beethoven is responsible for the existence of his Sonata. It is a set. It contains a sonic structure. That sonic structure is dazzlingly beautiful. But Beethoven isn't responsible for the dazzling beauty of the sonic structure in question, even if he *is* responsible for the existence of the set that it joins.

*Tatjana:* Isn't this like arguing as follows:

1 Margot and Juan are responsible for the existence of Lana.
2 Lana is a successful engineer; therefore,
3 Margot and Juan are responsible for Lana's success.

I think we can agree that 3 is false, and this argument has nothing to do with sets. I'm happy to agree that Margot and Juan brought someone into existence who is a successful engineer. But what makes Lana successful are not their parents or what they have done. Similarly, Beethoven brought something dazzling beautiful into existence but what makes it dazzling beautiful is not Beethoven or him creating it.

*Sam:* Right. But, I take it that one of the ambitions of impure Platonism is to be able to attribute the dazzling beauty to Beethoven, somehow. Platonism can't do this, because Beethoven merely discovered the beauty. He didn't make it. Impure Platonism, as Mag Udhir understands it, was designed precisely to allow for us to see Beethoven as somehow responsible for the beauty. Mag Udhir thinks it fails in this central ambition. Beethoven is no more responsible for the beauty of his Sonata than Mag Udhir is responsible for the number 2 being prime. That's what Mag Udhir claims.

On the other hand, I agree with you, Tatjana. I think that it's enough for the impure Platonist to respond: "Yeah, but what we've been able to do, which the Platonist can't do, is to make sense of the claim that Beethoven actually created something beautiful. He did! Even if he didn't create the beauty of the thing that he created!"

Beethoven is no more responsible for the beauty of the sonic structure than Mag Uidhir is responsible for the fact that the number 2, which just happens to be the amount of members had by his set of doghouses, is *prime*. Sure, Mag Uidhir is responsible for the set having that number of members, but he's not responsible for the properties that that number has.

George Orwell might be responsible for the choice of sentences that *Animal Farm* contains, but he is not responsible for their being a biting critique of Stalinism. They had that property (at least they did by that point in history) all on their own.

The reason that the impure Platonist fought so hard to make sense of artists creating their art works – something that pure Platonism fails to respect – was to make artists responsible for various *qualities* of their artworks. Mag Uidhir's point is this: impure sets can be brought into existence by human beings, but that doesn't help us to do justice to our pre-philosophical notion of artistic and literary creativity.

If we wanted to make Beethoven responsible for the dazzling beauty of his sonatas, and Orwell for the biting satire of his prose, impure Platonism has failed us.

I would respond to Mag Uidhir as follows. No one ever meant to claim that Beethoven is responsible for making the sonic structure of his composition beautiful. They only claim that he is responsible for creating a sonata *with* a beautiful sonic structure. That's enough.

*Tatjana:* Agreed!

*Sam:* Great! I think this just unpacks, basically, the little discussion we had previously.

Orwell wrote *Animal Farm*, and thus he's responsible for creating a novel with the properties that it has. Once again: that's enough. We *have* done justice to what we're trying to praise when we praise the creativity of an artist. But our worries aren't over.

Ben Caplan and Carl Matheson raise a concern with impure Platonism (Caplan & Matheson 2004). If we think of *Animal Farm* as a set that contains (1) an ordered set of English sentences and (2) an historical doing, then yes, the set comes to exist only at a certain point in time – namely, at the point at which the act of writing began – but won't it also *cease to exist* as soon as Orwell finished his work? Does *Animal Farm* no longer exist?

Now, we *could* argue that impure sets exist for as long as they have any members *remaining*, and since one of the members of our set is completely abstract (i.e. the ordered set of sentences), *Animal Farm* is a set that will continue to exist forever.

But, if that's the case, then we seem to have undone the advantage we had sought over pure Platonism. The advantage was that impure sets can come into existence; they can be created by human beings. But, if one member of the set's existing is enough for the set to exist, then the set in question will always exist. It's existed forever (or at least for as long as the relevant English words have existed). Orwell didn't bring it into being.

*Tatjana:* But doesn't the *doing* have to happen at some point for there to be a novel? So, no novel without a doing but once the doing has been done, the set that consists of it and the set of sentences keep it in existence.

*Sam:* Yes, I think that's a legitimate response to Caplan and Matheson. But there are lots of complicated questions in the background here about the existence of sets, and also about the philosophy of time.

You might think that, before the *doing*, the set can't exist because one of its members has never existed at all, and that after the doing has happened, the set can continue to exist, even though the doing no longer exists, because, at the very least, the doing – so to speak – exists in the past.

But, if a member of a set existing in the past is enough for the set to exist, then why isn't its existing in the *future* enough for a set to exist? And, if existing in the future is enough for a set to exist, then every work of art that ever will be created already exists.

Now, your attempt to escape this conclusion, I think, requires an asymmetrical conception of time, according to which past things really do exist (perhaps in some place called, "the past") – such that sets (some or all of) whose members are in the past, can continue to exist; but that future things don't exist (perhaps because there is

> no place called "the future"; the future doesn't exist), such that sets cannot exist if any of their members are wholly in the future! This asymmetrical theory of time is known as the *Growing Block theory* of time. But some people, called *eternalists*, think that all times already exist. The future is as real as the past. If you're an eternalist, then Caplan and Matheson's concern will have real bite to it. If you're an eternalist, future things exist in the future, just as past things exist in the past. So, if members existing in the past is enough to give sets existence in the present, then members existing in the future should be sufficient to give sets existence in the present too. This is why philosophy of fiction is so awesome, but also why it's so hard. It connects to so many different sub-fields of philosophy.

Caplan and Matheson point out that there are ways to escape the problem. Take the sentences out of the set. Deny that they're a part of *Animal Farm*. Likewise, take the sonic structure out of the sonata. Deny that they're a part of Beethoven's work of art. Instead, say that *Animal Farm* is the set that contains Orwell's acts of writing, in addition, not to some set of words, but to every copy ever made of the work. Likewise, say that the sonata is a set that contains Beethoven's act of writing, in addition, not to a sonic structure, but to every copy and performance ever made of the work. A set need only exist for as long as any of its members do. This way, a work of art will not exist *before* it was written, but it also won't disappear as soon as the writing of it has finished!

But problems remain. Do we really want to banish the actual words of the story from the object itself? Do we really want to banish the notes from the sonata? Aren't we ejecting the very thing that we so often most admire about works of art? Haven't we stumbled back into the problem that faces the performance theory? On that theory, remember, we can't ever appreciate a *story* when we appreciate *Animal Farm*. We can only appreciate something that George Orwell did.

Now, some impure Platonists would deny that *Animal Farm* is a set at all. They'd just say that it's a *thing*. It's a thing that came to exist when George Orwell started writing. It has words associated with it, of course – but the work isn't a *set*, and so those words are not *members* of it, even if they might be *essentially* associated with it. It's just a thing that's kind of abstract but still dependent for its existence on certain concrete facts.

I have some sympathy with this view, but it might be accused of being a little mysterious. What is *Animal Farm*, you may ask, and all we're saying in response is that it's some sort of thing that's not quite concrete and not quite abstract, that it's not a set, and that it doesn't have members; that it's a cultural artefact, with words somehow essentially stuck on to it. It comes into existence when writers write and continues to exist for as long as copies of the work, or memories of it, remain. Despite my sympathy for this view, if you feel that you haven't actually received an *answer* to your question, I have some sympathy for you too.

## The Disappointing Truth

Here's my opinion, just in case you're interested.

I don't think that there is any single thing called *Animal Farm*. I'm sorry to have hidden it until now. I think the whole question of this chapter is a little bit misguided. The question itself assumes that, for any work of literature, there exists some single thing that we can identify as *the work itself*. I don't think that's true.

I think that there are lots of different entities that are relevant to our discussion of *Animal Farm*, and – depending upon what we happen to be interested in, at any given moment – any one of those entities might be the entity we're talking about when we claim to be talking about *the work of fiction itself*.

Sometimes we're merely interested in coming to an uneducated or decontextualized appreciation of the content of a work of art or literature – "Gosh this work is beautiful". In those situations the Platonist is often right. The object of our interest is likely the pictorial form, or the sonic structure, or a set of words.

Sometimes we're interested in the work as a cultural phenomenon – "This work is a national treasure", and then I think the impure Platonist is right – we are dealing with something that's kind of abstract, which has a life beyond the activities of its creators, but which nonetheless depends for its existence on them, among other things (like the continued existence of copies of the work).

Sometimes we're concerned with the physical work: "Help me lift this statue, I need to move it out of the way!"

Finally, sometimes, if we're interested in the achievement of the work, or in coming to an educated appreciation of it, and its place in art history, the object of our interest will be the generative performance of the artist.

In fact, just to show you how deep the ambiguity runs, and how many different objects there are, any one of which can sometimes legitimately claim to be *the work of fiction*, consider the ordered set of English sentences that make up *Animal Farm*.

If you're interested in the book's use of the English language, then that set might be your focus. But what happens if you read the book via a Latvian translation? Then you won't be relating to the work as a set of English sentences. Are you reading the same book?

Perhaps, in such situations, you're relating to the book as an ordered set of *propositions*. Propositions are the meanings of sentences. But it's not just sentence meanings that you appreciate, even if you're reading a translation. You also appreciate the way in which those meanings have been expressed.

Take the following two sentences, for example:

- "It ain't half hot in here."
- "The temperature in here is high."

Each sentence seems to express the same proposition. But they do so with all sorts of difference in tone and style.

When a translator translates a work, she tries not merely to swap sentences of the original text with sentences in a different language that merely express the same proposition. She's also trying to capture something of the tone and style of the original sentences with her choice of translation.

Perhaps there exists something called a *translation relation* that holds between sentences when they do more than merely express the same proposition. The translation relation holds between two sentences, in a given context, if they both express the same proposition, in that context, with sufficiently similar style and tone.

So, perhaps, when you appreciate *Animal Farm* through a translation, you're relating to the work as a set of *translation relations*.

Sometimes you're interested in the use of the English language. Sometimes you're interested in the propositions expressed. Sometimes you're interested in what a particular author did. Sometimes you're interested in a cultural phenomenon. All of these things deserve, in different circumstances, to be called *the work of fiction* (I argue for this conclusion at greater length in Lebens 2015).

But even if I'm right, and the question of this chapter was somehow misguided, I think our survey of possible answers has still been extremely productive. Even if there's no single thing that gets to be called the work of fiction, all of the theories that we've seen will have helped us to discover certain sorts of objects.

*Tatjana:* I find this pretty unsatisfying but I admit that I am the kind of person who always wants definite answers.

So, mightn't it be possible that a work of fiction is all of what you describe above and that when we talk about its cultural value, its beauty, or its physicality, we are talking merely about particular aspects/part of the work?

Just like we are talking about different aspects or parts of a person when we describe them as tall, kind, or a member of the poodle club. (Then again, what is a person, right?)

*Sam:* Well, first of all, sometimes the truth is unsatisfying! But, more to the point, I don't see what's added, by constructing some extra entity, made up of all of the varied entities we've discussed, such that each way of talking about *Animal Farm* can be construed as talking about one of its varied aspects. I suppose it's something we *could* do. I suppose it has a certain theoretical virtue in that it groups all of our various ways of talking about *Animal Farm* together, and making them all, in some respect, about the same object, even if only by being about different parts of that object. On the other hand, it comes at the theoretical cost of requiring more objects, not just all of the entities I've described in this chapter, but also, the extra entity that, together, they are part of.

On the other other hand, I suppose you might think that this entity already exists, for free – especially if you subscribe to a certain view in mereology (the study of parts and wholes), according to which whenever you have two entities, there always exist a third entity, the one that the two entities comprise. But that's a somewhat wacky view (however widely held it may be among philosophers). On this view, it turns out that because your ear exists, and my nose exists, then there exists a third object called ear-nose, or something like that, whose parts – thankfully for both of us, I guess – are spread out very widely in space, but which exists in its own right, in addition to your nose and my ear. Or perhaps you're just thinking of a set. Sets exist pretty much for free. As soon as you have some objects, there exists the set of those objects. But we've discussed some problems that emerge for thinking of works of art as it they're sets.

So, there are lots of different considerations to weight up here. I guess I'll leave it to our readers to draw their own conclusions, based on their own philosophical sensibilities!

Perhaps all of those objects, even if none of them is the one and only thing that gets to be called *the work of fiction*, are sometimes what we're interested in when we engage with, appreciate, criticize, and otherwise think about fiction. And thus this search wasn't futile. It helped us to appreciate better the varied things that we appreciate when we appreciate fiction!

## Works Cited

Caplan, B. & Matheson, C. (2004) Can a Musical Work Be Created? *British Journal of Aesthetics*, 44(2): 113–134.

Davies, D. (2004) *Art as Performance*. Malden, MA: Blackwell.

Dilworth, J. (2005) Review of David Davies, *Art as Performance*. *The Journal of Aesthetics and Art Criticism*, 63(1): 77–80.

Lebens, S. (2015) Would this Paper Exist if I Hadn't Written it? *Philosophical Studies*, 172: 3059–3080.

Lessing, A. (1995) What Is Wrong with a Forgery? In A. Neil & A. Ridley (eds), *Arguing about Art*. New York: McGraw-Hill.

Levinson, J. (1990) *Music, Art and Metaphysics*. Ithaca, NY: Cornell University Press.
Lewis, D. (1986) *On the Plurality of Worlds*. Oxford: Blackwell.
Maddy, P. (1992) *Realism in Mathematics*. Oxford: Clarendon Press.
Mag Uidhir, C. (2013) *Art and Art-Attempts*. Oxford: Oxford University Press.
Thomasson, A. (1999) *Fiction and Metaphysics*. Cambridge: Cambridge University Press.
Wolterstorff, N. (1991) Review of *An Ontology of Art*. *The Journal of Aesthetics and Art Criticism*, 49(1), 75–77.

## Further Reading

Alward, P. (2004) The Spoken Work. *The Journal of Aesthetics and Art Criticism* 62(4): 331–337.
Cameron, R. P. (2008) There are No Things that Are Musical Works. *The British Journal of Aesthetics*, 48(3): 295–314.
Cox, R. (1985) Are Musical Works Discovered? *The Journal of Aesthetics and Art Criticism*, 43(4): 367–374.
Currie, G. (1989) *An Ontology of Art*. London: Macmillan.
Dodd, J. (2007) *Works of Music: An Essay in Ontology*. Oxford: Oxford University Press.
Goodman, N. & Elgin C. Z. (1986) Interpretation and Identity: Can the Work Survive the World? *Critical Inquiry*, 12(3): 564–576.
Hick, D. H. (2011) Toward an Ontology of Authored Works. *The British Journal of Aesthetics*, 51(2): 185–199.
Lamarque, P. (2010) *Work and Object*. Oxford: Oxford University Press.
Mag Uidhir, C., (ed.). (2012) *Art & Abstract Objects*. Oxford: Oxford University Press.
Rohrbaugh, G. (2003) Artworks as Historical Individuals. *The European Journal of Philosophy*, 11(2): 177–205.
Walters, L. (2013) Repeatable Artworks as Created Types. *The British Journal of Aesthetics*, 53(4): 461–477.
Wollheim, R. (1980) *Art and its Objects: An Introduction to Aesthetics*. New York: Harper & Row.
Wolterstorff, N. (1980) *Works and Worlds of Art*. Oxford: Clarendon Press.

Chapter 3

# What Are Fictional Characters?

*Tatjana*

Fictional characters are awkward creatures. They are edgy women or shy boys, witty cats, or courageous wizards. They fall in love, suffer, get angry, feel lonely, or get lucky – just like we do.

But who has ever shook hands with Superman or had waffles for breakfast with *Parks and Recreation*'s Leslie Knope? No one, of course. Fictional characters are just not the kind of objects we can hang out with. Marvel's Jessica Jones or *Harry Potter*'s Hermione Granger don't live, eat, and breathe somewhere on planet earth. Neither could we find them in some remote corner of the galaxy. We won't ever be able to visit them, no matter how advanced our technology will become one day. And Hermione can't do much to you. She can't meet you for coffee, submit your assignments for you, or donate one of her kidneys to you. She can, at best, inspire you, upset you, or haunt you in your dreams. All in all, your relationship with Hermione is pretty asymmetric and rather one-sided.

But wait, we *can* shake hands with Superman – all we need to do is travel to LA to meet Superman outside the Chinese Theater in Hollywood. And surely someone who had breakfast with Amy Poehler could rightly shout out, "I had breakfast with Leslie Knope!" They couldn't be accused of lying.

Well, you can meet an actor *impersonating* Superman. But they won't be *the* Superman. The real Superman can fly, lift buses, and live on another planet without an oxygen mask. This should be an indicator.

*Sam:* Hold on a minute! You're making it sound as if there is a real Superman, even if we can't meet him!

*Amy:* I mean "real" as in "original". But, yes, I suppose there is at least some sense in which there is the real Superman and then there are many fakes. Anyone who wears the Superman costume but who cannot fly or lift a crowded bus with one hand is a fake, for sure.

*Sam:* Okay. I'll bear that in mind!

DOI: 10.4324/9781003126102-4

Now, Leslie Knope is a normal person, so Amy Poehler could well do most of the things that Leslie does. But it still wouldn't make Amy identical to Leslie. Amy is different from Leslie because Leslie originated in fiction. Leslie was created by Greg Daniels and Michael Schur through an act of imagining. Amy, however, was created by her parents (if it makes sense to say that parents create their children). A fictional character can never be identical to the actress who plays her. Their origins are fundamentally different. Fictional characters originate in fictional stories, while the actors playing them originate in nature.

If fictional characters originate in fiction, then real people or places mentioned in fictional works aren't fictional characters. Stories often take place in cities or countries we are familiar with. We might have located them with our finger on a map, or we might have paid them a visit. We might even inhabit the place mentioned in the novel, TV show, or film. Jessica Jones lives and works in New York City. Sherlock Holmes inhabits a flat on London's Baker Street. Leslie Knope visits Washington DC. These are not fictional places. It wouldn't make much sense to call them "fictional". If we did, then how could we distinguish the status of NYC, London, and Washington DC from the status of places like Pawnee, Krypton, or Atlantis?

Real people also sometimes immigrate into fictional worlds. Napoleon appears in *War and Peace*. Madeleine Albright has coffee with Leslie Knope in *Parks and Recreation*.

There is something funny about watching the real Madeleine Albright chatting with the fictional Leslie (played, of course, by the real Amy Poehler). But you get this sense of funny only when you realize that Albright is a real politician. If you thought that she was a fictional character, if you didn't know that the person on your screen was Albright, or you didn't know that there was a real politician called "Madeleine Albright", then the scene would be lost on you. You might even question the point of the scene. But if you realize that Leslie is talking to a real Former United States Secretary of State, the whole scene becomes an amusing intermezzo; a charming reminder that some fictional worlds are ways the world could have been.

*Sam:* Some have assumed that Madeleine Albright simply cannot enjoy beverages with a fictional person and that the scene you're reporting doesn't really contain Albright at all. Instead, it contains a fictional character who is a fictional representation of Albright, who just happens to be played by Albright as an actress. In the same way, I think that Napoleon really does appear in *War and Peace*. But what do you think?

*Tatjana:* I'm inclined to say that Madeleine Albright isn't really having coffee with Leslie. It just seems to me a somewhat loose way of talking about what happens on the TV show. I don't think we can have coffee with fictional characters because to do so, we would have to meet them and we simply can't. Albright was playing herself, but what this means is just that she appeared on the film set and made-believe that she was having coffee with fellow politician Leslie Knope. I'll return to this point later.

*Sam:* Just to be clear, I don't think that Albright *really* had coffee with Leslie. I think that it is true of Albright, in the fiction, that she had coffee with Leslie. Rather, what I would want to deny is that there exists some *further* thing, called "the fictional representation of Madeleine Albright" which had coffee with Leslie. I'd rather say that it was the *real* Albright, herself, who – in the fiction, but not in real life – had coffee with Leslie.

*Tatjana:* It seems to me that we are in agreement.

Here's something puzzling though: How come Madeleine Albright can enjoy beverages with Leslie Knope but you can't? Is there anything special about Albright that allows her but not the average Jane, Joe, or Jessie, to bump into fictional characters? That's a great question. To answer it, we must dig deeper into the question of what kinds of things fictional characters are.

## Ways the World Might Have Been

What are Harry Potter and Leslie Knope? What do they have in common with Lady Macbeth and SpongeBob SquarePants? They all seem to live in worlds not like our world. Some of these worlds are very similar to our world. Leslie's world of local politics in US America appears almost identical to our world. In fact, if you didn't know that *Parks and Recreation* is a mockumentary, you might watch the TV show thinking it was a *documentary*. But Leslie's world is not identical to our world. Our world doesn't contain a politician called "Leslie Knope" who obtained an honorary degree from IU Indiana Bloomington.

On 9 February 2016, IU Bloomington cleverly tweeted, after announcing a symposium on *Parks and Recreation in Public Health*: "Leslie Knope is not expected to attend." That's only funny if you know, and you know that IU knows, that Leslie isn't the kind of thing that could ever attend a real academic event in our world. Leslie's world is very similar to our world, to reality, if you will. Lady Macbeth's world of royalty and intrigues is still reasonably similar to our world, but not to the world we live in now. It's more like a stroll through an alternative history. But some of these worlds of fiction are very different from ours. SpongeBob's world of talking sea creatures and Hermione's world of wizards and demons is magically removed from our world. The idea that we could meet SpongeBob is clearly wilder than the proposition that we might meet Leslie. Still, neither of them inhabit the same world as we do.

Should we take talk about different worlds seriously? Is it possible that Leslie, Lady Macbeth, Hermione and SpongeBob live in different worlds, in parallel universes? Let's explore this idea. Some philosophers are drawn to the view that reality doesn't just contain our world – our earth, our galaxy, and other galaxies we could travel to if only we had the technology and enough time to make the long journey. These philosophers believe that there are possible worlds that are just as real as our actual world. Their view is called *modal realism*. Modal realist David Lewis, whom you'll remember from Chapter 2, thinks that possible worlds represent "ways things could have been" (Lewis, 1973, p. 84).

There are myriad ways things could have been. I could have scratched my nose before writing the previous sentence (but I didn't). Then the past would have been slightly different from how it actually is. This alternative world, in which I scratched my nose, is not the actual world. In the actual world, I didn't touch my face at all while writing that entire previous paragraph. But it certainly was a possibility. Setting aside questions of determinism and free will, it was possible for me to lift my hand, stretch out my index finger and scratch away. The modal realist will say, therefore, that there *is* a possible world in which I scratched my nose. And that possible world is just as real as this world in which I didn't.

Now, the possible world in which I scratched my nose but nothing else is different is almost identical to the actual world. But not every merely possible world is that similar to our actual world. There are possible worlds in which cats are blue and pigs fly. There are possible worlds in which you and I and everyone else walk on their hands all of the time.

*Sam:* Strictly speaking, a modal realist like David Lewis (i.e. someone who believes in the existence of these worlds as real places), would deny that you and I exist in other possible worlds. There are even possible worlds in which none of us, indeed, no human animals exist.

After all, we can only be in one place at a time, and these worlds are real places. Instead, they'd say that there are possible worlds in which you and I have "counterparts", people who are very similar to us (perhaps even practically identical to us), who walk on their hands all of the time.

*Tatjana:* Yes, strictly speaking, no one can exist in multiple different worlds. They are just copies of each other which bear very strong similarities. But I guess what's comforting is that your copy, your counterpart in a different possible world, has a very intimate relationship to you. It's more intimate than to any other creature in the actual world.

The world we live in is also a possible world – it's a way that things could have been ... and are! That's what makes our world special: it's the actual world. But it's only special from our viewpoint. Being actual is a matter of perspective. And, thus, for the blue cats in another possible world, their world is actual, from their point of view. You might have noticed it already, but "actual", in this context, is a technical term. It means that something is (or is part of) the possible world whose viewpoint we are considering. That's why the world you and I live in is the actual one, and that's why you and I are actual people.

For modal realists, there is a crucial difference between being real or existing and being actual. A vast number of things exist. Every possible world and all of its inhabitants do. But only a subset of real things are actual from a world's viewpoint. It's only our world and its inhabitants that are actual for us. And possible worlds are not only real but also concrete. It's not that they are just ideas in our heads. They are extended in space and time – just like our world. Their inhabitants are equally concrete. People in other possible worlds bump into each other just like we do in our world.

So, can we travel to these other possible worlds? Are they some faraway galaxies? Unfortunately not. Even far away galaxies still count as part of our world. They are located very far away from us, but we could, with sufficiently advanced technology and enough time, visit them. But we cannot ever visit other possible worlds. They are inaccessible for us to visit them.

*Sam:* Right. They are spatial and temporal, because they are concrete. But they are not spatially connected to our universe, so there's no way of getting to them from here.

*Tatjana:* Yes, exactly, they are not located anywhere from our world. It's not like you could travel 9.25 billion kilometres west and 2.1 billion kilometres north and there they are.

## Fictional Characters as Non-Actual Things

So, how does all this talk about possible worlds help us? One of the few philosophers who have applied modal realism explicitly to argue for the existence of fictional characters is Robert Howell. In one article (Howell, 1979), he skillfully develops the view, which is often called "non-actualism about fictional characters", or "non-actualism" for short (it's also sometimes called "possibilism about fictional characters"). In what follows, I won't be discussing Howell's particular view (though I strongly recommend reading his article). Instead, I'll guide you through the non-actualist view of fictional characters more generally.

There are some worlds in which things are exactly the way they are in the TV show, the play, or the novel. In some worlds, there is a politician named

"Leslie Knope" who is passionate about local government, who has an honorary degree from the University of Indiana and a friend called "Ron Swanson", and so on – whatever else *Parks and Recreation* tells us about Leslie. In other worlds, there is a wizard that goes by the name of "Hermione Granger" who is a very smart muggle and student at Hogwarts, and so on. In all of the possible worlds in which things are as the books describe them to be, Hermione is a real flesh-and-blood human being, she is just not actual from your and my viewpoint. Fictional characters are non-actual, concrete creatures, or things that genuinely exist, but inhabit other possible, and for us spatially inaccessible, worlds.

Why are we talking about "some possible worlds"? Why is there not just one world in which everything is the way the show describes? Possible worlds are complete. Think of our world. It's one among many possible worlds. In our world, for every possible state of affairs, it either occurs or it doesn't. You either have a cat named "Munchkin" or you don't. You either live on Mars or you don't. Serena Williams either is president of the United States or she isn't. Aeroplanes fly faster than paper planes or they don't. I either wear shoe size 6 or I don't. But fictional works are *descriptions* of possible worlds. And descriptions are notoriously incomplete. They don't tell you of every single state of affairs whether it obtains or not. *Parks and Recreation* doesn't inform you whether Leslie likes koala bears, or whether Ron's blood type is AB negative. The TV show keeps mum about Ben's favourite ice cream flavour, or whether Anne would rather holiday on the Seychelles or the Maldives. And there are various possible worlds that are entirely compatible with what the TV show shows us, but quite different from one another. There's a world in which Leslie likes koala bears, Ron's blood type is AB negative, and Anne likes the Maldives. There's another world in which Leslie hates koala bears, Ron's blood type is 0, and Anne dislikes all tropical islands equally. I hope you can see how there are many, many possible worlds in which things are as we are told they are on the TV show. And none of these possible worlds is clearly the one that the TV show presents to us.

Now, the incompleteness of fictions causes a challenge for the non-actualist. If there are many possible worlds in which things are as a fictional work describes them to be, then there are also many possible worlds in which there are Hermiones and Leslies who look and behave just the way *Harry Potter* or *Parks and Recreation* describe Hermione or Leslie. But which Leslie, in what possible world, is the one we are referring to when we say that Leslie is the heroine of a critically acclaimed 2010s' TV show? There are so many candidates! It could be any Leslie in any possible world in which things are exactly as the show depicts them. There doesn't seem to be one Leslie who is a better candidate than all of the other Leslies. One solution the non-actualist can offer at this point is to say that when we talk about Leslie Knope, we refer to all of the possible candidates simultaneously. This solution may seem a bit strange. After all, when I say that Leslie is a TV character, I seem to be talking about just one Leslie, not a multitude of Leslie-candidates. A more attractive answer to the challenge of multiple candidates may be to say that the name "Leslie Knope" refers indeterminately to one Leslie in one of the possible worlds that match the TV show's depiction. Either way, the non-actualist has options.

## What about Impossible Fictions?

Possible worlds are ways the world could have been. Harry and Hermione fight demons and dark wizards. That's improbable – the novels describe a world very different from ours – but it's not outright impossible. Some of the stories written by magical realist Jorge Luis Borges are great examples of metaphysical impossibilities. In *The Circular Ruins,* a wizard dreams up a man who, somehow, leaves the boundaries of the dream world and lives among real people. I find it difficult to even describe what is going on in that short story. Regardless, it seems that the dreamed-up man can either be a dream character or a real man. No one can walk out of a dream into reality. It's just not a way, not even a very unlikely way, that the world could have been. In *Alice in Wonderland,* the Cheshire Cat disappears in his entirety – teeth and lips included – before his smile disappears. That doesn't just seem improbable, it seems impossible: without mouths there are no smiles.

Since some fictions, like *The Circular Ruins* and *Alice in Wonderland,* describe impossibilities, there are no *possible* worlds in which things are as the fictions describe them to be. This poses a problem for the Non-Actualist who argues that fictional characters are creatures inhabiting other possible worlds. What is the Cheshire Cat if not a fictional character? Some philosophers, such as Graham Priest, resort to an obvious solution: the postulation of *im*possible worlds. If there are ways the world could have been, there are also ways the world could not have been. The view that there are impossible worlds faces its own challenges (in particular, challenges to do with philosophical logic), but it's not an *ad hoc* solution to the problem of impossible fictions. Philosophers who embrace impossible worlds usually have further independent reasons for doing so.

## Fictionalising You and Leslie

So, why can't you have breakfast waffles with Leslie? Enjoying meals is the kind of thing you can only do with actual people; that is, people who inhabit your actual world. Leslie can only have waffles with actual people, too, and from her point of view you are non-actual. That's why she has to make do with her actual friends Ron and Ben.

Some possible worlds don't merely contain Leslie, Ron and Ben, they also contain a counterpart of you. Counterparts of you are not quite you but they share a very intimate connection with you. There is certainly no one in the actual world you could ever be more closely related to than your other-worldly counterpart. Think of all of the Dr. Stranges in Sam Raimi's *Doctor Strange in the Universe of Madness* (2022) but without the possibility of their ever visiting or otherwise contacting other universes. What this means is that in some possible world there is now a counterpart of you having waffles with Leslie Knope. Still pretty exciting, isn't it?

But there is an even more exciting thought. What the non-actualist means by a fictional character is someone or something in *another* possible world, that an author in *our* world has written about. Being a fictional character is relative to a viewpoint. Now, given the vast number of possible possible worlds, there is also a possible world in which an author has written a story about you. Yes, that's right, the story is not about your counterpart, it's about you! Well, it's indeterminately about you and your counterparts. But you're in the mix! It's all about perspective from within a possible world. From the point of view of the author in this other possible world that you do not inhabit it's you who is non-actual. So we may tentatively conclude that we are all fictional characters from the viewpoints of some merely possible worlds. Still, fictional works are incomplete and therefore might refer to you or one of your many counterparts. But don't let this challenge to non-actualism dampen your excitement. (If you don't like the competition with your many counterparts, then hold your breath – Sam presents a different way in which we might be fictional characters in Chapter 12).

But there is a consequence of non-actualism that does not sit quite right with many people. The non-actualist can't agree that fictional characters originate in fictions. She doesn't believe that authors really create fictional characters. After all, in the possible worlds that contain Leslie Knope, Hermione Granger, or Jessica Jones, these characters are actual people. And people are born to other people; they are not created by ink and a pen. Rather, what the authors and creators of fictions do is to "fictionalise" Leslie, Hermione, or Jessica. They spun these non-actual people into stories; stories that describe other possible worlds. In the same way, the author who wrote a story about us in another possible world only fictionalised us; they didn't create you or me.

Non-actualism seems a rather attractive construct, at least once you buy into the whole idea that there are concrete possible worlds, competing with our actual world. But you might find the claim that authors do not create fictional characters implausible. Writing of Tolstoy's Anna Karenina, Howell acknowledges that there may be a problem for non-actualism:

> [The] most natural construal of [merely possible] worlds – as existing, with their contained objects, antecedently to the novelist's creative activities – [do not] happily mesh with our belief that Anna Karenina first comes into existence through Tolstoy's creative activities.
>
> (Howell, 1979, p. 279)

There are, after all, a handful of pre-theoretic beliefs we all have about fictional characters. And one of them is that authors create them. Indeed, this appears to be a very robust belief that most of us share. And what would be the alternative to genuine creation? If fictional characters exist independently of authors and film-makers then the most these can be said to do is to discover fictional characters. But talk of discovery seems to greatly undersell the creative achievement of fiction creators. Authors don't just discover their heroines and heroes; they make them from scratch.

As Peter van Inwagen, a defender of a view we will examine next, points out, denying authors the genuine creation of their fictional characters "makes the creativity of the novelist seem very like the 'creativity' of the flower-arranger" (van Inwagen, 1977, p. 308). Authors and film-makers use their imagination and originality to actively create fictional characters with unique personalities, appearances, backgrounds, and motivations. They make choices to shape each character and their role in the story, and this, to me, suggests active creation rather than passive discovery. Fiction-makers exercise artistic control over their characters, revising and refining them to suit the story's needs or achieve a desired effect. The uniqueness of individual fictional characters, which often distinguishes them from real people, seems a testament to the author's genuine creativity rather than sheer discovery.

Now, the artistic process is complex. Novelists and film-makers may sometimes describe it as a sort of discovery. They seem to be alluding to intuition or inspiration that feels external to them, or they may feel a sense of the characters "coming to life" and dictating their own actions. But I think their talk of discovery is rather metaphorical than literal. What fiction creators literally do is create fictional characters.

If you are suspicious of the idea that authors don't genuinely create fictional characters but only fictionalise or discover them, then you might find the next view exciting. Tellingly, the view is often called *fictional creationism*.

## Fictional Characters as Abstract Things

In Chapter 2, Sam showed that there is a difference between a novel (e.g. *The Colour Purple*) and a copy of the novel (e.g. the book I own). The copy is concrete. That's why I was able to place it on my shelf. The novel itself is not, and in that, according to some philosophers, it resembles Hermione Granger and Leslie Knope. If we cannot bump into Hermione or Leslie maybe it's not because they inhabit different possible worlds, but because they are not made of flesh and blood as we are. That's what the fictional creationist believes. If she were to paint a picture of the fictional character Lady Macbeth, and frame it, the result would look like this:

*Figure 3.1*

You don't see anything in the frame? Well, that's because Lady Macbeth is not extended in space, so the creationist will say. And she's not just not extended in space; unlike unextended points in space, she's also not *located* anywhere in space. Not in our space, not in another possible world's space – nowhere. This makes Lady Macbeth fundamentally different from you and me. It might seem like she shares important features with us – being a human, living on planet earth, speaking a language – but, in fact, she has none of these qualities. Indeed, she has more in common with the number 9, the legal principle *in dubio pro reo*, or the property *love* than she has in common with you and me: they are all abstract entities, we are not. Of course you can scribble "9" on a piece of paper, I can type "9" into my iPhone, and Kate Winslet can shout "9" from her rooftop. What your scribble, my typing, and Kate's shout have in common is that they are concrete manifestations of *the number 9*. These manifestations are concrete. But *the number 9*, of which they are manifestations, is abstract. It's not located anywhere in space. What about the actors who play Lady Macbeth on stage or in films, you may ask. Just like your scribble of "9" is not *the* number 9, but merely a concrete manifestation of it, an actress playing Lady Macbeth is not *the* Lady Macbeth, but merely a concrete manifestation of the fictional character.

The fictional character is nowhere to be found because she *is* nowhere. That's the kind of object she is – not located or extended in space. In other words, Lady Macbeth is abstract. I should say that there are many different understandings of what it means to be abstract in philosophy, but here all we require is that an object not be spatially located. To say that fictional characters are abstract is not the same as saying that they don't exist. The fictional creationist firmly believes that Hermione, Leslie, and Lady Macbeth are part of the "furniture of our world", to use a popular philosophical metaphor. Fictional characters exist as abstract objects.

What's more, the fictional creationist says, fictional characters are created by authors, story tellers, screenwriters, or whoever creates the fiction in which they originate. You might be surprised to hear that fictional creationism has many defenders among those philosophers who think about fiction. The details of their views differ. For example, Amy Thomasson describes fictional characters as cultural artefacts, created by human animals for human animals. As such, they belong to a group that contains such varied members as marriages, contracts, promises, and, indeed, fictions themselves. Peter van Inwagen thinks of fictional characters as theoretical entities of literary criticism. The differences are subtle here, and unless they truly matter to catching the general idea of fictional creationism, I will gloss over them.

## Properties of Abstract Objects

If Lady Macbeth is abstract then she's not only very different from you, she's also very different from how you imagine her. I bet you imagine her as a woman, dressed in elegant but somewhat outdated clothing. But fictional characters are just as unable to wear robes as numbers are unable to wear platform sneakers (and not just because platform sneakers are hideous, and, yes, I totally tried to pull them off during the 90s). Strictly speaking, we shouldn't refer to Lady Macbeth using the pronoun "she", because Lady Macbeth is not the kind of thing that *could* even have a gender. As an abstract object, Lady Macbeth is more like the number 9 than she is like Lady Gaga.[1]

Are fictional characters at all what we think they are? Yes. Some qualities we ascribe to fictional characters are entirely appropriate to ascribe to abstract objects. Here are some things Leslie Knope *is* besides being abstract: a fictional character, created by Greg Daniels and Michael Schur, the main character of *Parks and Recreation*, a character in a TV show, played by Amy Poehler, better known than Duarte "Boxer" Silva (a fictional character in the TV show *White Lines*), loved more than most real politicians. She's also a *person in Parks and Recreation*, but that does not make her a real person; it only makes her a fictional person.

In *Parks and Recreation,* Leslie is a politician, a friend, and a passionate citizen. In other words, Leslie is, according to *Parks and Recreation,* a politician, a friend, and a passionate citizen. To say this much does not mean that we are ascribing to Leslie properties she cannot have as an abstract thing. Celebrities notoriously are many things according to some magazine articles that they are not in reality. Now, unlike magazine writers, fiction creators don't want us to believe their stories. But both present people or objects as being a certain way. Whether the representation matches reality is a different question. Fiction creators don't standardly aim at correct representations.

But why, then, do we imagine Harry Potter as a flesh-and-blood boy, when Harry Potter is an abstract object? Maybe it's because when we are first introduced to Harry, it's through the novels or films that depict the character as a boy. From the moment we meet the character we are encouraged to imagine Harry as a person, a wizard, a friend, and so on. And first introductions are powerful. Suppose someone introduced your brand new acquaintance as the lizard king. Once you've formed an image of the person as a lizard king (and why shouldn't you, what a fun game!) it's difficult not to imagine a lizard king every time you hear their name.

Being a person, a wizard, an animal, a politician, or the governess of Candyland are also much more exciting properties than being abstract, being created by an author, or being modelled on a real person. Maybe that's why we imagine fictional characters the way they are in their fictions rather than how they are in reality. And how would you even imagine an abstract object? Our imaginations typically have a spatial component. We imagine something that's extended in space; something with arms and a head or with visible sides. But abstract things are not extended in space. You can't create a mental picture of something abstract. Pictures have, by their very nature, spatial dimensions. But since engaging with fiction frequently involves visual sensory imagining, also called visualising, it's natural that we imagine our fictional characters as they are represented in the fictions (more on the role of imagining when engaging with fiction in Chapter 5).

## Talking about Stories

So, are we making a big mistake when we say "Leslie is a politician" or "Harry Potter has two best friends"? Not at all! "Leslie is a politician" may structurally look the same as "Sam is a philosopher", but looks can be deceptive. Some philosophers of fiction believe that reports about the content of novels or TV shows and other fictions are elliptical. "Harry Potter has two best friends" is simply an abbreviation of the longer claim, "according to the *Harry Potter* novels, Harry Potter has two best friends" or "Harry Potter has, according to the *Harry Potter* novels, two best friends". Since it's usually clear to our audience that we are talking about fiction when we make claims such as "Jessica Jones lives in NYC" or "Lady Edith Crawley owns a magazine", it's perfectly acceptable that we drop the phrase "according to [the fiction]".

Peter van Inwagen (1977) even believes that there is a special relation in which fictional characters stand to the properties that they are said to have in fictions. He calls this special relation *holding* and it contrasts with *having* (or, to use a more technical term, *exemplifying*), the standard relation between objects and their properties. Leslie *has* the property of being a fictional character, but she *holds* the property of being a government employee – a property that Leslie's husband Ben *holds* as well, but does not *have*. The sentence "Harry Potter has two best friends" is ambiguous, so van Inwagen claims, between both readings: that Harry has two best friends and that Harry holds having two best friends. But it's usually clear in the context of the utterance which reading is intended. Naturally, if you and I discuss the contents of the *Harry Potter* novels it's clear to both of us that we are talking about properties that Harry Potter holds rather than has.

Other philosophers think that we are not really asserting anything when we say "Jessica Jones killed Kilgrave". To assert a claim is to put it forward as being true. But when we report the content of *Jessica Jones* (2015–2019) we are not saying that it's true that Jessica Jones killed Kilgrave. Yet, it's appropriate to utter "Jessica Jones killed Kilgrave" when we talk about the content of the fiction. It's appropriate because this utterance, unlike "Jessica killed her French teacher", is faithful to the story. I am also not lying when I utter "Jessica Jones killed Kilgrave". I am merely pretending or make-believing that Jessica killed a man, and I rely on your knowing that I merely pretend or make-believe. That's why neither of us calls the police to report a murder. You'll read more about this view in the next chapter, since it is often combined with the claim that there *aren't* any fictional characters; that fictional characters don't exist. In any case, whether we are saying something true or merely something faithful, when we utter "Leslie Knope is a politician", we don't need to commit to the problematic view that people are making mistakes when reporting on the content of fictions.

## Creating Fictional Characters

Fictional creationism looks like a pretty smooth theory, doesn't it? Many philosophers who write and think about fiction are attracted to fictional creationism. The view matches our intuition that fictional characters are genuinely created by their authors. But creationism's advantage also poses a challenge. How *do* authors create fictional characters? Amie Thomasson (1998: 12) writes that:

> because characters are created by being written about by their authors, Jane Austen creates the fictional character Emma Woodhouse and brings her into existence (assuming she did not exist before) in writing the sentence:
>
> Emma Woodhouse, handsome, clever, and rich, with a comfortable home and happy disposition, seemed to unite some of the best blessings of existence, and had lived nearly twenty-one years in the world with very little to distress or vex her.

Thomasson's passage seems to suggest an answer to two questions, namely, *how* fictional characters are created, and *when* fictional characters are created. Jane Austen brought Emma into existence when she first used the name "Emma Woodhouse" in her writings about Emma.

So, can we say that fictional characters are created when authors use their names for the first time in their written work? Not quite. Not all works of fiction are written pieces or are based upon written work. There was a time when fairy tales were only orally passed on from generation to generation. While we don't have any records telling us who created Snow White or

Rumpelstiltskin, someone created these characters. They did so by *talking* rather than *writing* about them. And it's, of course, entirely possible (even if seldom advisable) to make a film without any sort of script written prior to filming. Moreover, not every fictional character we encounter is referred to by a name in the relevant work of fiction. We can refer to people, pets, and places without using their names. I can refer to Angela Merkel with her name but also by using the definite description "the first female chancellor of Germany". Her husband will sometimes refer to Merkel as "my wife", and in the context of his utterance it will be clear to his audience who he is talking about. Similarly, fictional characters can be referred to by using a name or by using a definite description.

We never learn the names of the Irish man and the Czech woman in the Oscar-winning indie musical film *Once* (2007). Maybe the screenwriter never had any names for them in mind, and might have simply used the expressions "the guy" and "the girl" in the script. Yet, he created these characters. If anything, we should say that fictional characters are created when authors use their name *or the definite description* that will refer to them for the first time in their work – whether that work is written, oral or visual.

Okay, suppose I start writing a novel that features Angelface, a crime solving tapir. Halfway through my novel writing process, I change my mind about my tapir. "Angelface" isn't really a suitable name for a tapir; "Jean Claude" is a much better fit. And tapirs aren't crime solvers, they are CEOs. A while later, I decide that Jean Claude, the CEO, is not a tapir but a gibbon. Clearly, my main character has changed significantly during the course of writing the novel. Or, did it not change, and I rather created a new fictional character every time I changed a major feature? Changing species is a big deal, I would imagine. If you changed species, no doubt you wouldn't be you anymore.

*Sam:* That's no doubt true, although you get funny cases about fictional people changing species in their fictional world.

Kafka's *Metamorphosis* is a story in which the main character was a human but woke up a bug. Having said that, it was a bug with very human-like thoughts, memories, and personality. Perhaps a creature like that isn't really a bug at all!

*Tatjana:* I suppose Kafka intended to create one single character who changes from a human into a bug. But had he changed his mind halfway through the novella and had Gregor change into a seahorse and live in a house under water, I'd be inclined to say that Kafka decided to create a new character, albeit similar in many regards.

But then again, a change of species alone might not change the fictional character if the narrative remains pretty much the same. There's a Japanese animated adaption of Sherlock Holmes in which Sherlock Holmes and Watson are dogs. But we have no problem identifying the dogs as Holmes and Watson. Holmes does what Holmes does – dog or not. If dog Holmes is the one and only Holmes, i.e. the fictional character created by Arthur Conan Doyle, then why not say that turning a fictional tapir into a fictional gibbon is just making changes to a fictional character, rather than creating a new one?

## Meeting Madeleine Albright

At the beginning of this chapter, we were wondering how it's possible for Leslie Knope to meet up with Madeleine Albright if fictional characters are not the kind of entities we can bump into. I hope you can now see why you can't have waffles with Leslie. She either eats waffles in her own possible world instead of our actual world, or she's abstract and doesn't have a body, let alone a digestive system.

If Leslie is an abstract object, as the fictional creationist holds, then she simply cannot have coffee; not with Madeleine Albright, not with anyone. Even if we thought that the real Albright was not identical to the Albright character in *Parks and Recreation* and that, indeed, the Albright character was an abstract object, Leslie still couldn't have coffee with the Albright character. Drinking coffee is just not the kind of thing that abstract entities do.

But both the abstract Leslie and the concrete Albright can be *presented* as having coffee together. Leslie Knope and Madeleine Albright, according to *Parks and Recreation*, enjoy a cup of java in each other's company. Or, put slightly differently, the (abstract) fictional character Leslie Knope, and the (concrete) real-world politician Madeleine Albright, are depicted in the TV show as having coffee together.

In the depiction, Leslie is portrayed by Amy Poehler while Albright plays herself. Albright is a character in *Parks and Recreation*, but she's not a fictional character. She does not originate in the fiction but rather in real life.

*Sam:* This is actually one of the things that makes creationism attractive to me. I can explain all the phenomena without recourse to two Madeleines – the *real* one portraying the *fictional* one. Rather, I can say that there's only one Madeleine, but just like fictional characters can *have* but also *hold* properties, it turns out that real people can also *hold* properties relative to a story. Accordingly, Madeleine portrays herself. Even though no person of flesh and blood can *have* the property of drinking coffee with a fictional character, a person of flesh and blood can *hold* that property. And that's what happened to Albright, when she came to play herself in *Parks and Recreation*. She came to hold properties that she doesn't have.

Now, having said that, sometimes a character who is based on a real person may plausibly be classified as a fictional character. Netflix's *Manhunt: Unabomber* presents the fictionalised FBI account of the pursuit of the Unabomber. The miniseries depicts FBI profiler Jim Fitzgerald as the person who more or less single-handedly solved the case. But the real Jim Fitzgerald was apparently only part of a team of profilers that helped to crack the case. Here, I think it would be fair to say that *Manhunt*'s Jim Fitzgerald is a fictional character, or maybe semi-fictional character, who at least partly originated in the fiction.

Similarly, the comedy film *Look Who's Back* asks us to imagine that Hitler wakes up in the twenty-first century. Of course, we need to know who the historical figure Adolf Hitler is to grasp the humour of the film. But in many ways, the film's Hitler is so different from the historical one that we might find it a stretch to say that they are not separate characters, albeit the fictional being heavily based on the historical Hitler. In any case, for the fictional creationist, the short answer to the question of how Albright can hang out with a fictional character is: she can't. That's rather bad news for anyone who's ever been infatuated with a fictional hero or heroine.

## "Hermione Granger Doesn't Exist!"

Alright, so we think that Hermione is a clever student, a fictional character, and possibly non-actual or abstract. But we also say things like "Hermione doesn't exist" or "There is no Hermione". I'll assume, as is standard, that both sentences mean the same thing, that is, to *exist* (or to not exist) just is to *be* (or to not be).

Sentences that seemingly predicate the lack of existence of fictional characters – negative existentials (about fictional characters) – are notoriously challenging. They simply don't seem to allow for a literal interpretation. In Chapter 4, I will introduce you to views that deny that fictional characters exist What seems like an easy solution to the interpretation of negative existentials is far from easy. Of whom or what are we predicating a lack of existence when we say that "Hermione doesn't exist"? Some will say that Hermione is just what she seems to be, a non-existent wizard. Others will look for different ways to interpret negative existentials. And, if you accept the existence of fictional characters, interpreting negative existentials poses even more of a challenge. After all, both the non-actualist and the fictional creationist *do* argue that fictional characters exist. So what on earth is going on when we seem to be saying truly that they don't?

Take a moment to think about the context in which we say that a fictional character doesn't exist. It's usually said to correct someone's false belief. "No, Timmy, you cannot play mud pie baking with SpongeBob. SpongeBob doesn't exist." Or, "Oh, did you not know Leslie Knope is made up? There is no Leslie, she's not a real politician." What people seem to be up to in these examples is that they want to deny that SpongeBob is a concrete, walking, talking creature that can go on playdates, or that Lesie is a human politician, capable of one day being the first female president of the United States of America. So, people may use the phrase "doesn't exist" but that does not automatically mean that they literally think that SpongeBob or Leslie do not exist. They mean something slightly different.

Rather, what I think is going on, is that we use negative existentials to deny that a particular fictional character belongs to a particular *kind* of thing (von Solodkoff 2014). So, when people seemingly say of a particular fictional character that they don't exist, what they really mean is that the fictional character is not the kind of object that it is said to be in the fiction. Leslie Knope is depicted as a person and as a politician but, in reality, she's neither. In reality, she's not even a "she", because Leslie is an abstract object. And abstract objects couldn't possibly have a gender. My view is inspired by an observation that Amie Thomasson makes: "statements like 'there is no Lear' [are] quite naturally interpretable as [claiming] that … 'there is no (real) person who is Lear'" (1998, p. 112). This is a step in the right direction, but I don't think it's far enough. When you say "King Lear doesn't exist" you are not only ruling out that Lear is a real person. You are also ruling out that Lear is a pet, a tree, or a sleigh.

How can we account for this all-around denial if we are a creationist? Rather than tying the kind in question to a narrow kind, like "person" or "pet", we interpret negative existentials with the help of the kinds *non-pretend object* (as opposed to pretend object) and *concrete object*. The sentence "Hermione doesn't exist" is true because Hermione isn't a concrete or non-pretend object. Or, in other words, because Hermione is a non-concrete (i.e. abstract) or pretend object. Arguably, not every non-concrete or pretend object is a fictional character (your imaginary childhood friend is the former but not the latter), but in Hermione's case she is correctly described as a non-concrete or pretend object *because* she is a fictional character. I envisioned my view to be particularly helpful for the creationist but the non-actualist can make use of it too. The non-actualist could claim that the relevant kind is *actual object* or maybe *non-merely possible object*. So, "Hermione doesn't exist" is true – not because she doesn't exist at all but – because Hermione is a non-actual object, or is a merely possible object.

## Concluding Thoughts

In this chapter, we've asked a metaphysical question: what is the nature of fictional characters? I've discussed two kinds of answers. First, fictional characters are non-actual flesh-and-blood creatures that inhabit other possible worlds. And, second, fictional characters are abstract things in our world. Where do I stand? I am not convinced that authors do not genuinely create their characters. I don't think the idea that authors fictionalise non-actual people, pets, or places is a satisfying answer to our pre-theoretical belief that fictional characters are created by their authors. So, my sympathies lie with the creationist.

Now, here's the thing with pre-theoretical beliefs: some of them are just wrong. It makes perfect sense to conclude that the earth is rather flat, or that the sun revolves around our planet, given what we can see and feel. It rings true that you are more likely to get help when being attacked by someone if you are surrounded by a large group of people than when there are only a few strangers witnessing the attack. Yet, we know that these pre-theoretical beliefs are false. So, why do we care about pre-theoretical beliefs, common sense, or intuitions, in philosophy? Philosophy is not an empirical discipline and so, as philosophers, we rarely conduct proper scientific experiments. And in any case, how would we go about to empirically decide between non-actualism and fictional creationism? But that philosophy is not an empirical science is only part of the answer.

Reasonable pre-theoretical beliefs fit into our wider belief system. To give up a pre-theoretical belief often means giving up on a whole set of related beliefs that are affected by the change. We need a good reason for spending all this energy to revise part of our belief system. One reason for revising a belief is that it will lead us to better navigate the world around us. Another reason is that doing so will resolve inconsistencies in our belief-system. Yet another reason is that revising a pre-theoretical belief is just a small price to pay in exchange for a set of beliefs that together constitute a much more plausible view. And, of course, being inconsistent with scientific facts is another reason for revising one's pre-theoretical belief. Do we have any good reasons to jettison the belief that fictional characters are genuinely created? I don't think so. Or, at least we don't find it in non-actualism. I do believe, however, that there are reasons to be suspicious of the idea that fictional characters are anything at all – either non-actual or abstract. If that's awoken your curiosity, turn to the next chapter.

## Note

1 Having said that, for as long as I can think, the numbers 1–20 have had genders and personalities for me. For instance, the number 9 is a docile and compassionate character with a soft voice and gentle manners who acts as a mediator between the more hot-headed numbers, such as 4 and 7. This isn't as crazy as it sounds. Or maybe it is. But it's not that uncommon. There is a form of synaesthesia, called "ordinal-linguistic personification", that involves what I just described. While I can't further indulge in the discussion of this form of synaesthesia here, I do wonder whether the fictional creationist can say that similar mechanism are at play when we think of Lady Macbeth as wearing shoes.

## Works Cited

Howell, R. (1979) Fictional Objects: How they Are and How they Aren't. *Poetics*, 8: 129–177.

Lewis, D. (1973) *Counterfactuals*. Cambridge, MA: Blackwell.

Thomasson, A. L. (1998) *Fiction and Metaphysics*. Cambridge: Cambridge University Press.

van Inwagen, P. (1977) Creatures of Fiction. *American Philosophical Quarterly*, 14(4): 299–308.

von Solodkoff, T. (2014) Fictional Realism and Negative Existentials, in Manuel García-Carpintero & Genoveva Martí (eds.), *Empty Representations: Reference and Non-Existence*. Oxford: Oxford University Press, pp. 333–352.

## Further Reading

Braun, D. (2005) Empty Names, Fictional Names, Mythical Names. *Noûs*, 39(4): 596–631.

Everett, A. (2005) Against Fictional Realism. *Journal of Philosophy*, 102(12): 624–649.

Everett, A. (2007) Pretense, Existence, and Fictional Objects. *Philosophy and Phenomenological Research*, 74(1): 56–80. *Anthony Everett is an avid critic of the view that fictional characters are anything at all.*

Friend, S. (2007) Fictional Characters. *Philosophy Compass*, 2(2): 141–156. *Stacie Friend offers an excellent overview of the debate about fictional characters in this paper.*

Goodman, J. (2004) A Defense of Creationism in Fiction. *Grazer Philosophische Studien*, 67(1): 131–155.

Kripke, S. (2013) *Reference and Existence: The John Locke Lectures*. Oxford: Oxford University Press.

Priest, G. (2005) *Towards Non-Being: The Logic and Metaphysics of Intentionality*. Oxford: Clarendon Press.

Salmon, N. (1998) Nonexistence. *Noûs*, 32(3): 277–319. *In Nathan Salmon's article, there is a line that has become famous among philosophers who think about the metaphysics of fictional characters. Salmon compares fictional characters to a sportscar and urges us to not be stingy when it comes to using them. Otherwise, it would be "like buying a luxurious Italian sports car only to keep it garaged. I do not advocate driving recklessly, but I do advise that having paid for the car one should permit oneself to drive it, at least on special occasions" (p. 299). What a fun simile!*

# Chapter 4

# Do Fictional Characters Really Exist?

## *Tatjana*

This might seem like a trick question. Have we not just discussed what fictional characters are? We have. And doesn't any discussion about fictional characters presuppose that they exist? Your question makes a lot of sense. But the answer is not as obvious as you might think it is. Some philosophers, I will call them the *anti-realists* (about fictional characters), think that fictional characters are neither abstract, nor non-actual – they are nothing at all. This sounds paradoxical, but we can put it in a less puzzling way: anti-realists think that there are no such things as fictional characters. Wait, what? But there are obviously novels and fiction films that feature characters, and since these characters originate from fictional works, there are *fictional* characters. The Joker, Elizabeth Bennett, Harry Potter, Minnie Mouse, and their ilk – why would anyone deny that they exist?

Let me back up a little to put the question into a wider context. The question of whether fictional characters exist and, if they do, what they are like, falls into the philosophical discipline of metaphysics. Metaphysics is the philosophical study of reality. Metaphysicians investigate the most general features of reality using philosophical methods. One central sub-discipline of metaphysics is ontology. Ontology searches for answers to what there is. And quite literally the existence of any kind of entity is up for grabs to ontologists. Are there tables? Cats? People? Facts? Nature? Laws of physics? Electrons? Theories? Agreeableness? Grades? Possible Worlds? Numbers? Necessary beings? Viruses? Values? Relations? And of course, are there fictional characters?

*Sam:* I think some readers might fairly ask: how can some of these things be up for grabs? "Of course tables exist", they might say, "I put stuff on them." Or, "Of course cats exist, I have a pet one!" How can these things seriously be up for grabs?

*Tatjana:* Some philosophers argue that the world only contains simples: the smallest, indivisible physical entities. Simples can be arranged in various ways. Some are arranged table-wise – they are arranged in

DOI: 10.4324/9781003126102-5

such a way that to us they appear as what we conventionally call "table". That there are no tables follows from the more general claim this view makes that there are no composed objects, only "mereological simples". Such a view might seem exotic at first, but the reasons for subscribing to it are intriguing. Interestingly, some (though few) philosophers are convinced that while your table doesn't exist, your cat does. Why? Simply put, that's because there are no composed objects except for *organisms*. Anyone intrigued by this conclusion should read Peter van Inwagen's masterpiece *Material Beings* (1990).

While the philosophical study of what there is is called ontology, there is no unique name for the philosophical study of what things are like. It's just called "metaphysics". And in any case, any distinction between ontology and the rest of metaphysics is somewhat artificial. Suppose someone is trying to convince you that there are demons. Will they convince you? You might think, "no way"! But what if the person told you that demons exist because all they are are figments of our imagination and, of course, figments of imagination exist. Do you agree now? Maybe. Because it's much easier to wrap your head around the idea that figments of imagination exist than around the idea that there are supernatural beings. How plausible it is that some things exist, depends a lot on what they are supposed to be. This is why it makes little sense to ask what there is, without also asking the follow-up question, "and what is it like?"

You might have noticed that I have listed *kinds* of things above rather than individual entities. That's because metaphysics is concerned with big-picture questions. Metaphysicians sometimes say that they study the most fundamental or most general features of reality. They don't wonder, "the Beatles exist, but what about the Rolling Stones?", or "Mum is part of reality, but what about Dad?" Rather, they ask, "do bands exist, and what makes a collection of people a band?", or "do people exist?" I hope you can see how these are big-picture questions and why I talk about *kinds* of things rather than particular objects.

## Choosing between Theories

Now, how do philosophers choose between competing metaphysical theories? How should you go about choosing between a realist and an anti-realist view about fictional characters? Metaphysical musings usually start with a particular phenomenon we all seem to observe or an experience we universally have. We first describe the phenomenon as objectively as we can and then try to explain it using philosophical methods. Here is how we might describe the phenomenon we observe in the debate about fictional characters. Authors and filmmakers describe to us people in their work, and these people don't walk, and never have walked, this earth. We say things like "Hannibal Lecter is a cannibal" and think that Holly Golightly is eccentric. We agree that Jessica Jones displays symptoms of post-traumatic stress and shake our heads in disbelief when someone claims that King Kong's secret identity is James Bond.

It seems impossible to describe a phenomenon without revealing some of our background beliefs. The way we talk and think about fictional characters reveals the background belief that there are fictional characters; that they exist. Any philosophical view that explains the phenomenon that entails that there are fictional characters will be intuitively plausible to us. Why? Because it matches our background beliefs. Background beliefs, pre-theoretic intuition, or common sense – they all roughly refer to the same kind of beliefs. And they are valued guides in philosophical debates. Not because common sense is infallible. We all know it fails regularly. But if most people, across different cultures, share a pre-theoretic intuition, there must be a reason for that. There must be, for example, a reason why people think there are fictional characters rather than just books and films. It cannot be a coincidence. That's why we cannot ignore universally shared background beliefs.

*Sam:* Is it not a virtue in the sciences? Quantum physics can seem pretty counterintuitive. But still …

If a scientist has two theories to choose between, and each is equally good at explaining the data, but one of them is more intuitively plausible, will the scientist not prefer that theory? Is metaphysics here any different to other disciplines or sciences? Maybe because fiction is a human creation our intuitions about fiction are more reliable or important. What do you think?

*Tatjana:* That's a good point. Aligning with common sense is not just a *prima facie* theoretical virtue in metaphysics but also in any other armchair (sub)discipline.

Very crudely, in empirical disciplines, our data are measurable, qualifiable observations. In armchair disciplines, our data come from various sources, including pre-theoretic conceptions of the world and its mechanisms. The latter isn't standardly a source of data for the empirical sciences. So, I don't think this particular virtue matters in the sciences.

Amie Thomasson would agree with you that our intuitions about fiction and fictional characters should have significant weight when it comes to the metaphysics of fiction and its characters. And it's, as you mention, because fictional works are human-created artifacts.

If you want to deny a common-sense belief, you have your work cut out for yourself. Pre-theoretic intuitions matter when it comes to choosing one theory over another. Philosophers will often view it as a plus that a theory advances many intuitive and few or no counterintuitive claims. Aligning with our pre-theoretic intuitions is a theoretical virtue for metaphysical theories.

But it's not the only theoretical virtue that matters when you choose between competing views. Theories can have theoretical vices as well. And you need to weigh the theoretical virtues against the vices a theory has.

*Sam:* So, I guess, if someone wants to deny that fictional characters exist, then they'll have to explain to us why it is that so many people make the mistake of thinking that they do. Likewise, if someone wants to convince me that my table is made up of little atoms, each of which have electrons zooming around them, they'll have to explain to me why I don't see the moving parts. Right?

*Tatjana:* Exactly. The wonderful thing about philosophy, as I view the discipline, is that it attempts to reconcile universal truths about the world with how we relate to this world. So, the philosopher shouldn't argue that common sense errs and leave it at that. They owe us an explanation of why things appear to us to be one way when they really are another. I have to admit, I am a fan of many revisionary theories – theories that crucially deviate from common sense. But if a particular theory does not, in the end, reconcile its claims with our pre-theoretic intuitions, I am left intellectually unsatisfied.

Theoretical virtues and vices don't tell us whether a theory is true or false. Theoretical virtues have less to do with truth and more to do with what it is rational to believe. What is true and what is rational to believe may come apart. It may be rational for you to believe that you will not get caught stealing 10 Euros out of the tip bowl, but your belief might be false, and you do get caught. But hopefully, more often than not, when it is rational to believe a proposition, that proposition is also true. Theoretical virtues, then, are guides to rational beliefs. And since we hope rational beliefs guide us towards true theories, theoretical virtues are indirect guides towards the truth.

Two theoretical virtues any theory worthy of consideration must exhibit are internal consistency and explanatory adequacy. A theory should not forward or entail claims that contradict each other. A theory that claims that only physical objects exist, but also entails that ghosts exist, is not internally consistent. So too, if your theory claims that there are no fictional characters but also that Elizabeth Bennett and her ilk are abstract objects. Your theory would be internally inconsistent and, hence, it wouldn't be rational for you to believe in it, once you realise the inconsistency.

*Sam:* Can something not be abstract while also not existing?

*Tatjana:* Well, some philosophers say that there are things that don't exist. I am going to mention this view called "Meinongianism", later in this chapter. But they would still say that there are fictional characters. I cannot really make sense of the idea that there are no fictional things, and yet that some fictional things are abstract.

Can you?

*Sam:* No. I can't make sense of that position either, but I know that some philosophers have made such claims. I was just asking ... for a friend!

A theory should also explain the phenomenon it set out to explain. If we expect a theory to explain what fictional characters are but instead it only explains what stories are, it's not a valid candidate for the best metaphysical theory of fictional characters. Such a theory is not explanatorily adequate.

Explanatory power is a further theoretical virtue. Suppose you're an anti-realist and you think that fictional characters don't exist. If your arguments can show that not only is reality free of fictional characters but that there are also no failed posits of science (e.g. Vulcan or Aether) then your view has increased explanatory power.

But the theoretical virtue that will concern us most in this chapter is simplicity. Theoretical simplicity can take different forms. I bet you have heard of Ockham's razor. It is the best-known principle of simplicity. Ockham's razor says that we must not multiply entities beyond necessity. For example, if creaking noises in old houses can be explained by the structure of the wood and the wind, then a theory that holds ghosts accountable for the sound would seem to violate Ockham's razor. After all, even the theorist who believes in ghosts is likely to believe in objects such as wood and wind. And if these things are enough to explain the creaking, there is no need to postulate ghosts to explain the noise. Thus, assuming ghosts to explain the creaking in addition to the structure of the wood, the wind, and the laws of physics would mean multiplying entities beyond necessity. Of course, there may be another reason for believing in ghosts. But a belief in such extra entities cannot be justified by a phenomenon that is perfectly well explained by things we already believe in, that is, wood, wind, and the laws of physics. A theory that postulates fewer kinds of things is ontologically more parsimonious than a theory that claims there are more kinds of entities in the world. I hope you can see how ontological parsimony matters when the realist and the anti-realist debate. Since the anti-realist thinks that there are no fictional characters, their view is ontologically more parsimonious when it comes to fictional people, pets, or places, than the realist's view that claims such things really exist.

Another way a theory can be simpler – or more elegant – than a rival one is by requiring us to accept fewer controversial claims. For instance, a creationist cannot simply claim that Holly, Hermione, and Hannibal exist; they also have to explain what kind of thing a fictional character is. As we've seen, they will say that fictional characters are abstract and created – two claims that need further explanation. And so, creationism appears to be more complex and, hence, less simple, than a theory that rejects fictional characters (although you'll see shortly that this is debatable).

The theoretical virtues I've mentioned in this chapter are these. Alignment with common sense, internal consistency, explanatory adequacy, explanatory power, and simplicity. Conversely, theoretical vices are these. Being counter-intuitive, exhibiting internal inconsistency, not being explanatorily adequate, lacking explanatory power, being ontologically indulgent, and being unnecessarily complex. Think of theoretical virtues and theoretical vices as pros and cons for a theory. If a philosophical theory existed that had only theoretical virtues and no theoretical vices, then there would be no debate and everyone would recognise it as rational to accept the theory as true. But the interesting thing about philosophical debates is that *all* theories have both virtues and vices. Unfortunately, it's impossible to offer a formula of how to calculate the attractiveness of every theory. Some theoretical virtues weigh more than others in some debates, and to some philosophers. And the same is true of the theoretical vices. Philosophers will try to convince us that the theoretical virtues of their preferred view outweigh the theory's vices. They might also try to show that the theoretical vices of their view are merely sheep disguised as wolves, and that biting the bullet and accepting the theory with its vices isn't too much of a cost.

So, when you learn about different views to a philosophical issue and you want to know which one would be most rational to believe in, ask yourself: What is the phenomenon that requires explanation? What does common sense have to say about the phenomenon? Are the competing theories explanatorily adequate? Are they internally consistent? If one of them isn't, discard it. Which theory is ontologically more parsimonious? Which one offers simpler explanations? Are some virtues or vices more crucial than others when it comes to developing a theory to solve this particular philosophical issue? Do some virtues greatly outweigh the vices of a theory? Are the vices maybe not as bad as we might initially think? I hope my detour gives you a better idea of how to decide between anti-realism and realism about fictional characters, and even between different versions of anti-realism or different versions of realism.

*Sam:* Perhaps I'm jumping the gun here. But how can there be multiple versions of anti-realism?

I understand how there can be multiple versions of realism. All realists will agree that fictional characters really exist. But they might disagree as to what they're like, what they are, whether they can be created, or whether they exist eternally, and more. But if you're an anti-realist, you'll have concluded that they don't exist at all. And so, anti-realists won't be able to have further debates about what fictional characters are like. How then can there be multiple versions of anti-realism?

*Tatjana:* I guess the way I think about it is this. A theory is realist or anti-realist about a kind of object, the *F*s, by virtue of what ontological status they assign to the *F*s. So, a theory counts as realist about the *F*s if and because it holds that *F*s are real, that is, that they are part of the real world. Now, we should note that it is standardly assumed that being real, existing, and having being, are all the same quality. Under this assumption, a theory counts as realism about the *F*s, if and because it holds that *F*s are real/exist/have being (for most of this chapter, I am making this assumption, although my own view is that being real is not the same as existing, and I will also introduce readers to a view that distinguishes existing from having being). A theory counts as anti-realism about the *F*s, if and because it holds that there are no *F*s/*F*s are not real/*F*s do not exist.

Just as there are different realist theories about fictional characters because they differ in their explanation of what fictional characters are, there are different anti-realist theories about fictional characters, because they differ in their explanations of what is going on if – *contra* everyday parlance – there are no such things as fictional characters. I hope this makes sense.

*Sam:* Yes. That helps. You're saying that there can be different sorts of anti-realists because there can be different sorts of explanations as to how to make sense of our talking about the *F*s, on the assumption that, in actual fact, there are no *F*s. So, all the anti-realists about the *F*s will agree that there are no *F*s, but they might offer very different explanations as to how to explain all of our common-sense talk about the *F*s.

*Tatjana:* Right!

## Realism or Anti-Realism?

Now, since the anti-realist holds that fictional characters do not exist, their view is ontologically more parsimonious than the realist's view. For some, this is the main draw to anti-realism. If the phenomenon we want to explain can be explained without postulating the existence of fictional characters, then Ockham's Razor advises us to do without the offending entities. Holding onto them regardless would be irrational. On the flip side, the burden of proof is on the anti-realist to show that we don't need fictional characters to make sense of talk and thought that is seemingly about them.

The anti-realist can pull another card from their sleeve. I said that it's a universal background belief that there are fictional characters. But that was hasty. For, you see, we also utter sentences such as "Hannibal Lecter does not exist". In fact, we treat fictional characters as *paradigmatic examples* of things that don't exist. (And when we say that some things don't exist, we mean that there are no such things). It seems that our background beliefs about fictional characters point in different directions, and are therefore somewhat muddled. Go ahead and decide for yourself which pre-theoretic intuition is stronger. The realist and anti-realist are both on similar grounds here. To undermine the realist's motivation to postulate fictional characters, the anti-realist must argue that we should not only take sentences such as "Hannibal Lecter is manipulative" (i.e. sentences which seem to be true within a fiction) at face value. They must also argue that we should take sentences such as "Lecter is one of the best known villains in film history" (i.e. sentences about fictional characters that even seem to be true outside of any fiction) at face value.

Finally, the anti-realist might argue that fictional characters, if they existed, as realists claim they do, would be obscure things. They would be either abstract or non-actual, which is not how we typically think of characters like Hannibal Lecter or Jessica Jones when we imagine them in their respective stories. When we contemplate fictional characters we standardly think of them as concrete people, pets, or places. What does it mean that they are abstract or non-actual? The realist has to do a lot of explaining; and this compromises the realist view's simplicity. Also, it's true that there seems to be a robust pre-theoretic intuition that fictional characters (if they exist) are created by authors and filmmakers. But how exactly do you create an abstract object? To create something, you usually have to cause it to exist. This means that you enter into a cause-and-effect relationship with your creation. However, if you are creating an abstract object, it is unclear how you, as an object with a spatiotemporal location, could enter into a cause-and-effect relationship with an object that has no spatial location. Things are even worse for the non-actualist. As we've seen, the non-actualist cannot say that fictional characters are literally created, at best they can hold that Hannibal and his ilk are discovered. But this is counterintuitive. Common sense does not tell us that fictional characters are discovered. Here, the burden of proof is on the realist to show that their view is not as complicated as it may seem and that many of their claims are more intuitive than they seem at first. This is what I tried to portray in Chapter 3.

I hope you can see how challenging choosing between competing theories is. When you disagree with a particular viewpoint, it's not enough to simply point out the problems with it. You also need to offer a detailed explanation of your own view and argue that it provides a better balance between theoretical virtues to vices than the alternatives. And it's not as simple as explaining your own view. You also must show why your preferred view is better than the other options available.

So without further ado, let's see what the anti-realist has to say. We surely *talk* as if there are fictional characters. We say that Hermione Granger appears in more than one novel, that Dorian Gray is more narcissistic than Jay Gatsby, or that some fictional characters are more famous than their creators. But the anti-realist will say that none of these characters are *really* part of the inventory that makes up reality; they don't belong to "the furniture of the world", as a metaphor popular among metaphysicians has it. Consider the claim that the average Irish household consists of 2.7 people. I hope you agree with me that there are households and that there are people, but that no household has two people plus a fraction of a person. The average Irish household is not a *thing*; it's just a useful and convenient way of talking.

When you and I agree that Hannibal Lecter is manipulative, it certainly appears that we are talking about a fictional character. Moreover, it appears that we are agreeing on a proposition that is objectively true. The realist about fictional characters holds that things don't just appear this way, but that we actually *are* saying true things about *fictional characters*. But the anti-realist will insist that it only appears as if we are making true claims about fictional characters.

*Sam:* Just as we appear to be talking about something called the average Irish household, even though there's no such thing.

*Tatjana:* Yes, exactly. A household is composed of living people. But average households are said to have two and a half, or one point three people. I am ready to bet that you've never seen one point three living people.

Now, when theorists maintain that some appearances are deceptive, they owe us a two-fold explanation: First, what is really going on behind the appearance, and second, why do common people intentionally or unintentionally keep up the appearance?

## Truth and Description

Some anti-realists hold onto our pre-theoretic intuition that sentences such as "Celie Harris survived multiple sexual assaults" or "Hermione Granger is smarter than Daisy Buchanan" are true. After all, if you chose "Derek Zoolander" instead of "Hermione Granger" in an exam on English fiction as your answer to the question who's smarter than Daisy Buchanan, you'd lose points.

But how can we explain the truth of the above claims, if we don't think that there are fictional characters? Well, one way is to argue that our talk seemingly about fictional characters is true, but that it isn't actually about fictional characters. You might think that, for instance "Daisy Buchanan is charming but shallow", is a short cut. When it comes to human communication, we use short cuts all the time. Suppose you are at your favourite café and order "some coffee". You'd be shocked if the barista simply poured coffee from the pot onto your hands, and furious if they responded to your stare by scolding you that if you wanted it in a mug, you should have said so. This is not how communication works. Fortunately, any barista will know that "some coffee" is short for "*a cup* of coffee". Similarly, when you say "Daisy Buchanan is charming but shallow", what your utterance really expresses is that *according to The Great Gatsby*, Daisy Buchanan has those qualities.

Let's call any phrase of the form "according to fiction [*Title*]" and similar formulations, the *story operator*. We've got an elegant and thoroughly plausible solution for the anti-realist here, don't we? After all, when discussing Daisy Buchanan's charm and shallowness, we *are* talking about the content of a fictional work – or so the defender of the story-operator view will say. And yet, the approach that relies on the use of the story operator to explain the truth of sentences about fictional characters faces serious challenges. Here's a big one: when you utter "according to *The Great Gatsby*, Daisy Buchanan is charming but shallow", you still appear to be talking about a fictional character. You appear to be saying *of* Daisy that she is charming but shallow according to the novel. That's not what the anti-realist wanted. The entire point of the story-operator solution was to show that we don't need fictional characters to explain how sentences like "Daisy Buchanan is charming but shallow" can be true.

But maybe we do not *really* talk about Daisy when we take a deeper breath and utter the longer sentence "according to *The Great Gatsby*, Daisy Buchanan is charming but shallow". Maybe our utterance expresses the proposition that *according to* The Great Gatsby, *there is a unique person named "Daisy Buchanan" who is charming but shallow*. Now, if the latter is what the original sentence expresses, then we can indeed hold that we're not talking about a fictional character but about what is happening in the novel.

A view that develops this idea in greater detail is *descriptivism about names*. Bertrand Russell (1905) thought that ordinary proper names, such as "Daisy Buchanan" and "Angela Merkel", are abbreviations for definite descriptions. For example, "the unique person named 'Daisy Buchanan'" is a definite description that picks out a specific individual based on their characteristics. If we were to take a moment and use this full description, it's what we would say instead of simply saying "Daisy Buchanan". A descriptivist about names holds that names are disguised definite descriptions. A definite description describes a particular individual. Definite descriptions contrast with general descriptions, such as "dogs". The name "Emmanuel Macron" is a disguise for the definite description "the person who was president of France in 2023, who came into office in 2017, who is French, who studied Philosophy." Now, this description picks out an individual in our world and only one individual – that's why the description is called "definite". Similarly, the name "Sam Lebens", when I use it, uniquely picks out the philosopher who in 2023 was a professor at the University of Haifa, is married, has three children, and likes the colour purple. Now, I certainly don't know everything that there is to know about Sam. But it's enough to describe one particular person in this world.

Things are simpler when it comes to fictional names. Fictional works are pretty limited descriptions of fictional worlds and their inhabitants. Sure, it would take a while to list all of *Silence of the Lambs*'s Hannibal Lecter's properties, but you and I together could get it done over a weekend. (Let's not do that though. You get the gist.) But we don't need to produce a complete description. The description only needs to be definite; it needs to pick out one individual and only one.

Here's an example of a description of Hannibal Lecter that is *not* definite: "the man who killed and ate his victims". Shockingly, there are a whole bunch of murdering cannibals out there: Jeffrey Dahmer, Armin Meiwes, Issei Sagawa, to name a few. The description does not pick out one of them uniquely. Thus, the description is not definite. But there *are* definite descriptions that uniquely pick out Dahmer, Meiwes, or Sagawa, and that's all the descriptivist needs to make their point.

Russell also thought that sentences containing definite descriptions really stand for sentences that don't contain any definite descriptions, but quantificational expressions instead. What this means is that we must analyse the sentence, "The unique person called "Daisy Buchanan" is charming but shallow" as follows: "There is at least and at most one thing that is a person called "Daisy Buchanan" and that thing is charming but shallow". Now, if you're a fictional anti-realist like Russell, you don't think that there is such a thing. Moreover, because there is no thing that fits the description, the sentence turns out to be false. But that's nothing over which a descriptivist anti-realist loses sleep. For the sentence "there is at least and at most one thing that is a person called "Daisy Buchanan" and that thing is charming but shallow" is just a shorthand for the longer sentence "according to *The Great Gatsby*, there is at least and at most one thing that is a person called "Daisy Buchanan" and that thing is charming but shallow". And while the embedded sentence is false, the claim that it is *true according to the novel* is true.

The descriptivist anti-realist can argue that when you say "Hannibal Lecter is manipulative," you're not expressing the false proposition that there is only one Lithuanian-American male serial killer who used to be a forensic psychiatrist, eats his victims, and now helps the FBI catch a killer and he is manipulative. Rather, your utterance expresses the proposition that according to *Silence of the Lambs*, there is exactly one person who fits that description And that proposition *is* true. Such an elegant solution, isn't it?

Alas, descriptivist anti-realism also encounters issues. One is due to the descriptivist part of the view. Definitive descriptions pick out at most one individual. Now imagine the following scenario: in a few years from now an anonymous source leaks top secret FBI information that there was indeed an incarcerated male serial killer of Lithuanian-American descent who ate his victims, used to be a forensic psychiatrist, and helped the FBI catch a killer. And the public, including the author and filmmakers, knew nothing about him. It's a jaw-dropping coincidence. The scenario is highly unlikely to happen. But it *is* possible and that is all that's needed to land the descriptivist anti-realist in a pickle. If the name "Hannibal Lecter" expresses a definite description and that description does pick out an individual, then it would seem that we were talking about that individual, the real cannibal, all along. But that's implausible. When you talked about *Silence of the Lambs*'s Hannibal Lecter with your friends last time, you were talking about a creation by author Thomas Harris. You were not talking about a real man whose existence you, your friends, and Thomas Harris knew nothing about. This thought experiment should give you reason to doubt whether a fictional name really means the same thing as some definite description.

The second issue that the descriptivist anti-realist faces when they adopt the story-operator solution, is that it does not work for all the various kinds of talk about fictional characters. In particular, it cannot account for our *critical* talk about fictional characters. When you say "Holly Golightly is the main character in Truman Capote's 1958 novella *Breakfast at Tiffany's*", you're not just summarising what the book says. Your sentence is not an abbreviation for "According to Capote's *Breakfast at Tiffany's*, Holly Golightly is the main character'. After all, in the world of the fiction, Holly is a real person, not just a character who has been created by storytellers. And when I say "some fictional characters are more famous than their authors", I am not talking about a specific story so there isn't even a clear story operator that can be applied to the proposition. Yet, it's an example of critical talk about fictional characters that seems true to common sense.

*Sam:* Right. I'd say that what's puzzling here for the anti-realist is that there are things which we would tend to classify as non-fictional truths about fictional characters. The idea that some characters are more famous than their authors, for example, seems like a non-fictional truth; as do many of the truths that we utter as literary critics. Moreover, how will the anti-realist deal with comparisons between multiple stories? Which story operator are we using when we say that Sherlock Holmes is more intelligent than James Bond?

*Tatjana:* What you call "non-fictional truths" and I call "critical talk about fictional characters" is also sometimes called "external talk about fictional characters" in the literature. It's hard to make the story-operator view work for this kind of talk, although it is a strategy that Stuart Brock (2010) employs. Mind you, Brock's "story operator" is not what you expect.

Now, there is a way for the anti-realist defender of the story operator to deal with transfictional comparisons. They could, for example, hold that the sentence "Sherlock Holmes is more intelligent than James Bond" is true because according to the Holmes stories, Holmes is intelligent to a certain degree *n* and in the Bond stories, Bond is intelligent to a certain degree *m*, and $n > m$. So there are strategies to be explored to meet the challenges.

If various sentences seemingly about fictional characters turn out to be false on the descriptivist anti-realist account, the view loses points when it comes to how well it matches our pre-theoretic intuitions. Remember, deviating from common sense in some ways is almost inevitable. And maybe the right approach is to say that talk about fictional characters is never true. But there should be very good reasons for embracing the story-operator solution as an anti-realist, independently of your desire to do without fictional characters. Anything else would be *ad hoc.*

## Pretence Through and Through

The issues I flagged with the descriptivist view about fictional names might be resolvable but at this point I'd like to introduce you to a more popular anti-realist view. We started out by considering a theory that confirms our intuition that a lot of the things we say about fictional characters are true – albeit not really about fictional characters. Let me now introduce you to a view that throws that commonsensical idea overboard and holds that talk about fictional characters is *never* true. The view sounds more absurd than it is. It doesn't mean that we should give up talking about Hermione Granger and Norman Bates. That would be too radical. After all, talk about fictional characters is useful when we want to discuss a fictional story, compare different stories, or discuss the impact of a fictional work on us and society. And so, because talk about fictional characters is useful, we *should* continue talking about fictional characters in the same way as we have been doing.

Talk about fictional characters is not the only kind of talk we hold on to because it's useful, even though it is false or untrue. Recall the average Irish household has 2.7 members. Talk of average households is, strictly speaking, not true (since there is no average household) but it is still a very useful way of talking about the ratio between members in one household and the overall number of households.

*Sam:* But surely there's a disanalogy here. You're right that, taken literally, a claim about an average Irish household will be false, but we recognise that what we're really saying is a useful short-hand way for saying something else, and that this something else is true!

But what your anti-realist wants to say now is that all of our talk about fictional characters, even when we've unpacked all of the short-hand figures of speech, is false. We only ever pretend that it's true.

*Tatjana:* Talk about average households is, strictly speaking, false, because there are no average households. But it's useful talk because it's a handy way to express other propositions that are true. The fictionalist can say that the same applies to talk about fictional characters. It's strictly speaking not true (in other words, ultimately false) but it is useful talk because it's a handy way to express other propositions that are true – propositions that are not about fictional characters; propositions that are instead about storytellers, audiences, and our conventions surrounding works of fiction.

The strategy of declaring one domain of discourse to be useful but ultimately not true is often called *fictionalism*. And when you say that talk about Gregor Samsa and his ilk is not true but useful, you subscribe to fictionalism about fictional characters. (Although I will save words in the remainder of this chapter by dropping the "about fictional characters" and simply write "fictionalism".)

The most popular fictionalist version amongst anti-realists about fictional characters is what I shall call *pretence fictionalism*. One of the first who developed a detailed pretence fictionalist account about fictional characters is Kendall Walton. Walton argues (1990, Part Four) that when we engage in talk about the content of fictional works (e.g. *Silence of the Lambs*), we typically *pretend* that there's a real serial killer called "Hannibal Lecter" who eats his victims and consults the FBI. Engaging with fiction wouldn't be much fun if all you did was to coldly note that the story has it that there is a Hannibal Lecter or that Anthony Hopkins acts as if he has murdered people. That's not very gripping. If you want to immerse yourself in the story, it seems that you have to pretend or imagine for the length of the story that Hannibal is real.

Further, the pretence fictionalist holds that when you say "Hannibal Lecter is manipulative", your sentence simply expresses a falsehood. After all, Hannibal Lecter doesn't exist. But that's ok, your sentence is still appropriate or proper or correct because you are uttering it while pretending that there is a Hannibal Lecter. You are playing a popular and widely recognised game of make-believe. Talking about the content of a story is pretty similar to playing a board game (which is also a fiction, one in which you take an active role). You conclude "Miss Scarlett murdered Professor Green in the kitchen with the rope", though, of course, no one really died. The professor only died in the board game. You don't really mean what you're saying; which would imply that there's a dead body lying on your kitchen floor. You are just pretending that this is what happened, as part of the game you are playing. Keep going.

What's more, when you say things such as "Hannibal Lecter is dangerous", you are pretending to express a *truth*. But in order to pretend that you are speaking truly by uttering this sentence, there need not be any real individual in this world that 'Hannibal Lecter' refers to. After all, the person you pretend to talk about does not exist.

Even if we are only pretending to speak truly when uttering the sentence "Elizabeth Bennett is strong-willed", we still need to explain why it is correct to pretend one way but not another. Suppose you are reading *Pride and Prejudice* and pretend that Elizabeth Bennett is an enormous-sized rabbit. You would be doing something wrong. Walton's explanation for why one pretence is proper and the other improper is based on his broader theory of fiction. He thinks that just as we are not free to believe as we please, we are not free to imagine, that is, pretend when we engage with fiction. It is only proper to pretend what is fictionally true. (Sam provides an in-depth analysis of truth in fiction in Chapter 6.) And it is certainly not true in *Pride and Prejudice* that Elizabeth is an oversized rabbit. On the other hand, when you are pretending that Elizabeth is strong-willed, you are doing exactly what the fictional work prescribes you to do. In short, it is appropriate to imagine that Elizabeth Bennett is strong-willed and that Hannibal Lecter is a serial killer but inappropriate to pretend that Elizabeth is a gigantic rabbit or that Hannibal is a vegetarian.

Now, it's one thing to think or say out loud "Elizabeth Bennett is strong-willed" while reading *Pride and Prejudice*, but what about the times we talk – *seemingly* talk – about fictional characters outside of reading or watching the fictional work? The central aspect of Walton's approach to talk about the content of a fiction is based on the idea that participation in games of make-believe, games in which we pretend things are a certain way, is widespread:

> Verbal participation may be much more prevalent than one might have thought. Even when it is perfectly obvious that a speaker is making serious claims about a fictional world, we need not deny that he is participating verbally in a game of make-believe.
>
> (Walton, 1990, p. 394)

Suppose, for example, that you are reading *Pride and Prejudice* to your young niece and you utter the sentence "Elizabeth's astonishment was beyond expression. She stared, coloured, doubted, and was silent." In doing so, you are engaged in a game of make-believe, pretending to describe real people. And now contrast this with a case in which you and I are discussing the novel and I say "Elizabeth froze and blushed", a sentence that one cannot find written in the novel. On the face of things, we are not engaged in a game of make-believe;

it seems that we are taking a more critical, a more detached stance and describing the fictional world of *Pride and Prejudice*. So whereas in the original case you were only pretending to describe the real world, in this case I seem to be really describing the pretend world. However, according to the pretence fictionalist, this is not what is actually happening.

When I say "Elizabeth froze and blushed", I am not truthfully describing the world of Austen's novel. Rather, I am pretending that the world – the *real* world we live in – is as it is portrayed in *Pride and Prejudice*. I am pretending to describe the real world rather than actually describing the pretend world. I pretend that the real world, our world, contains a woman named "Elizabeth Bennett" who, on one occasion, froze and blushed. So even though it may seem as if no pretence is happening, claims the pretence fictionalist, we still are playing a game of make-believe when we talk about the content of a fiction in a rather critical setting.

*Sam:* Okay. But, am I playing some game of make-believe when I say that some characters are more famous than their authors?

That seems like a non-fictional truth about fictional characters. What, according to the pretence fictionalist, am I doing when I utter things like that? Relatedly, how would a pretence fictionalist make sense of my claim that Arthur Conan Doyle created Sherlock Holmes?

*Tatjana:* When you utter "some characters are more famous than their authors" or "Doyle created Holmes" you are playing a game of make-believe in which fictional characters live side by side with their authors in the same, real world. But bear with me, I'll get to critical or, as you call them, non-fictional truths in a bit.

What makes "Hannibal Lecter is manipulative" an appropriate sentence? Walton points out that it is the fact that *Silence of the Lambs* the story is such that pretending to speak truly by uttering "Hannibal Lecter is manipulative" in an authorized game of make-believe is to speak truly in that game. In simpler words, when you're saying "Hannibal Lecter is manipulative" when talking about *Silence of the Lambs*, then you're doing something right. An authorised game is one in which you follow the novel's or film's prescriptions to pretend. What, then, makes "Hannibal Lecter is vegetarian" an inappropriate pretence? It's the fact that no authorised pretence involves you pretending that Lecter is a vegetarian. The crucial point is that the properness of disengaged, critical uses of sentences like "Elizabeth Bennett is strong-willed" only requires real world objects (that is, works of fiction), and the pretend games they authorize. It doesn't require fictional characters.

The pretence fictionalist can explain why fictional characters are not necessary to account for our untrue useful talk and thought about the content of a fictional work. And since they are not necessary, we don't have a good reason to believe in them. (Remember Ockham's Razor!) It's pretty plausible that some sort of pretence is happening when we talk or think about what is true in the fictional world. But since the pretence fictionalist thinks fictional characters do not exist, they also need to account for the other kinds of talk and thought we engage in that appear to involve fictional characters. Take the sentence "Elizabeth Bennett's social skills are better than those of Sheldon Cooper". Here, it appears that we are comparing the main character of *Pride and Prejudice* with one of the main characters of *The Big Bang Theory*. Yet, what's really going on, so says the pretence fictionalist, is that we are only pretending to speak truly when we utter the sentence.

But since there is no fictional work that is a combination of *Pride and Prejudice* and *The Big Bang Theory*, there are no authorised games that would make pretending to speak truly when saying "Elizabeth Bennett's social skills are better than those of Sheldon Cooper" appropriate. It seems that in order to judge the appropriateness of this utterance we need to pretend that Bennett and Cooper are real things inhabiting *one* fictional world and then compare their respective social abilities in that fictional world. And the pretence we are engaging in, when we are pretending to say something true with such a sentence, is what Walton calls an *unofficial* game of make-believe.

Why is it appropriate to say that Bennett's social skills are better than Cooper's? It's appropriate because *Pride and Prejudice* and *The Big Bang Theory* are such that pretending to speak truly by uttering "Elizabeth Bennett's social skills are better than Sheldon Cooper's" in an unofficial game of make-believe based on the two fictional works is to speak truly within that unofficial game. In much simpler terms, you're doing the right thing in your unofficial game when you say "Elizabeth Bennett's social skills are better than those of Sheldon Cooper", given how things are in the respective fictional works.

But pretence fictionalism about fictional characters comes under pressure when we consider utterances with which we seem to quantify directly over fictional characters. Take the sentence "some fictional characters are better developed than others". The sentence doesn't specify any particular fictional characters or fictional works. We are overtly saying certain things about fictional characters and it seems what we are saying is true about the real world. This kind of talk appears to be purely critical, detached from the make-believe games we are playing when we are engaging with a particular work (or even several works) of fiction. It appears that, if we accept that this sentence expresses a truth, we commit ourselves to the belief that there are fictional characters.

The pretence fictionalist has two options now: they can either claim that overtalk about fictional characters is simply false. But then they still need to explain why "some fictional characters are our neighbours" is, well, somehow more wrong.

This is a dead end. So, the fictionalist might want to say instead that some games of make-believe include both real people, pets, and places, *and fictional* people, pets, and places. Consequently, an utterance of "some fictional characters are better developed than others" can be interpreted as a move within such a game. The game will be unofficial, of course, but the utterance will be appropriate whenever it is made within a pretence that fuses the real world with all of the fictional worlds. But this seems like an odd idea. For while it does indeed appear as though we are pretending when we say things like "Elizabeth Bennett's social skills are better than those of Sheldon Cooper", it's much more difficult to see why I would be pretending if I said "Sheldon Cooper is a fictional character". Likewise, I don't take myself to be pretending when I say "some fictional characters are better developed than others". For all intents and purposes, I am dead serious.

*Sam:* It certainly doesn't feel as if I'm pretending anything when I say that Bennett's social skills are better than Cooper's. Moreover, it certainly doesn't seem as if I'm pretending that these two people are real people living in the same world.

*Tatjana:* One reply to your worry is that make-believe is much more pervasive in everyday life than we normally think. Walton argues for this claim in the first chapter of his ground-breaking book *Mimesis as Make-Believe*. Maybe we just haven't noticed the pretence before reading about it.

I'm not the only one who finds this pretence fictionalist treatment of quantified talk overtly about fictional characters a little bizarre. If pretence fictionalism about fictional characters attracts you, you have your work cut out for you. To explain how talk in which we overtly quantify over fictional characters can be appropriate will be your biggest challenge.

## Non-Existent Being

No metaphysical discussion about the nature of fictional characters would be complete without at least mentioning *Meinongianism*, named after the Austrian philosopher Alexis Meinong. I'll keep my discussion on Meinongianism short for two reasons. The first reason is not because the view isn't interesting or is easy to dismiss, but because it's significantly different from the other views we've talked about in Chapter 3 and this chapter. Unlike non-actualism, creationism, and the forms of anti-realism I discussed here, Meinongianism entails a much more exotic view on existence itself. Throughout both chapters, I haven't drawn a distinction between existence and being. It's a standard assumption in contemporary metaphysics to equate the two: to exist is nothing else than to be; and vice versa. There are ghosts if and only if ghosts exist. To say that Sam has existence is to say that Sam has being and to say that I have being is just to say that I exist. But not everyone agrees that everything that has being also exists. Meinongians believe that it is one thing to have being and quite another thing to exist. Things that exist are special. You, Sam, and I, our pets and our smartphones exist *and* have being. But Hermione Granger and *Marvel*'s Loki, the cure for the common cold, and the poison in your drink only enjoy being – not existence. Sam will provide more detail on Meinongianism in Chapter 6.

The second reason why I am keeping the discussion about Meinongianism short is that the view isn't just applied to fictional characters and similar creatures. So, there is a whole bunch of other further commitments that one subscribes to if one subscribes to Meinongianism. In fact, according to Meinongians, to any set of properties, there corresponds an object. And this object has being. Take the properties being a giraffe, wearing a bowtie, and studying philosophy: there is an object that has these and *only* these three properties, the Meinongian argues. But the object doesn't exist, of course, because nothing in reality has only three properties. Notice that, corresponding to every property, there is the property of not having that property. So, if you don't have the property of having been born in Frankfurt am Main, then you have the property of not having been born in Frankfurt am Main. This way, the list of properties that you and everything else that exists have is endless. There's also an object that is a universal cure for death. Nice, eh? Too bad it only has being but no existence and is, hence, pretty useless to us those of us (myself included) who desire embodied immortality.

Meinongianism might seem somewhat crazy at first, but it has roots in the way we talk and think about things. The Meinongian holds that when people use negative existentials about fictional characters, such as "Hermione Granger doesn't exist", they literally express the truth that Hermione has the property of non-existence. Just as we are predicating the property of not speaking Indonesian to Sam when we say "Sam doesn't speak Indonesian", we are predicating the property of not existing to Hermione when we say "Hermione Granger doesn't exist". And just as having the property of not speaking Indonesian means *lacking* the property of speaking Indonesian, having the property of non-existence amounts to lacking existence. Existence, just like speaking Indonesian, is a *discriminatory property*, according to Meinongianism. Some objects have it but not all.

A considerable advantage of Meinongianism as it applies to fictional characters is that it provides us with an object of reference; an object to think and talk *about*. Holly Golightly is available to be discussed, admired, copied, or adapted. This is an advantage that Meinongianism shares with realism about fictional characters. It also shares the advantage with anti-realism about fictional characters that we don't need to accept the existence of fictional characters to make sense of our talk and thought.

Just like non-actualism, Meinongianism cannot say that fictional characters are created by authors. Since any set of properties corresponds to something that has being, the set of properties that Holly Golightly has in the novel corresponded to something long before Truman Capote picked up a pen. In fact, it never started to exist – it exists timelessly. And according to Meinongianism, it's no surprise that you cannot meet and greet Loki – since Loki doesn't exist and you can only bump into things that exist.

Meinongians typically hold that the properties fictional characters have are the ones they have according to fictions. So, the non-existent Hannibal Lecter really has the property of being a cannibal who murders rude people. The non-existent Holly Golightly really is a socialite. But what about being a fictional character or appearing in more than one novel? Just like the realists I discussed in Chapter 3, the Meinongians need to distinguish between properties fictional characters have according to a fiction and those they have outside of the fiction. Without any distinction, fictional characters will have inconsistent properties. For example, Hermione would have the property of appearing in more than one novel but also the property of *not* appearing in *any* novels – since she's not described as appearing in novels in the fiction. Objects that have inconsistent properties are impossible. And impossible objects are rejected by most philosophers, even Meinongians.

In *Nonexistent Objects* (1980), Terence Parsons suggests that we distinguish between nuclear and extranuclear properties. Nuclear properties are those properties a character has within the story. Extranuclear properties are properties such as being a fictional character, appearing in more than one fiction, or having been created by David Lynch. Now, when it comes to the impossibility of an object, so the idea goes, all that matters are its extranuclear properties. An object is only impossible if its extranuclear properties are inconsistent. So as long as a fictional character's extranuclear properties are consistent, we're fine. Suppose that, according to a novel, a fictional character can transform from a human into a cat. Presumably, it's impossible to be a human who transforms into a cat. But since it is a nuclear property, that property does not render the fictional character impossible. Conversely, no object could have been created by Lynch and not been created by Lynch. These are extranuclear properties; they are not properties a character is attributed in a fiction. Extranuclear properties cannot be inconsistent. Sam will subject Parsons' distinction between nuclear and extranuclear properties to some further scrutiny in Chapter 6.

It's a bit tricky to characterise some of the general theoretical commitments Meinongianism has. Does the Meinongian believe that non-existent things are part of reality? If they are, then reality contains an awful lot of entities we usually don't think of as being out there. If non-existent things are *not* part of reality, then what realm do they inhabit? Is it just the place where all of the non-existent beings go? After all, Meinongians don't think that non-existent objects are nothing at all! The Meinongians have their work cut out for them.

Just to be clear, I believe Meinongianism is a challenging and interesting view that deserves a much more thorough discussion than I can offer in this chapter.

## Some Further Thoughts

I've discussed realist views about fictional characters in Chapter 3, and in this chapter, I introduced you to anti-realist theories. Which theory about fictional characters should you rationally subscribe to? Which one beats out all of the other views in terms of theoretical virtues vis à vis theoretical vices? There is no *obvious* answer to these questions. Realist theories, as well as Meinongianism, account for some of our strongest pre-theoretic intuitions. For example, the intuition that we talk and think *about fictional characters*. Unlike non-actualism and Meinongianism, creationism also respects the common-sense truth that Hannibal Lecter, Holly Golightly, and the rest of their ilk are created by authors or filmmakers. Creationism seems a particularly elegant theory, but its biggest challenge is to explain how exactly fictional characters are created.

All realist theories (and Meinongianism on one interpretation) lose out to anti-realism about fictional characters when it comes to ontological parsimony. Since anti-realist theories don't have us believe that there are fictional characters, there are fewer entities we need to accept, and, very importantly, characterise and explain.

My own view is somewhat complex and, like Meinongianism, requires its subscriber to deviate from widely accepted metaphysical views about existence. The widely accepted view in question here is the view that all things that exist are real. In a nutshell, I distinguish between what is real and what exists (von Solodkoff, 2019). The real things are those that are the subject of fundamental metaphysical facts. Metaphysical facts are facts about what there is and what those things are like. Fundamental metaphysical facts explain all other metaphysical facts, while not being explained by other facts themselves – that's what makes them fundamental. The entities the fundamental facts talk about are the fundamental entities.

Fictional characters, in my view, are not real because they are not fundamental. Yet, there are fictional characters, and Hermione Granger and Leslie Knope are two of them. As an example, you might think that the fact that there are fictional characters is further explained by the fact that there are authors or filmmakers and their audiences, and maybe ultimately explained by the fact that fundamental particles exist and behave the way they do. When it comes to ontological parsimony, which I called a theoretical virtue, the only entities that matter are the fundamental ones. So, accepting that there are fictional characters (or, in other words, that fictional characters exist) is not being indulgent. After all, they are not fundamental. Holding this view, let us call it the *Fundamentality View about Fictional Characters*, means that I can acknowledge various pre-theoretic intuitions about fictional characters, for instance, that they are created, and yet I can be ontologically parsimonious and say that reality only contains few kinds of things, fictional characters not being one of them.

*Sam:* Are you saying that fictional characters exist but that they're not real? They exist because, at the less fundamental levels of reality, they appear in the true things that we say, but they're not real because they appear in none of the fundamental metaphysical facts?

*Tatjana:* Yes, the fundamental metaphysical facts do not refer to or quantify over fictional characters. But there are numerous non-fundamental facts that do.

## Works Cited


Parsons, T. (1980) *Nonexistent Objects*. New Haven, CT: Yale University Press.

Russell, B. (1905) On Denoting. *Mind*, 14(56): 479–493.

van Inwagen, P. (1990) *Material Beings*. Ithaca, NY: Cornell University Press.

von Solodkoff, T. (2019) Explaining Fictional Characters. *Ergo: An Open Access Journal of Philosophy*, 6.

Walton, K. (1990) *Mimesis as Make-Believe: On the Foundations of the Representational Arts*. Cambridge, MA: Harvard University Press.


## Further Reading


Brock, S. (2010) The Creationist Fiction: The Case against Creationism about Fictional Characters. *Philosophical Review*, 119(3): 337–364. *Brock defends a different kind of Fictionalism about fictional characters, one we might call* operator fictionalism.

Eagle, A. (2007) Telling Tales. *Proceedings of the Aristotelian Society*, 107(1pt2): 125–147. *Eagle defends an anti-realist view about fictional characters.*

Everett, A. (2005) Against Fictional Realism. *Journal of Philosophy*, 102(12): 624–649. *Everett is not convinced that fictional characters exist. In this and the next paper he tries to undermine some of the motivations for being a fictional realist.*

Everett, A. (2007) Pretense, Existence, and Fictional Objects. *Philosophy and Phenomenological Research*, 74(1): 56–80.

Everett, A. (2013) *The Nonexistent*. Oxford: Oxford University Press. *Contrary to what the title of this book suggests, Everett defends a kind of pretence fictionalism about fictional characters.*

Parsons, T. (1975) A Meinongian Analysis of Fictional Objects. *Grazer Philosophische Studien*, 1(1): 73–86.

Sainsbury, R. M. (2009) *Fiction and Fictionalism*. New York: Routledge. *Sainsbury discusses a variety of theories about fictional characters and concludes the discussion with his own anti-realist view.*

Salis, F. (2013) Fictional Names and the Problem of Intersubjective Identification. *Dialectica*, 67(3): 283–301.

Chapter 5

# Imagination and Fiction

*Tatjana*

Fictions are magical. They introduce us to worlds, places, people, and events that we are unlikely to visit, encounter, or experience in real life. Sometimes they transport us to places unreachable for us, such as faraway galaxies, or to events impossible for us to witness, like the beginnings of our universe. They introduce us to characters none of us could ever possibly meet, including talking cats or medieval monks. And how do they achieve all of this? By inspiring and directing our imagination.

There is something special about imagining in response to fiction, about *fiction-imagining*, as we might call it. When we read a novel or watch a film, our imaginative activity is deliberate, unlike when we dream. And unlike imagining in the context of dreaming, daydreaming, or worrying, fiction-imagining is guided. The novel you're reading or film you're watching tells you what to imagine. Fiction-imagining is also a distinctively social activity. You can engage in it simultaneously with thousands of other readers or viewers. Dreaming, however, is notoriously private. Sam, you, and I cannot dream together. But if the three of us decided to simultaneously watch *Blade Runner* what we would imagine would significantly overlap. For instance, you'd imagine that Nexus-6 replicant Pris is "retired" by blade runner, Rick Deckard, and so would Sam and I. This shared experience is possible because we are engaging with the same fiction that uniformly prescribes to its viewers what to imagine. Imagining in response to fiction is deliberate and it's guided.

Neither deliberate nor guided imagining is unique to fiction-imagining. As we saw in Chapter 1, defining fiction in terms of imagination comes with some serious challenges. And I don't want to claim that imagining is crucial *only* to fiction. Pick up a newspaper and you will find various non-fiction articles that contain prescriptions to imagine. An article on sex trafficking may ask you to imagine the torture and terror of its victims. But arguably, it's not a *requirement* of proper engagement with a non-fictional work that you imagine anything. You don't need to imagine that or how sex trafficking leads to suffering for its victims; if you end up believing that it does, the article will have fulfilled its purpose. Proper engagement with an article on sex trafficking or a

DOI: 10.4324/9781003126102-6

documentary on hate crimes requires your willingness or at least openness to believe the content of these works. Imagining is optional.

But when it comes to fiction, many of us will agree that imagination plays an immensely important role in our engagement with it. Indeed, most philosophers of fiction would subscribe to what I will name the *imagining thesis*; the claim that imagining is necessary and crucial to our engagement with fiction. It's this kind of imagining – guided and deliberate imagining in response to fiction – that we'll talk about in this chapter. We'll think about how imagining, as an activity, matters to our full and proper engagement with fictional works. Although my primary focus in this chapter will be on novels and films, I believe our discussion about imagination will also provide insights into other forms of fiction, such as songs, theater performances, video games, and poems.

## A Mental Activity Like No Other

Imagining is ubiquitous in our lives. Daydreaming about life on a tropical island, dreaming that you are losing all of your teeth, worrying about the future, reading Stephen King's *The Shining* – all of these are imaginative activities. What exactly imagining amounts to has been the topic of a long debate in the philosophy of fiction and imagination, and there does not seem to be an end to it in sight any time soon. Most likely imagining cannot be broken down into other cognitive states and attitudes such as believing or desiring. Imagination is a phenomenon in its own right. I will not offer a definition of what it is to imagine, but we can make some interesting observations that contrast imagining with other forms of mental activities, and we can draw some helpful distinctions between different forms of imagining. Doing so will hopefully help us to better understand the role imagination plays in our proper engagement with fiction.

Imagining is an activity we engage in, something we do: we imagine. When we imagine something, we mentally represent it. If I imagine a tropical island, I might do something that resembles what I do when I perceive an object. Of course the object of my "perception" is in my head rather than part of the external world. Yet, there is a sense in which I see the tropical island in my mind's eye. This kind of talk is, of course, metaphorical, and we don't really have eyes in our minds that see. Rather, imagining this way means *visualising* the object in question.

Not all imagining is visualising though. Instead of seeing an apple in your mind's eye, you might hear the apple in your mind's ear. Can you imagine the sound of an apple cracking when you take the first bite? In addition to seeing a tropical island in your mind's eye, you might be lucky enough to also smell it in your mind's nose. Maybe what you imagine is the smell of sunscreen lotion and piña coladas (FYI, if your mind's nose is refined enough to "smell" tropical scents, I am very envious of you). We certainly use our minds' eyes more frequently than our minds' other "sense organs". Well, chances are that up until now you've never read the expression "the mind's nose" or "the mind's taste buds". But we don't always prioritize vision. When I imagine listening to Pulp's "Common People", I'm imagining the melody and the lyrics. I don't visualise a performance of the song, the song's notes, or myself listening to the song. So, to acknowledge all the various inner senses that can be involved when imagining an object, I'll use the term *sensory imagining*. Visualising then, is only one form of sensory imagining, even if it is the most popular form of imagining an object.

It's tempting to try and analyse sensory imagining in terms of perception. After all, both sensory imagining and perception involve our senses. Well, sensory imagining doesn't involve our real senses, of course, but rather our minds' "senses". In any case, we should resist the temptation to assimilate sensory imagining too much to perception. Our behaviours and responses differ if we perceive an object or if we imagine it. If I perceive a tropical island, I might start applying sunscreen or changing into swim clothes. These behaviours are not rational if I only imagine a tropical island. If you see a robbery take place, you better call the police to let them know. If you only visualise a robbery taking place, better keep your phone in your handbag.

Not all sensory imagining is visualising but not all imagining is sensory imagining either. When we imagine a proposition we engage in *propositional imagining*. Propositional imagining is imagining-*that*; *that* unicorns live in dark forests in Sweden, *that* Watson is Holmes's sidekick or *that* the weather on your perfect tropical island will be warm. Propositional imagining is somewhat similar to believing. Just like imagining, believing is a mental attitude that involves mentally representing a proposition. But unlike imagining, believing means mentally representing a proposition as being true.

*Sam:* I'm fully in agreement with you that sensory imagining is different from propositional imagining and that the two phenomena come apart. But it's a little difficult to draw the distinction clearly in my mind because, whenever I try to imagine that a proposition is true (just for the sake of imagining), I find that I also engage in sensory imagining. So, when you ask me to imagine that unicorns live in dark forests in Sweden, there are images that go through my mind; so too when you ask me to imagine that Watson is Holmes's sidekick. So, since the two sorts of imagining seem to come together so often, what more might you be able to say to make it clear that these are two separate phenomena?

*Tatjana:* I know what you mean. I don't seem to be able to imagine something about dark forests without visualising a dark forest. But sensory imagining and propositional imagining are not just theoretically different concepts. As we'll see shortly propositional imagining without sensory imagining happens. And do you really visualise that there are unicorns in dark forests in *Sweden*? Unicorns – yes. Lots of dark trees – check. But located in Sweden? Well, I don't visualise that part. But it's an important piece of information, isn't it? Suppose a story asks you to imagine that unicorns inhabit the dark forests of Sweden *and no other place on the earth*. Should you conclude that in this fictional world, there are unicorns living in the Gobi Desert? Of course not. You should infer the opposite, that there are no unicorns in the Gobi Desert. However, merely visualising unicorns in a dark forest won't lead you to the conclusion that such creatures don't exist in the desert. After all, your visualisation is not about the Gobi Desert; it's about a dark forest.

Our behaviours and responses to propositions we believe are markedly different from propositions we only imagine. If you believe that you are meeting your friends in Berlin tomorrow morning, then you better make your way to Germany. But if you imagine that you are meeting Eleven in fictional town of Hawkins from Netflix's *Stranger Things*'s, then you better not spend your hard-earned money on a plane ticket to Indiana (unless you want to go to Indiana for some other reason, of course).

Can we believe and imagine the same proposition at the same time? Psychological research suggests we can. Shaun Nichols, a philosopher with a strong interest in psychology, describes an experiment by Alan Leslie:

> Leslie had young children watch as he pretended to pour tea into two (empty) cups. Then he picked up one of the cups, turned it over and shook it, turned it back right side up and placed it next to the other cup. The children were then asked to point at the "full cup" and at the "empty cup". Both cups were really empty throughout the entire procedure, but two-year-olds reliably indicated that the "empty cup" was the one that had been turned upside down and the "full cup" was the other one.
>
> (Nichols, 2006, p.460)

The children were able to distinguish between the cup they imagined to be full and the one they imagined to be empty. But, of course, both cups were empty and the children believed them to be empty. They imagined of the "empty cup" that it is empty but they also believed of the "empty cup" that it is empty. The experiment suggests that we can very well imagine and believe the same proposition at the same time. So, there's no barrier to your both imagining and believing that there are small towns in Indiana when you are watching *Stranger Things*. But here is where imagining and believing a proposition really come apart: If you only imagine that peculiar events are occuring in a small town in

Indiana, your imaginings will do little to influence your upcoming travel plans. But if you believe that there are strange things happening in Indiana, for example because you read a newspaper article, you will integrate this belief into your already existing belief system. You'll conclude that it may be better to stay clear of small towns in Indiana for a while – or to finally book that trip.

What we imagine does not typically motivate the same kind of behaviour that we would exhibit if we believed or perceived something. Yet, some responses will be similar, whether we imagine or believe or perceive things. Talking Heads' song "Wild Wild Life" puts me in a good mood no matter whether I hear it or I imagine hearing it in my mind's ear. Imagining that you are holidaying on a tropical island may give you a warm and fuzzy feeling similar to the one you'd get if you believed you were there. And imagining that one will take a trip to Berlin soon, just as much as believing that one will make the visit, may cause one to wonder – and to google – what Berlin's public transportation system is like.

You might be tempted to think of propositional imagining in terms of supposing or entertaining. Maybe when we imagine what it would be like if our pet could talk to us, we are really supposing or entertaining the thought that Molly, Rex, or Mr Fuzzyboots are complaining about our morning routine. It would seem that in both imagining and in supposing or entertaining we hold the proposition we are mentally representing lightly. We don't commit to its truth, yet, for the sake of the argument, the thought experiment, or the fiction, we accept the proposition. I say we hold the proposition lightly, because we don't show the various behaviours we would show if we thought the proposition were true. But, despite this similarity, it would be a mistake to equate propositional imagining with supposing or entertaining. The reason lies in how the mental attitudes affect our emotions differently.

Imagining things to be a certain way can evoke strong feelings in us. We sense a lump in our throat if we imagine what it would be like if we lost our loved ones. We feel excited if we imagine that we will travel to the Perhentian Islands next year. We feel heartbroken if we imagine that our fictional heroine succumbs to her injuries. But we don't seem to feel emotional to quite the same degree when we simply suppose or entertain a proposition as we do when we imagine it. Supposing or entertaining appears to be mostly stripped of emotional involvement. Its main purpose is to reason through a hypothetical scenario to arrive at a conclusion, for example, "suppose that I travel to a Malaysian island; I better pack swimming clothes and ask my GP for recommended shots".

Consider Hilary Putnam's (1981) famous thought experiment in which you are really just a brain in a vat, floating in a nutritious soup, hooked to cables, while scientists are making you (the brain) believe that you are taking a stroll in the park or talking to a friend. I might either ask you to *suppose* that you are a brain in a vat, for the sake of argument. Or I might request (as Putnam does) that you *imagine* that you are a brain in a vat. Does it amount to the very same request? It seems to me that asking someone to imagine (rather than suppose) a scenario is an invitation to indulge, to involve as many senses as possible, to fill in as many details as one can conceive. If I asked you what exactly it is that you are supposing when you are supposing you are a floating brain, and you replied that you are supposing that one of the scientists is wearing a green blouse, that would be confusing. Including details about the scientists' clothing seems to be a lot more natural when the request is to *imagine* being a brain in the vat. Supposing or entertaining a scenario makes questions of relevance seem salient in a way that imagining a scenario doesn't. Imagining, unlike supposing and entertaining, invites us to fill in as many details as we want, to go above and beyond the aspects of the scenario that are most directly relevant.

We've considered the possibility that imagining could be spelled out in terms of other mental attitudes such as believing, perceiving, or supposing or entertaining. While I haven't considered all the possible options, it's likely that we cannot reduce propositional imagining or sensory imagining to other mental attitudes. Imagining is quite plausibly a mental activity like no other.

## Imagining for Proper Engagement

The Imagining Thesis says that imagining is essential if we want to properly and fully engage with a novel or a film. Two of the most prominent accounts of the role imagining plays in our engagement with fiction are Kendall Walton's make-believe account and Gregory Currie's simulation account. For the purposes of this chapter, the differences between Currie's and Walton's accounts don't really matter. Both emphasize the role of imagining to engaged reading and viewing of fiction. Both hold that fictional works prescribe imaginings, and that engaged audiences follow suit by imagining as prescribed. Let's briefly look at their individual accounts.

As you will remember from Chapters 1 and 4, Kendall Walton, in his seminal book *Mimesis as Make-Believe* (1990), compares our engagement with works of fiction to children's games of make-believe. As children, we crossed wooden sticks with our friends, pretending we were crossing swords. We let stuffed dogs bark, stick people talk, and plastic dinosaurs roar. Toys and plastic objects were cars and crowns in our games of make-believe. Even *we* were props in our imaginative activities; we were princes or doctors, police officers or samurais. Engaged reading and viewing of fiction, so Walton argues, is continuous with children's games of make-believe. Whether we're re-enacting a sword fight with our children or immersing ourselves in a novel, we're participating in games of make-believe where various props guide our imagination. Jamie pokes Jameela with a wooden stick and they both make-believe that Jameela was stabbed by a sword. Jameela's wooden stick breaks in two and the children make-believe that the sword has broken in two. The wooden sticks are props in the children's game that, through their material, shape, and movements, tell Jamie and Jameela what to imagine in their sword fight. Similarly, your copy of *Harry Potter and the Philosopher's Stone* serves you as a prop in the game of make-believe that you enter when you pick up the book and start reading. You imagine that Harry meets Hermione for the first time on a train, or that Snape teaches classes on poisons because these events are described within the book's written content. Fictional works, for Walton, are props that mandate us to imagine various things, and that we correctly respond to by make-believing these things. We propositionally imagine, but typically also sensorily imagine, when we engage with fiction.

Gregory Currie argues in *The Nature of Fiction* (1990) that imagining in response to fiction means simulating the mental states, attitudes, beliefs, and desires of another person. We imagine ourselves in the fictional situations and experiencing the mental states of the characters. Simulating the mental states of the characters in the story helps us understand how we might respond if we were in similar situations. By putting ourselves in the characters' shoes, we can explore our feelings and thoughts in the context of the fictional situation. Our simulations are run "offline", without the real environmental stimuli (such as an actual threat by an alien) and without the same behavioural responses (fleeing the scene, for example). In engaging with fiction, we form different types of imaginings. We create propositional imaginings and sensory imaginings but we also form imaginary beliefs, which are the outcomes of simulating the beliefs we might hold if the fictional events were real. When watching *District 9* we simulate what it would be like if we transformed into a prawn. This simulation helps us imagine the fear and helplessness we would feel if we were in Wikus van de Merwe's place. But of course, we do not create a GoFundMe page to connect the victim with world-class specialists, since we do not really believe that such a transformation took place; or that Wikus van de Merwe exists, for that matter. This is because our simulations lead to imaginings rather than to beliefs.

Understanding a fictional work is not just a matter of grasping the meaning of the words or images in front of you. Even to understand the unfolding of events in a fictional work at a rather basic level, we need to fill in various details. Imagining helps us to interpret the fictional story beyond the meaning of the words it is composed of. Pick up Philip Pullman's novel *Northern Lights*, and you'll read: "Lord Asriel was a tall man with powerful shoulders, a fierce dark face, and eyes that seemed to flash and glitter with savage laughter." As engaged readers, we allow this brief passage to guide our imaginings. We imagine that there is a tall man called "Lord Asriel", and that that man has a certain apperance based on the description provided in the passage. When you read the above passage, you learned that in the fictional world of *Northern Lights* there is a person called Lord Asriel. But is he more than 5 feet tall? Is Lord Asriel's head on his shoulders or between his legs? The novel does not mention the location of his head or tell us his height. Yet, in the fictional world of *The Northern Lights* there are definite answers to these questions. Lord Asriel is either more or less or exactly 5 feet tall. His head is resting on his shoulders or located elsewhere (or nowhere).

But you'll probably agree that the man is taller than 5 feet, and that his head rests on his shoulders rather than between his legs. Why? You successfully used a heuristic device sometimes called the *reality principle*. The reality principle posits that the fictional world of a work is pretty similar to our actual world. That's how we start off when we read a novel or watch a movie. We typically presume that the story tracks the actual world, the world we live in. Of course, the worlds are not identical. Many of the events that are described in fictional works don't occur in reality and the characters portrayed usually don't exist in the real world. But unless we truly have a reason to think that a fictional world is *nothing* like ours, it's sensible to assume that they share many unmentioned details. The novel doesn't mention the location of Lord Asriel's head. But in reality, the heads of living humans rest on their shoulders. Assuming that the fictional world that the Lord inhabits is similar to ours regarding human anatomy, it's reasonable for us to conclude that the man's head is on his shoulders. And people aren't considered tall in our world if they are 5 feet. So, applying the reality principle, you can conclude that Lord Asriel, described as a tall man, measures over 5 feet in height.

Similarly, in reality, one can only make it from Dublin, Ireland, to Haifa, Israel, within 24 hours by flying on a plane. So, if a character is in Dublin one day and in Haifa the next day, we reason that she has travelled by plane, even if the method of travel is never explicitly mentioned (Possibilities of how the character has travelled may increase if the fictional work belongs to the science fiction genre). Thus, imagining the explicit content of a fiction – what we read or see in front of us – helps us figure out what else is going on in the fictional world. And the more open we are to embracing the imaginings required by a fictional work, the more we can uncover about the world it portrays. Engaging our imagination is crucial for correctly interpreting and deeply immersing ourselves in the fictional realms of novels and films.

## Emotional Engagement

Have you ever cried when the hero dies in a novel? Or felt elated when the fictional character you've been rooting for finally gets the life they deserve? In other words, have you reacted emotionally to fictional scenes? One of the biggest perks of fiction is that it makes us feel things without having to deal with the same real-life consequences. I am devastated when I read the final pages of *Never Let Me Go* but, thankfully, in reality there are no clones who are being used as organ donors. I am delighted for Phil Connors when his days stop repeating in *Groundhog Day*, but I don't start researching the phenomenon of day-repetition. Imagining can influence our emotions in powerful ways. If I imagine that my partner is cheating on me, I become upset, even if I firmly believe that they are not cheating. And the more vividly I imagine my partner's transgression, the more upset I become. Some people with phobias such as arachnophobia or coulrophobia can significantly reduce the distress they are feeling by repeatedly imagining the frightening stimulus, such as a spider or a clown, and employing some calming techniques at the same time. More generally, studies have repeatedly shown that our brains can react to imagination a lot like they do when confronted with reality. And as a consequence, the emotional effects of imagining can sometimes be just as strong as the emotional effects of believing.

But not everyone agrees that to be emotionally engaged with a fiction film requires of us that we imagine its content. Derek Matravers denies that we need to *imagine* that (spoiler alert!) one of the main characters, Ruth, dies of terminal cancer in Jon Avnet's *Fried Green Tomatoes* (1991) to feel devastated. It's enough that we believe that it's true in *Fried Green Tomatoes* that Ruth dies to have an emotional reaction. Do you agree? I don't. Note that the belief that it's true in *Fried Green Tomatoes* that Ruth dies is a belief about the *film*. But it's not my belief about the *film* that makes me tear up. I'm distraught because I treat Ruth's death as something that is or has really happened, even though I know the story is fictional. The best way I can think of to describe my mental activity is to say that I imagine or make-believe that Ruth is dead while watching the film.

But Matravers isn't convinced:

> I might witness a relative of mine drinking a cup of tea and remain wholly unmoved. However, we could add some relevant context. Perhaps she has just suffered some grievous loss, had her confidence destroyed, looked as if she was unable to go on. In such circumstances, I might find her quiet engagement with a domestic ritual extremely moving. Clearly, the latter case is not the former with a dose of the imagination; it is only that in different circumstances, different features move us. It is certainly true that to be moved at all, we need to be engaged – it might be that I am so cold to the world that the plight of my relatives does nothing to move me, whatever their circumstances. However, again, whether or not we are engaged with a situation (given to us via a representation or happening in our immediate environment) is not a matter of whether or not we are imagining it.
>
> (Matravers, 2010, pp. 195–196)

Matravers' point is that our emotional responses to situations can be heavily influenced by context and our level of engagement. His example is supposed to illustrate that it is not the power of imagination that impacts our emotions, but rather the specific circumstances and our engagement with the situation, i.e. whether we let ourselves moved by it. I must confess, I don't find it immediately clear that the act of imagining isn't a factor in determining whether we feel emotionally moved or indifferent when observing a relative drinking a cup of tea. The reason, it seems to me, that Matravers might be moved by a tea-drinking relative in distress is because he would empathise with his relative's situation. Empathising involves imagining – envisioning what one would feel if one were in similar circumstances. This process of putting ourselves in another person's shoes can help deepen our emotional connection and understanding of another creature's situation, thereby making us more likely to be emotionally moved by it. The knowledge of his relative's situation alone does not seem to suffice to move Matravers after all; rather, it's imagining the relative's suffering.

Is it *possible* to read a novel or watch a film without engaging in any propositional or sensory imagining? Maybe so. We could simply understand the words and grasp the propositions expressed in a novel or we could process moving images at a minimal level. We could refrain from exploring the fictional world a work is describing and remain detached from the fates of its inhabitants. It's possible, I suppose. But I think this would be a rather disengaged consumption of a fictional work.

*Sam:* I agree, and I'd probably go further than you and say that, whatever it is they're doing, they're not really consuming the fiction as fiction.

*Tatjana:* Yes, that's a good point. I am saying that reading or watching fiction without any imaginings is disengaged consumption. You just let the moving images entertain you (maybe you just enjoy looking at that one actor) or you are simply interested in the style of language a book is written in. But maybe, if that's all you're doing, you are not even consuming fiction. Maybe you are just consuming moving images or written words – that's all.

And remember that proper and full engagement with fiction is what we are after. Full engagement with fiction, I think this much has become clear, requires us to imagine. Well, at the very least, it requires us to propositionally imagine. But what about imagining sensorily?

## Is Sensory Imagining Necessary?

Now, if you are anything like me, when you read Pullman's description of Lord Asriel above, you will have done more than just imagine that there's a tall man who goes by that name. You will also have formed a more or less detailed mental image of a tall, strong-built man in your mind's eye, that is, you will have visualised the fictional character. In other words, you did not just propositionally imagine, you also sensorily imagined the character. But what if instead of reading *Northern Lights* you watched the cinematic adaptation of the novel, *The Golden Compass* (dir. Chris Weitz, 2007)? Did you imagine Lord Asriel with dark-blonde hair, piercing blue eyes, and a beard? Well, that's what he looks like in the film adaptation of the book.

Up until now, I've glossed over any difference between our imaginative engagement with literary fiction and film fiction. Yet, there are significant differences between watching moving images on a screen and reading words in a book. Your brain has to work hard to translate black dots that look like ant footprints on a page into meaningful content about tall men, chatty cats, or kissing friends. Moving images are more direct; it almost seems as if you see the story's content with your own eyes, no major translating required. One seeming consequence of this dissimilarity between novels and films is that sensory imagining is much less involved when it comes to engaged viewing of fiction compared to reading.

To visualise Clarissa Dalloway or Lord Asriel, we translate the novels' words into mental images and fill in the unwritten details thereby creating a more complete visualisation. We get to create our own version of beloved fictional characters. But moving images take this chance at creativity away from us. There's not much to visualise when it comes to the physical appearance of Dr. Ryan Stone while watching *Gravity* (dir. Alfonso Cuarón, 2013). After all, the looks of the actor who's portraying her, Sandra Bullock, don't leave much unspecified. While a description of a tall, slim, dark-haired woman in a novel allows for many different visualisations visual presentations through actors and features of the film-set leave very little room for variation.

We don't need to visually (and auditorily) imagine what it looks (and sounds) like when Wikus van de Merwe turns into a shrimp-like looking creature in *District 9*; after all, the actors and various film-set technicians show us exactly what it looks like. Our visual and auditory imagination may run wild when we read that a human turned into some sort of shrimp. But there's very little room to sensorily imagine anything different from what we perceive when we watch the transformation in the film *District 9*. Now, that doesn't mean that we don't visualise Dr. Stone, or visually and auditorily imagine anything when watching *Gravity* or *District 9*. Just as we can believe and imagine the same proposition at the same time, it's plausible that we can perceive and sensorily imagine the same object at the same time. We can see Sandra Bullock portraying Dr. Stone on the screen and also "see" Dr. Stone in our head with our mind's eye. But both times, we see and "see" a woman who looks identical to Sandra Bullock. That's pretty annoying, if you envisioned Dr. Stone to look more like Zoe Saldaña.

As Wolfgang Iser points out, the discrepancy between what we imagined a fictional character to look like while reading a novel and what we perceive him to look like when we watch a film adaptation of the novel can be frustrating:

> [T]he reader of *Tom Jones* is able to visualize the hero virtually for himself, and so his imagination senses the vast number of possibilities; the moment these possibilities are narrowed down to one complete and immutable picture [when watching a film adaptation of the novel], the imagination is put out of action, and we feel we have somehow been cheated... With the novel the reader must use his imagination to synthesize the information given to him, and so his perception is simultaneously richer and more private; with

> the film he is confined merely to physical perception, and so whatever he remembers of the world he had pictured is brutally cancelled out.
>
> (Iser, 1978, p. 283)

I think Iser makes a valid point. Audio-visual depictions of fictional events and characters fill in many gaps that usually exist in their written counterparts. There are a myriad of ways in which we could imagine the physical appearance of Lord Asriel that are compatible with the novel's content. We can imagine him with a strong jaw line or a double chin, a wide face or a narrow one, blonde hair and blue eyes, or with dark hair and a dark complexion, with huge claws or dainty small hands. But when we watch *The Golden Compass*, we cannot imagine anymore that Lord Asriel has a double chin. If we did, we would not be properly engaging with the film. Audio-visual fiction can afford a more detailed depiction of what fictional characters and events *look and sound* like.

*Sam:* That's interesting. You're right that, watching the film, I imagine the character to look just like the actor. But, then again, it doesn't *have* to be that way. In the Broadway musical, *Hamliton*, an intentional decision was made to cast actors from a wide variety of ethnicities and races to play actual historical persons who may have had a different racial or ethnic identity. For example, the role of George Washington was played by an African American. But, it was still part of the imaginative reconstruction of history, that we might call the story of the play, that Washington was white.

*Tatjana:* That's a very interesting example. So, do you think that we are asked to imagine a white man in our mind's eye while seeing a black man on stage? I find myself unable to do it. Do I imagine an entirely different man? A picture of the historical Washington? Or just the actor as a white person? What I can imagine, propositionally imagine, is that Washington is white while watching a black actor portray him, but I won't be sensorily imagining a white man.

*Sam:* Right. I don't think, when watching *Hamilton*, I visualise Washington as white. I visualise him as looking like the actor. But at the level of propositional imagination, I think I assume that he's white. After all, the characters talk about slavery. It's not like it's set in an alternate history where there was no racial oppression. But, I suppose what makes it an interesting example is that it's uncommon. Normally, we're invited to imagine that a character looks exactly as the actor looks.

*Tatjana:* Interesting. I imagine the novelty in the depiction leads different people to visually and propositionally imagine different things.

But I disagree that because we see and hear the fictional characters and events, as Iser says above, "the imagination is put out of action". Does the fact that sensory imagining appears to be limited and less important in the experience of watching fiction imply that the Imagining Thesis is false, particularly when it is applied to audio-visual fiction? Only if sensory imagining were the only way that we imagine in response to fiction. Even if sensory imagining is not vital to our engagement with fiction, it still leaves us with propositional imagining. More on this later. It may seem as if no visualising beyond what we perceive is happening when we watch a film. But that's not so. Some visualisations in response to watching a fiction film are not entirely fed to us through our perception of the moving images. A character mentions that she grew up in a large mansion set in a luscious garden. The mansion is never shown, yet you might visualise the vast estate. A scene merely shows a shadow of a woman holding a knife. You fill in the unshown details – that there is a woman holding a knife in the dark – and visualise the woman wielding the murder weapon. A silent film shows a man opening and closing his mouth, the words "I am running late" written at the bottom of the screen, and you auditorily imagine the man uttering the phrase. So, even when we engage with film fiction, we often sensorily imagine above and beyond what we perceive on the screen.

Does proper engagement with film *require* that we visualise more than what we see? No, it doesn't. In fact, we have a reason for thinking that not even written fiction requires us to visualise or, more genrally, to sensorily imagine. Doubts come from burgeoning research into a fascinating human variation to imaginative engagement called *aphantasia*. People with aphantasia do not visualise (see e.g. Dawes et al., 2020). They don't just fail to visualise when they read a novel or watch a movie; they also don't visualise very real but not currently present apples, birthday cakes or loved ones. When an aphantasic person reads *Northern Lights*, they do not visualise a tall man with powerful shoulders and a fierce face. Their mind's eye doesn't "see" anything (or they might be best described as not having a mind's eye).

For people with aphantasia it's naturally hard to imagine what visualising a tall man or a grinning cat looks like. Similarly, people without this variation can struggle to understand how aphantasic people engage with novels. Research on aphantasia is still in its infancy. But anecdotal evidence (thank you, Reddit) suggests that aphantasic people enjoy reading novels just as much as non-aphantasic people. If engaged reading required visualising then people with aphantasia would take significantly less pleasure in reading novels than people without aphantasia. Since there is no indication that this is so, I am inclined to conclude that we don't need to visualise (or otherwise sensorily imagine) anything to fully engage with a fictional work. Propositional imagining is sufficient to access and fill in details about the fictional world and to emotionally engage with a fictional work.

There are two more reasons for thinking that sensory imagining is not necessary for engaged reading or watching of fictional works. Sometimes people without aphantasia cannot visualise an object or an event either. This is the case when a fiction contains an impossibility. Impossible stories present us with interpretative challenges, as Sam will show you in Chapter 6. In Robbe-Grillet's nouveau roman, *La Maison de Rendez-vous* (1953), a dog is described as being a stuffed animal and (therefore) inanimate, and a few sentences later as drooling from his mouth and (therefore) animated. We cannot visualise a dog who is both animate and inanimate at the same time, which is exactly what the novel seems to describe. (I suspect what you imagined is a dog who was stuffed first and alive a second later instead.)

Here's a different example of a fictional story that prescribes you to imagine an impossibility. Lewis Carroll's Cheshire Cat in *Alice in Wonderland* gradually vanishes until only his grin is left. The grin is supposed to be still intact while the mouth of the cat has already faded away. But this just doesn't seem possible. A grin is just something a mouth does. When it comes to imagining impossibilities, we are in the same boat as people with aphantasia; we simply cannot visualise what the fiction prescribes us to imagine. But that doesn't mean that we cannot properly respond to the fiction's prescription to imagine. We can imagine that a dog is both stuffed and alive in response to reading *La Maison de Rendezvous*, and we can imagine that a cat's mouth disappears before his grin disappears when reading *Alice in Wonderland*. That is to say, we respond by propositionally imagining. We imagine *that* something is true, even if we are not able to picture it.

And what about other forms of sensory imagining and their role in our engagement with novels and films? We see, and often hear, the actors on screen. But we cannot touch them. We don't know what Sandra Bullock or Dr. Stone smell like. We can't taste the sweaty air during van de Merwe's transformation. Imagining with all of our inner senses would undoubtedly enhance our experience. Yet, we usually focus on our mental eye and, to a lesser degree, ear. This focus is not unique to fiction. Most of us mainly notice what we see or hear. We don't pay the same degree of attention to what we smell, feel, or taste.

*Sam:* They have cinemas in some places that they call 4D. They bring lighting effects in the room, move your seats with the movement of the camera, and even pump smells into the room, and control the climate in there, to enhance the experience. I tried it once. It kind of made me feel sick!

*Tatjana:* It sounds like my kind of experience! I'm not certain how much I would enjoy it while in the theatre. But I'd expect to greatly value the experience - afterwards. *Perceiving* the movement or smell may be uncomfortable, but I suppose just *imagining* the movement or the smell would be great fun. After all, you have some level of control over your imaginings and can always stop imagining the smell of the pile of garbage or the feeling of the sizzling hot air.

*Sam:* Fictions written by dogs might be different, since their sense of smell is so much more pronounced.

*Tatjana:* Apparently, bunnies have many more taste buds than humans. Assuming that the point of having more taste buds is to be able to distinguish between more tastes, then books written by bunnies would probably be confusing for us humans. Or for dogs. Dogs have even fewer taste buds than people.

Films present us with visual and auditory information, and we rarely feel the need to fill in olfactory gustatory, or tactile details. It might be interesting to smell Dr. Stone or taste the air of a fictional scene, yet it does not seem necessary to do so to fully appreciate the fiction. If you can imagine Dr. Stone's smell or imagine the taste of the air around van de Merwe when he transforms into a prawn, I'd recommend you do so while watching the films for a deeper immersion.

We don't usually generate propositional imaginings about the ways a character smells or a fictional meal tastes either. Does Lord Asriel smell of cotton candy? We don't know the answer to this question, of course, but it seems more in line with *Northern Lights* and what we know about men of his kind in reality to assume that he does not smell of sweets. Two lovers are saying their final goodbyes at the beach. It seems to make sense to imagine that the air tastes salty. And yet, we rarely have imaginings about taste, smell or touch, neither sensory nor propositional imaginings. It would be quite a stretch to say that fictional works require us to imagine the smells, tastes, or tactile sensations of a scenario they describe. Prescriptions to imagine are usually presented in visual terms (e.g. "he was tall with broad shoulders"), sometimes in auditive terms (e.g. "her voice broke"), and often in emotional terms (e.g. "they were scared").

But occasionally fictions do describe smells, tastes, and tactile experiences. Patrick Süskind's 1985 novel *Perfume: The Story of a Murderer* made the sense of smell its main topic. And in *Polyester* (John Waters, 1981), the narrator encourages us to smell scratch-and-sniff cards created for the film and distributed by theatres to follow the smells in the fictional world. In William Faulkner's *The Unvanquished* (1938), we read:

> the scent of the verbena in her hair seemed to have increased a hundred times, to have got a hundred times stronger, to be everywhere in the dusk in which something was about to happen which [he] had never dreamed of.

Now, as a smell aficionado I am pretty confident that I would recognize the smell of verbena. But I cannot olfactorily imagine it. In fact, I don't think I can ever imagine olfactorily. It seems I don't have a mental nose. I can't even olfactorily imagine what are often considered the most recognizable scents – the smell of coffee and of freshly baked bread. Certainly, my enjoyment of Faulkner's story would increase if I went through the trouble of finding myself some verbena twigs to sniff while reading the passage. But I am very well capable of enjoying the novel without either the real or the imagined smell of verbena. I cannot even begin to imagine how much more I'd get out of reading *Perfume* if I were able to imagine all of the smells described in the fictional work.

*Sam:* Or maybe it would be too distracting, like my 4D cinema experience!

*Tatjana:* I think it would be a really intense experience, especially because there are also some truly disgusting smells involved. It would be amazing if I could deliberately olfactorily imagine the smell of Grenouille's final creation while also deliberately refraining from imagining the smell of the fish market. But I fear it would only come in a double pack. Even if I were able to imagine the smell of Grenouille's perfume, I would also inevitably end up imagining the smell of the fish market, even if I didn't want to.

If proper engagement with some fictional works requires me to olfactorily imagine, in response to detailed descriptions of smells, then I cannot ever properly engage with works containing such descriptions. But that's not an acceptable outcome. Many people struggle to imagine smells, tastes, or feels. It would be implausible to say that only a very few lucky ones can fully appreciate *The Unvanquished* or *Perfume*. Instead, we should conclude that to the extent that imagination is necessary to the consumption of fiction, it is propositional imagination that counts; the various modes of sensory imagination are, by contrast, an additional bonus.

## Objection to Imagining: The Belief-Action Paradox

Earlier in this chapter I indicated that Derek Matravers isn't convinced by the Imagining Thesis; the claim that imagining is necessary to our engagement with fiction. His general strategy is to undermine the reasons that are thought to support the Imagining Thesis. I have discussed one of his objections to the idea that emotional engagement with works of fiction requires imagining their content. Now, I'd like to discuss another argument that Matravers considers and subsequently counters. Very briefly, the argument is that we don't believe the content of fiction films, so our mental attitude towards it must be that of imagining. Here's the reasoning behind this inference:

1 If the audience did believe what they were watching, then they would be motivated to act.
2 The audience is not motivated to act.
3 Therefore, the audience does not believe what they are watching.

(Matravers 2010, p.191)

In other words, the argument suggests that our non-reactivity when watching fiction is rooted in the fact that we are only imagining certain propositions to be true. The argument is a non-starter because, as Matravers points out, audiences of documentaries and other audio-visual works of non-fiction *do* believe what they are watching and yet, they don't act. Thus, so the thought goes, the above argument cannot support the prescription to imagine thesis.

Should you agree with Matravers? Well, I think Matravers gets something right about premise 1. But I also believe there is something he gets wrong. So, here's what's right. A lack of motivation to call the police or to run for cover isn't a phenomenon exclusive to works of fiction. You don't call the police or move as far away from Milwaukee as possible when you watch a documentary on the cannibalistic murderer Jeffrey Dahmer. Matravers thinks it's because in both cases – the fiction film and the documentary – what we watch are representations rather than real events. But that doesn't seem to be true to me. The reason why we aren't motivated to act when watching David Fincher's *Seven* (1995), or a documentary on Dahmer, is that neither depict current events to which we *can* directly react by calling the police or running away.

The murders in *Seven* are not currently happening and neither are the murders in the documentary (of course, we might still feel motivated to act less directly, such as by being wary of strangers or by researching racial bias in the US police force). So, the kinds of beliefs we should consider in premise 1 are beliefs about what is happening now and, depending on the event, happening close to us. When they believe something they watch can directly affect their lives, many people are motivated to act (even if they choose not to). Suppose you are watching a live-streaming of a tornado approaching your town. What you are watching is a representation and yet, I suspect, you would be very motivated to jump off your couch and look for shelter. Now, this only goes to show that the reason we're not responding in certain ways when we watch fiction is not because what we see are representations but because what we see is not directly affecting our lives at the moment of watching. Note that this observation does nothing to support the Imagining Thesis. Premise 1 is true, I argued, because people *are* motivated to act if they believe what they are watching on the small or the big screen might have important and direct consequences for their lives. When audiences lack a motivation to act, it's because they don't fear such consequences. It's not because they only imagine (without believing) the content of a fiction film.

## Concluding Remarks

We've seen that imagining is a fascinating mental activity where we internally create and manipulate representations of propositions or objects. When we propositionally imagine, we imagine that certain things are true, that such-and-such is the case. Sensory imagining allows us to mentally construct and experience an object's visual appearance, sound, feel, taste, or smell in our mind. So here's what I think: while sensory imagining is not required for a proper engagement with fiction, it no doubt adds a layer of enjoyment to our experience. Moreover, it would be exciting if we could also utilise our other inner senses when we immerse ourselves in a work of fiction, and thereby create a more complete mental representation of the world described. But these are bonuses. What is truly essential to properly and fully engage with novels or films is to propositionally imagine. We need to imagine that things are as the fictional work describes them to be. If you fail to imagine that Clarissa Dalloway is a member of London's high society when reading *Mrs Dalloway*, you are likely missing out on a significant portion of the intended experience. In doing so, you lose an opportunity to fully explore the intricacies of the fictional world and to truly engage emotionally with the narrative.

Now, we need to tread carefully and avoid overstating the role of imagining in reading or watching fiction. Non-fictional works such as newspaper articles or documentaries also encourage us to imagine various propositions. A self-help book on healthy relationships may present a fabricated dialogue between Juanita and Amir. The book does not require us to believe that Juanita and Amir are real. It may be useful for us to imagine that the conversation between them has really taken place to better understand a point the book is trying to make. But we wouldn't be disengaged readers if we decided to skip the dialogues and focus on the passages the book's author intends us to believe. Propositional imagining, I maintain, plays a pivotal role in our proper engagement with fictional works. But that doesn't mean that we are not also engaging in imaginings when reading or watching non-fiction.

## Works Cited


Currie, G. (1990) *The Nature of Fiction*. Cambridge: Cambridge University Press.

Dawes, A. J., *et al.* (2020) A Cognitive Profile of Multi-sensory Imagery, Memory and Dreaming in Aphantasia. *Science Reports*, 10: 10022.

Iser, W. (1978) *The Implied Reader: Patterns of Communication in Prose Fiction from Bunyan to Beckett*. Baltimore, MD: Johns Hopkins University Press.

Matravers, D. (2010) Why We Should Give Up on the Imagination. *Midwest Studies in Philosophy*, 34(1): 190–199.

Nichols, S. (2006) Just the Imagination: Why Imagining Doesn't Behave Like Believing. *Mind and Language*, 21(4): 459–474.

Putnam, H. (1981) *Reason, Truth and History*. Cambridge: Cambridge University Press.

Walton, K. L. (1990) *Mimesis as Make-Believe: On the Foundations of the Representational Arts*. Cambridge, MA: Harvard University Press.

## Further Reading

Kind, A. (2013) The Heterogeneity of the Imagination. *Erkenntnis*, 78(1): 141–159. *Kind explores imagination's role in four philosophical contexts and concludes that imagination is more diverse than previously understood, and no single mental activity can fully explain its role in all these contexts.*

Matravers, D. (2014) *Fiction and Narrative*. Oxford: Oxford University Press. *In this monograph, Matravers challenges the common belief that fictions rely on imagination, presenting a unique perspective on engaging with narratives.*

Sherman, N. (1998) Empathy and Imagination. *Midwest Studies in Philosophy*, 22(1): 82–119. *The article discusses how empathy and imagination play a significant role in shaping our moral understanding.*

Terrone, E. (2020) Imagination and Perception in Film Experience. *Ergo: An Open Access Journal of Philosophy* 7.

Weinberg, J. M. & Meskin, A. (2006) Imagine that! In M. Kieran (ed.), *Contemporary Debates in Aesthetics and the Philosophy of Art*. Oxford: Blackwell, pp. 222–235. *The authors examine the philosophical concept of imagination in relation to aesthetics and the philosophy of art.*

Chapter 6

# Interpreting Fiction

*Sam*

After all of this talk about fiction, I'm going to sit down to read a story. Let's start with Kurt Vonnegut's *Breakfast of Champions* – one of my favourites. Skipping the preface (which you should never do in a Vonnegut novel), I find myself confronted with these words:

> This is a tale of a meeting of two lonesome, skinny, fairly old white men on a planet which was dying fast.
>
> One of them was a science-fiction writer named Kilgore Trout. He was a nobody at the time, and he supposed his life was over. He was mistaken. As a consequence of the meeting, he became one of the most beloved and respected human beings in history.
>
> The man he met was an automobile dealer, a Pontiac dealer named Dwayne Hoover. Dwayne Hoover was on the brink of going insane.
>
> (Vonnegut, 1999, p. 7)

What I'm going to do now is to present a (non-exhaustive) list of things that I take myself to know, or at least to have good reason to believe, on the basis of these words. Then I'll explain how I take myself to know each of the items on the list. By that point, I think we'll have enough material to raise a whole host of philosophical questions.

1 The story is about two human beings, members of the species *Homo sapiens*.
2 The story takes place on earth.

*Tatjana:* The fact that it says in the passage "a planet which was dying fast" made me consider that it wasn't earth. After all, why be vague if it was earth?

*Sam:* That's a fair point. I'll explain my justification soon.

DOI: 10.4324/9781003126102-7

3 Kilgore Trout is a science-fiction writer.
4 Dwayne Hoover is a Pontiac dealer.
5 Dwayne Hoover is about to develop symptoms of ill mental health
6 Dwayne Hoover has a nose.
7 Kilgore Trout has two ears.
8 The story takes place in America.
9 Dwayne Hoover has hair.

*Tatjana:* Why couldn't he be bald?
*Sam:* He could be. I just mean that he has some hair somewhere, even if there's not all that much coverage over his scalp compared to others.

10 There is no specific number that numbers the hairs on Dwayne Hoover's head, but whatever the number is, it will be odd or even.

Why do I claim to know these things?

Well, some of the claims are pretty straightforward. The text tells us explicitly that Kilgore Trout is a science-fiction writer and that Dwayne Hoover is a Pontiac dealer on the verge of some sort of descent into insanity. I'm going to assume that the narrator is reliable (I'm going to leave the whole thorny question of narrators to Tatjana in the next chapter). So, we've already taken care of claims 3, 4, and 5.

But why do I assume that the action of the story takes place on earth? Perhaps, later on in the story, I'll discover otherwise. But, even though Vonnegut was a science-fiction writer who'd be happy to set a novel on another planet, it isn't standard fare, even in science-fiction, for there to be Pontiac dealerships on other planets. Moreover, Vonnegut is well-known, and well-loved, for his dry and cynical sense of humour. Given that fact, it's natural, I would think, to interpret his words "two lonesome, skinny, fairly old white men on a planet which was dying fast" to be describing two Caucasian *Homo sapiens* on earth, rather than two aliens on a planet in some other solar system. This is just the dry and cutting way in which Vonnegut would describe such things.

You're free to disagree, of course, and perhaps things will become clearer as the story unfolds further. But at least I've explained why I'm clinging onto claims 1 and 2, if only provisionally.

And, since Pontiac dealerships are not so common outside of America, and given Vonnegut's fascination with America, it seems fair to assume, also, that the story takes place there. That takes care of claim 8.

Later on in the story, a character called Lyle will suffer a broken nose. But nowhere in the story is the nose of Dwayne Hoover referred to. And yet, it seems as if the conventions of fiction consumption, so to speak, license me – and even encourage me – to assume that Hoover has a nose, even if the nose isn't mentioned in the text. He is, after all, a human being. Human beings tend to have noses. And if Hoover was a human being *without* a nose, that would be such an exceptional fact about him that one would expect the narrator to point it out. Accordingly, until, or unless the narrator tells me otherwise, or unless something in the story occurs to indicate otherwise, I'm going to assume that Hoover has a nose.

I'm going to assume, for exactly analogous reasons, that he has two ears. Moreover, given that he's a mammal, I'm even going to assume that he has hair (somewhere on his head). It would be remarkable if he didn't. And it is nowhere remarked that he didn't! This takes care of claims 6, 7, and 9.

But what's going on with 10? Well, the basic idea is this: we've established that Dwayne Hoover has hair. But you can't have hair without there being some number of hairs that he has. So, there must be a number. And that number must be either even or odd because all numbers are. But there's no *specific* number.

One reason for thinking that 10 is true is because the conventions of reading fiction, along with the text, simply don't settle the matter as to how many hairs are on that head. We might be invited to go beyond the details of the text to imagine that Hoover has a nose. But we're not invited, for any specific number, to imagine that that's the number of hairs that Hoover has. Stories sometimes have gaps in them. They leave things underspecified. For any number, *n*, it will neither be true nor false that *n* is the number of hairs that Hoover has on his head.

That's all very nice. We've derived ten claims that are, we imagine, true within this story, just from the first few sentences. This brings us to the philosophy. The philosophical question this all raises is *what does it mean* for these ten claims to be true? What *makes* them true?

You'll get a better grasp of the question that I'm asking once you hear some of the answers that philosophers have suggested.

## Meinongianism

Some philosophers make a distinction between existence and *being*. These thinkers are called Meinongians, after the Austrian philosophy and psychologist Alexius Meinong (and to be clear, I'm less interested in Meinong himself than in a number of later philosophers who developed some of his insights, even while disagreeing with other details of his view). According to Meinongians, you exist if you are a concrete being, located somewhere in space and time. But even if you don't exist, you'll still have *being*. Otherwise, how would we be able to talk about you? What would we be talking about, if you didn't have some location on the map of *being*? Contemporary Meinongians include Terrence Parsons (1975, 1980) and Edward Zalta (1983, 1988).

So, according to the Meinongian, Dwayne Hoover and Kilgore Trout have *being* even though they don't exist – that is to say: they have some sort of being that's less than fully fledged existence.

Even though Hoover and Trout don't exist, they *are* human beings. They're just *non-existent* human beings. That's what makes claim 1 true. What makes it true is that, even though they don't exist, Hoover and Trout really are *Homo sapiens;* non-existent *Homo sapiens.* You'd be wrong to say that they were elephants, and right to say that they were, "skinny, fairly old white men".

All of the events that take place in the *Breakfast of Champions* have *being*, even though these events don't exist. If you look for the events of the story on the timeline of the earth, you won't find them there. Again: they don't exist. But these events still have *being*. All of the non-existent events that take place in the story, really *do* involve the planet earth, and they really *do* involve the country of America. This is what makes claims 2 and 8 true – for the Meinongian.

Similarly, Kilgore Trout, even though he doesn't exist, *really is* a science-fiction writer; just a non-existent one. That's what makes claim 3 true. Trout isn't an investment banker. That's why it would be false to say that he is.

Trout also has two ears. He doesn't have three ears. His having two ears, rather than three, or any other number, even though he and his ears don't exist, is what makes claim 7 true.

Likewise, the Meinongian will say that Dwayne Hoover is a non-existent being. But, despite not having the property of existence, there are lots of other properties that he *does* have. For example: he is a Pontiac dealer; he is about to develop symptoms of ill mental health; he has a nose; and he has hair. This is what makes claims 4, 5, 6, and 9 true.

One especially weird thing about Meinongian non-existent beings is that they can have a kind of gappiness that existent beings cannot have. It's this strange form of gappiness that's going to explain the truth of claim 10.

For an existent being, if he has hair, there will always be a perfectly specific and precise number of hairs that he has. But non-existent beings aren't like that. They can be incomplete, or fuzzy, or under-determined. Accordingly, even though Dwayne Hoover has hair, and therefore, even though there must be a number of hairs that he has, and even though that number must be either odd or even, there is no *specific* number of hairs on his head. It's more like an undefined cloud of hair, perhaps!

And thus you get this really weird phenomenon according to which, it won't be true to say that Dwayne Hoover has an even number of hairs, and it won't be true to say that he has an odd number of hairs – since there is no specific number that numbers his hair – but it will still be true to say that he has *either* an odd or even number of hairs on his head – because every number, even non-specific ones, are either even or odd. Strange!

It's the gappiness (or perhaps fuzziness would be a better word) of Meinongian non-existent beings that makes strange claims like 10 true. It's this gappiness that leaves some claims about fictional characters neither true nor false, even though every similar claim about an *existent* being *will be* either true or false. To use the language of contemporary philosophy of language, fictional characters as Meinongians construe them are *incomplete* (which is what I've been describing in terms of gappiness or fuzziness).

## Problems with Meinong

So, apart from the weirdness of admitting that there are non-existent beings (which requires us to distinguish between the things that have *being* (which you might call the things that *are*) and the things that *exist*, which is a distinction that only Meinongians make), and apart from the weirdness of saying that non-existent beings can have really fuzzy and gappy properties (i.e. that they can be incomplete), why might we want to reject Meinongianism? Saying that something is weird is never a decisive reason to reject a theory. So, are there other reasons to reject it?

Let's look at three common objections. The first is that some things are true about a fictional character *within* the story, and other things might be true about the same fictional character *outside* of the story. For example, *outside* of the story, it's true that Sherlock Holmes is a fictional character. But it's not true *within* the story that Holmes is a fictional character. On the contrary, *within* the story, Holmes is non-fictional! Our first objection is that Meinongians can't respect this distinction: the distinction between what's true about a character *within* the story, and what's true about the character *outside* of the story.

If what makes it true, within the story, that Sherlock Holmes is a detective, is that he is a non-existent being who has the property of being a detective, then what makes it true outside of the story that he's a fictional character? If what makes it true that he's a fictional character is that the non-existent being called Sherlock Holmes has the property of being a fictional character, then what stops it from being true, *within* the story, that Holmes is fictional?

Our second objection is related to the first. Even if Sherlock Holmes is a non-existent being, it's still surely true *within* the story that Sherlock Holmes *exists*. But what makes it true within the story that Holmes exists? The fact that the non-existent detective is a detective is what makes it true in the story that he's a detective. But what makes it true in the story that he *exists*? And, if he's a non-existent being, then he has no location. So, how is it true in the story that he's located in London? Are we going to have to say that this non-existent being, despite being non-existent, also *exists*? And that this non-located being, even though he has no location, is located in London? Isn't that a flat-out contradiction?

This second objection leads us to our third, which is a more general worry that the Meinongian cannot avoid all sorts of contradictions. Conan Doyle was a great writer, but he made a number of mistakes. In fact, his stories contain an outright contradiction. At times, Watson is described as having a war wound in his leg (and not in his shoulder). At other times, Watson is described as having the same war wound in his shoulder (and not in his leg). Does that mean that Watson is a non-existent being who both does and doesn't have a war wound in his leg, and who both does and doesn't have that very same wound in his shoulder? Conan Doyle can contradict himself. He's only human. But can the actual world contain contradictory objects like this?

*Tatjana:* You might think contradictory objects are fine as long as they don't exist but only have *being*. After all, we can *talk* about contradictory objects, can't we? The cat who disappears before his smile does, the dog who's alive and stuffed, the round square, the number that falls in love, the man who's bigger than the tallest building and smaller than a mouse. All of these things we can talk about and, it seems, attribute at least one quality to them – non-existence.

*Sam:* Right. That's exactly how the Meinongian would respond to this concern (or, at least, the neo-Meinongian. Meinong himself is another story). But I suppose that the non-Meinongian feels queasy about this response. They think that you don't even need to have *being* in order not to exist. The non-existent, for them, aren't some group of beings that happen to fail to exist. The non-existent is a category that has no members, because nothing doesn't exist. And, thus we don't have to admit into our universe any actual non-existent beings. When you describe the cat who disappears before his smile does, they will say, you're not really describing anything at all. You just appear to be. But in actual fact, nothing at all corresponds to your description.

Terence Parsons (1980) escapes our first concern by distinguishing between what he calls nuclear properties and extra-nuclear properties. The nuclear properties would be ones like, being tall, being a man, and being a detective. The extra-nuclear properties would be ones like being possible, being fictional, and being created (or discovered) by Conan Doyle.

*Tatjana:* You worried earlier that the Meinongian has to say that this non-existent being, despite being non-existent, also exists.

Is Parsons's solution that Holmes's non-existence is an extra-nuclear property and that his existence is a nuclear one?

*Sam:* Well, it would be good for him if he could say that. He could say, "Oh, sure, Holmes has nuclear existence, but not non-nuclear existence." But, as we'll see, Parsons doesn't take that route. For Parsons, it's the nuclear properties that get to the heart of what a being is. Accordingly, he can't let existence in on the party. After all, if existence is in your nuclear core, so to speak, then you're not a mere being, but you actually exist!

According to this theory, whenever you say something about non-existent objects you're always saying something ambiguous. For example, you say that non-existent object X has property P (substitute any non-existent object or person you like for X, and any property you like for P). You *could* be saying that X has P as a *nuclear* property, or you could be saying that X has P as an *extra-nuclear* property. That will always be ambiguous, according to Parsons.

When we say that Holmes is a famous creation of Conan Doyle, we speak truly if and only if we mean that the property of being created (or discovered) by Conan Doyle is among Holmes's *extra-nuclear* properties. By contrast, when we say that Holmes is a detective, we speak truly if and only if we mean that the property of being a detective is among Holmes's *nuclear* properties.

But this theory is going to run into all sorts of problems if it wants to give an account as to what makes some properties nuclear and some properties extra-nuclear.

Edward Zalta (1983, 1988) doesn't distinguish between different sorts of properties but between different ways of having a property. This sounds very much like the distinction that Tatjana raised in Chapter 4 between *having* properties and *holding* properties. Zalta's distinction is between *encoding* a property and *exemplifying* a property.

On Zalta's account, a fictional object *encodes* the properties attributed to it by the fiction, but the object doesn't necessarily *exemplify* the properties that it encodes. Holmes, for example, encodes the property of being a detective, and he exemplifies the property of being a famous creation of Conan Doyle; he encodes the property of existing, but he doesn't exemplify that property.

According to Zalta, Holmes isn't really a detective in exactly the same way as is Jay J. Armes (the actual detective). Holmes is a non-existent entity that only *encodes* being a detective whereas Armes is an existent entity who *exemplifies* the property of being a detective. For Parsons, by contrast, the two are detectives in exactly the same way, it's just that one of them exists and one of them doesn't.

*Tatjana:* Does the distinction between exemplifying and encoding track the same properties as the distinction between nuclear and extra-nuclear properties? After all, both distinctions concern properties.

*Sam:* As I understand Parsons, he wants to say that some properties capture what the being really is. Those properties are nuclear. Some properties, by contrast, attach to a being but don't characterize what the being really is; they're more peripheral to its identity. Those are the non-nuclear properties. Indeed, that's why, as I'm just about to say in the body of the text, Parsons has no good answer to the question, which you raised earlier, about Sherlock Holmes existing in his stories. If Parsons makes existence a nuclear property, then he'd be saying that existence really characterizes the essence of his being. But if that's the case, then surely the being exists!

Now, you're right that Zalta's category of encoded properties maps neatly onto Parson's category of nuclear properties, but, because Zalta doesn't think that the encoded properties characterize the essence of the being, if anything, it's the exemplified properties (which correspond to Parson's non-nuclear properties) which, for Zalta, do that job, Zalta has no problem saying that Sherlock Holmes encodes existence. Since Holmes merely encodes existence, we can still say that he doesn't exist, because he doesn't *exemplify* existence.

Let's turn now to our second concern. If the story tells us that Holmes exists, does that mean that existence is among Holmes's nuclear properties? Surely not. You can't make something exist just by saying that it does. And indeed, Parsons's concedes that when we're dealing with non-existent beings, existence is always to be treated as an *extra-nuclear* property. But then, what makes it true *within the story*, that Holmes exists?

All that Parsons can say at this point is that fictional characters must have some "watered-down" nuclear property that corresponds to existence but isn't actually existence (Parsons, 1980, p. 44). It's because Sherlock Holmes has this watered-down nuclear property that we can truly say, relative to the story, that Holmes exists. Perhaps he also has a watered-down nuclear property that corresponds to location, allowing us to say, in the story, that he lives in London. If you're scratching your head, at this point, trying to figure out what this all means, all I can say is that you're not alone.

Zalta's solution is more elegant. Zalta can say, quite straightforwardly, that Holmes doesn't exist because he doesn't exemplify existence. But of course, he *encodes* existence. If it's true, in a story, that some object X has some property P, it's because X encodes P in that story. If it's true that X has P *outside* of a story, then it's because X exemplifies P. Holmes encodes, but he doesn't exemplify existence. In this way, our second objection is answered.

Moving on to our third problem: Parsons (1980, p. 21) is happy to accept that there are, among the things that don't exist, impossible objects. If the properties of Watson's war wound are somehow paradoxical, then Watson might just be an impossible person. Of course, impossible things don't *exist*, but Parsons isn't saying that impossible things *do* exist. He's merely saying that among the things that *don't* exist, there are some impossible things!

Likewise, Parsons accepts that fictional objects may be incomplete, indeterminate, and fuzzy in various ways. Now, just because all *existing* objects are complete, and precise, and non-fuzzy, we have no reason to suppose that all *non-existent* objects must *also* be complete! In a similar (but perhaps more elegant) vein, Zalta insists that the rules of completeness and not having contradictory properties apply only to the *exemplification* of properties, but not to the *encoding* of properties (he develops a logic of encoding in Zalta 1983 and 1988).

So, if you really want to stick with Meingongianism, there may be ways to avoid all of the objections. Although we've only sampled three of them. Other problems lie in wait. Can the Meinongian make sense of fictions within fictions? Does the Meinongian have to deny that authors *create* fictional characters? And though I said that being weird isn't a decisive argument against a theory, you might think that all things being equal we should *prefer* a theory that's less weird to a theory that's more weird. Fuzzy, non-existent beings are about as weird as it gets.

## David Lewis

David Lewis isn't generally thought to be the philosopher to flee towards if you're seeking to escape from weirdness. He's the guy who believes that all of the possible ways that the world could be actually exist as distinct and completely real universes. An infinite number of concrete and complete universes (which Lewis calls, "possible worlds") are a weird thing to believe in. Indeed, Lewis admits that his belief in the reality of possible worlds would tend to encourage "incredulous stares" (Lewis, 1986, §2.8). Fine. But note two things:

1 Yes, it's weird to think that, in addition to our own universe, there are an infinite number of other universes, but it still seems less weird than admitting that there are fuzzy and even contradictory non-existent beings sharing our own universe with us. It follows that Lewis's beliefs will actually count as a *reduction* in weirdness from Meinong!
2 You don't actually have to believe, alongside Lewis, that each possible world is a real place in order to adopt a broadly Lewisian approach to

> the philosophy of fiction. Instead of thinking of a possible world as a real universe, just think of each possible world as a complete description. A complete description is just a set of sentences which collectively describe some way that a universe could be. In order for our possible worlds to be complete and consistent, we can stipulate that a possible world is a set of propositions such that, for every single proposition *P*, the set either includes *P* or its negation.

Once you're fully armed with possible worlds, we can give an account of truth in a fiction without having to swallow any Meinongian pills. So, let's return to Kurt Vonnegut's *Breakfast of Champions* and the things I claim to have learnt from its opening sentences. How will Lewis explain what's going on?

In our world, the text of *Breakfast of Champions*, I imagine, is nowhere being read by a well-informed, trustworthy adult, as an honest to life report of known fact. But there are possible worlds, of course, in which this very text *is* read out by a well-informed, trustworthy adult as an honest to life report of known fact. Let's call all of those worlds the *B*-worlds.

The *B*-worlds are going to be really important in explaining what we're doing when we read this story. But the *B*-worlds won't be enough. We also have to talk about distance between worlds.

Possible worlds aren't connected in space. So, you can't walk from one to another, or even fly to one in a spaceship. In that sense of "distance", there is no distance between them. They are neither close to nor far away from one another. They're simply disconnected. But when Lewis talks about some possible worlds being closer to ours and some being further away, he's talking about how similar or dissimilar they are to our own.

As a rough and ready way to measure the distance, in this sense, between two possible worlds, you could think about how many things you'd have to change in one world to make it identical to the other world. Regarding how many facts or propositions do the two worlds differ? The higher the number, the more distant the worlds. The smaller the number, the closer the worlds.

Figure 6.1 has the actual world in the middle with the @ sign standing for "actual". If a world has a *B* in it, that means that it's one of the worlds in which the text of *Breakfast of Champions* is read out by a well-informed, trustworthy adult, as an honest report of known facts. Worlds that have no *B* in them are worlds, like our own, in which the text of *Breakfast of Champions* is never read out by a well-informed, trustworthy adult, as an honest report of known facts.

The spatial distance in the diagram between the worlds is supposed to represent how near or far those possible worlds are from each other (not in terms of spatial distance, of course, but in terms of similarity). So, with that in mind, take a look at Figure 6.1.

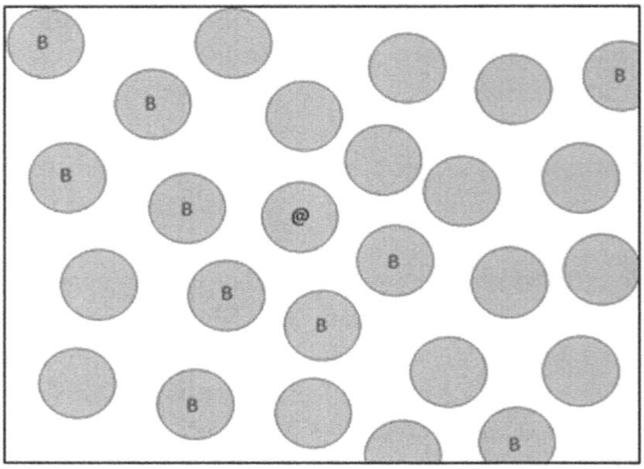


*Figure 6.1* The *B*-worlds.

Now, there *are* possible worlds in which human beings have three nostrils. Some of those worlds may even be *B*-worlds. The text of *Breakfast of Champions* is absolutely silent about the number of nostrils standardly had by human beings! But the worlds in which human beings have three nostrils are all going to be pretty far away from the actual world. What Lewis (1978) asks us to do, when trying to figure out what's true in a fiction like *Breakfast of Champions,* is to concentrate on the *B*-worlds that are at least as close as any other *B*-world is to the actual world, or to the single closest *B*-world to the actual world, if there is one. In our case, that means ignoring all of the worlds that I've blacked out in Figure 6.2.

The only worlds that are relevant to us are what we might call "the close *B*-worlds". When we say that something is true in the *Breakfast of Champions*, according to Lewis (1978), we mean that it's true in all of the close *B*-worlds. When we say that something is false in the *Breakfast of Champions* we mean that it's false in all of the close *B*-worlds. But there will be some propositions that are true in some of the close *B*-worlds, but false in other *B*-worlds, even though all of these worlds are equally close to the actual world. In cases where the close *B*-worlds disagree, a sentence will be neither true nor false in the story. This is a really clever analysis. It seems to give us everything we're looking for.

Let's walk through the list of things we know from the first few sentences of the story.

1 The story is about two human beings, members of the species *Homo sapiens*.
   - *That's right. A B-world in which the main characters are not* Homo sapiens *is going to have to be so different to the actual world as to fall altogether outside of the collection of close B-worlds. By contrast, in all of the close B-worlds, the narrator is telling a story about Homo sapiens.*

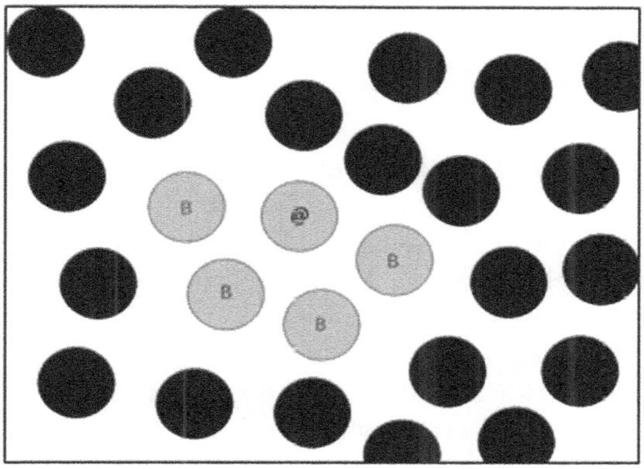


*Figure 6.2* The close *B*-worlds.

2 The story takes place on earth.
- *That's also going to follow from the fact that possible worlds in which Pontiac dealerships can be found on planets other than earth are going to be very far away indeed from the actual world. In all of the close B-worlds, the narrator is telling a story about events that transpire on earth.*

3 Kilgore Trout is a science-fiction writer.
- *Yes, because in every close world in which this text is read as known fact, it refers to a person called Kilgore Trout who is a science-fiction writer. Otherwise, the person reading the text would be lying!*

4 Dwayne Hoover is a Pontiac dealer.
- *Likewise, and for similar reasons, every close B-world is home to a person called Dwayne Hoover, and Hoover is a Pontiac dealer.*

5 Dwayne Hoover is about to develop symptoms of mental ill health.
- *In every close-by B-world, Dwayne Hoover is, given the reliability of the narrator, about to develop symptoms of mental ill health.*

6 Dwayne Hoover has a nose.
- *Worlds in which it's unremarkable for a human not to have a nose are very far away from the actual world. In every close B-world, the narrator doesn't mention Dwayne Hoover's nose because it's taken for granted that he has one.*

7 Kilgore Trout has two ears.
- *Likewise, worlds in which it's unremarkable for a human to have more or less than two ears are very far away. In every close B-world, the narrator doesn't mention that Trout has two ears because it's taken for granted that he does.*

8 The story takes place in America.
- *B-worlds in which Pontiac dealerships and the name Dwight are at all common outside of America are relatively distant to our world compared to B-worlds in*

*which these are distinctively American phenomena (as they are in the actual world). Accordingly, in all close B-worlds, the story that the text reports takes place in America.*

*Tatjana:* I'm not sure I get this. Surely, there are, at the very moment, Pontiac dealerships outside of America.

It may not be common, but it happens. And so does people being named Dwight outside of America. Maybe we should be more careful about claiming that the story takes place in America.

*Sam:* That's fair enough. I suppose that all ten of the claims I've inferred, are only provisional. All of them might get revised as we continue reading the story. I can only report that, as I read the story, I assume that it's in America, and I think that this has something to do with how typically American I find the names and the brand of car.

Sure, as I keep reading further, I may have to revise this judgement. And, in your own reading of the book – perhaps being less crude and judgmental than me, you may be slower to come to embrace claim 8.

Moreover, and as I'll try to explain later on, Lewis will actually allow me, in the final analysis, to use other factors to home in on the relevant worlds, not just proximity to our own world. Those extra factors will include details drawn from what I know of the genre of Kurt Vonnegut stories – a genre that has a preoccupation with America. Once those factors are in place, claim 8 will be better justified. But I haven't explained that bit yet!

9 Dwayne Hoover has hair.
   - *B-worlds in which the possession of no hair whatsoever by mammals is unremarkable are further away from the actual world than B-worlds in which the narrator doesn't mention that Hoover has hair simply because it's taken for granted that he does.*

10 There is no specific number that numbers the hairs on Dwayne Hoover's head, but whatever the number is, it will be odd or even.
   - *This is where Lewis's account really begins to shine. We don't have to believe, with the Meinongian, that there are (non-existent) people walking around who have hair without having a specific number of hairs. In the actual world, the average adult has approximately 100,000 hairs. In some possible worlds, the real and existing person called Dwayne Hoover named by the text of* Breakfast of Champions *has 100,001 hairs. That wouldn't be at all remarkable. In other possible worlds, the real and existing person called Dwayne Hoover named by the text of* Breakfast of Champions *has 99,999 hairs. But neither of these worlds need be any closer to the actual world than the other. So, every person (actual and*

> *possible) has an exact number of hairs, and every person (actual and possible) has either an odd or an even number of hairs. But the close B-worlds simply don't agree as to how many hairs Dwayne Hoover has. The close B-worlds agree that Hoover has either an even or an odd number of hairs, but there is no number* n *such that on all of the close B-worlds, the person called Dwayne Hoover by the text of* Breakfast of Champions *has* n *hairs on his head.*

And thus, according to Lewis, when we read a fiction, we're basically homing in upon a set of worlds that are as close to the actual world as the text of the fiction will allow. What we consider to be true in a fiction is just what's true in all of those worlds. What's false in a fiction is just what's false in all of those worlds. The reason why some things are neither true nor false in a story is simply because the worlds in question don't agree on all things.

Having presented this pretty ingenious account of what makes things true or false in a fiction, Lewis adds one further detail. Sometimes, when we read a story, we are informed not just by the relationship between the text and the actual world, and thus we're not just interested in the worlds of the text closest to the actual world. Sometimes, other worlds are relevant too.

For example, if I read a story that has an elf in it, I'm going to draw all sorts of conclusions about those elves. I'll draw these conclusions not just from the text, and not from the actual world either (since there are no elves in the actual world). Instead, it seems as if I'm also interested in worlds where other texts from the same genre are read as known fact.

So, when reading a story that has elves in it, I'm going to be interested in the worlds in which the text is read as known fact which are closest not just to our own world, but also to a collection of worlds that we might call, the fantasy worlds (where some fantasy story or other is read as known fact).

Indeed, in the ten facts that I derived from the opening of *Breakfast of Champions*, I was informed not just by my knowledge of the text, and of the actual world, but also my knowledge of other Kurt Vonnegut stories. So, perhaps, I'm not just interested in the *B*-worlds that are closest to the actual world, but to those *B*-worlds which are at once closest to the actual world, and to the set of Vonnegut worlds (i.e. worlds in which some Kurt Vonnegut story or other is told as known fact).

*Tatjana:* I don't see why it's the worlds in which his stories are told as known facts that matter. Isn't it the *actual* facts about Vonnegut that help you interpret the fiction, such as the fact that Vonnegut is obsessed with America?

*Sam:* I think you're right. When I introspect, it's the things I know about Vonnegut, rather than about worlds in which his stories are told as fact, that influence my reading, and my coming to embrace claim 8 as quickly as I did. But Lewis doesn't allow for those sorts of inferences to play a role in determining what's true and what's false. He only allows proximity to the actual world, and proximity to a set of worlds that are highlighted by a genre of fiction, to play a role. I think this renders his account artificial because, I agree with you, that it's facts about the actual Vonnegut that are influencing me here. The route that Lewis suggests feels more round-about than the route I actually use as a reader.

Finally, Lewis's account includes a subtle and elegant flexibility. He arrives at this flexibility in conversation with a real story by Conan Doyle. In that story, Sherlock Holmes solves a murder case on the assumption that a certain snake (most likely a Russell's viper) has the ability to climb a vertical rope. In the actual world, however, no snake that fits the description of the book could actually climb such a rope. Lewis (1978) concedes two things:

1 In the closest worlds in which the text of the story is reported as known fact, what actually happened is that Holmes and the narrator (called Watson) made a mistake. They think they've solved the murder, but since the relevant snake couldn't have climbed the relevant rope, the murder wasn't really solved.
2 The above conclusion probably wasn't Conan Doyle's intention. Conan Doyle had probably mistakenly thought that Russell's vipers *can* climb ropes.

But this is all fine. According to Lewis there are many ways in which we, as readers, might choose to engage with a text. If we're particularly historically conscious, and take the author's intention very seriously, then we might be interested in the world in which the text is read out as known fact which are closest, not to the actual world, but to the actual world as it was falsely believed to be by the author, or by the original audience of the story.

Alternatively, we might be less interested in what the author originally meant, or what original audiences would have assumed. If so, we might focus on the worlds in which the text is read out as known fact which are closest to the actual world as we, its contemporary audience, believe it to be. It's not that there's a right or wrong here. There are just multiple ways to read fiction. That seems right.

## Problems with Lewis

It wouldn't be fair, I think, to discount Lewis's approach to truth in fiction merely because you don't believe in the existence of real possible universes in addition to our own. Lewis's approach to truth in fiction works just as well if we treat possible worlds as sets of propositions, rather than real concrete universes. Nevertheless, there is one issue in particular, with which Lewis's account is known to struggle.

However flexible Lewis's suggestion may be, truth in fiction, for him, is always going to boil down to truth across some set or other of possible worlds. But the thing about possible worlds is that they're all possible! Not every story, by contrast, is possible.

Admittedly, some impossibilities are smuggled into a fiction by accident. The contradictory location of Watson's war wound is a case in point. Luckily for Lewis, when the impossibility in a story is very much incidental to the plot (as accidental impossibilities tend to be), there are various technical ways to fix Lewis's account. But sometimes there will be stories that have completely impossible plots, and which don't at all try to hide the impossibility, and which are such that the impossibilities are there completely on purpose, and are integral to the whole narrative.

Tamar Gendler (2000) tells the following story, titled "The Tower of Goldbach", to illustrate this point. The title of her story is a reference to the Tower of Babel, and though there's no tower in her story, the whole narrative is a pastiche of the Bible. Here's a summary of the story: Once upon a time, all of the mathematicians of the world were of common purpose. They came together and finally discovered a proof for Goldbach's conjecture (according to which every single even number greater than 2 is the sum of two prime numbers). God was shocked by their audacity. Accordingly, he took the number 12 and made it no longer the sum of 5 and 7. This ruined their proof. One mathematician was devastated by this development as it completely ruined their proof of Goldbach's conjecture. Accordingly, he prayed to God. "If I can find 5 righteous mathematicians, will you reverse your decree?" he beseeched his creator.

"Not even if you find me 5 righteous mathematicians," came the heavenly response.

"What if I can find you 7 righteous mathematicians?"

"Not even then."

In one last desperate effort, the righteous mathematician begged, "What if I can find you 12 righteous mathematicians?"

At this point, God conceded and said, "If you can find me 12 righteous mathematicians, I will reverse my decree, and I will restore 12 to being the sum of 5 and 7."

Unfortunately for the righteous man in question, he could only find 5 righteous mathematicians in one town, and 7 in another. Before the decree, this would have added up to 12, and would have been sufficient. But, because of the decree, it wasn't enough. This seemed especially unfair.

Accordingly, God and the mathematicians took their case to Solomon the wise. They explained that, before the decree, 5 + 7 mathematicians would have been sufficient to undo the decree, but because of the decree, 5 + 7 mathematicians is insufficient. Solomon could see the strength of both claims.

Accordingly, he decided that, from this day forth, 12 would both be the sum of 5 and 7 and also not the sum of 5 and 7, and everyone lived happily ever after.

Now, of course, there's a sense in which this story is utter nonsense. But there's another sense in which we can kind of follow what's going on. We find it amusing. And thus, there's a sense in which it sort of *works* as a story. You can probably even retell the story and in so doing respect the so-called facts of the story; that is, you have a sense of what's true in the story and what's false in the story, even though what's going on is completely and utterly impossible!

There are no possible worlds whatsoever in which 5 and 7 don't add up to 12. There are no possible worlds whatsoever in which Solomon could affect the sort of judgement he affects in this story. For that reason, and to the extent that this story is a kosher story, Lewis must be wrong. Truth in a fiction simply can't be a function of what's going on in some set of possible worlds because there are no possible worlds whatsoever in which the facts of Gendler's impossible story obtain.

Now you could try to save Lewis's account by appealing not just to possible worlds but also to impossible worlds. But even if I could accept that there are such things as impossible worlds (something like incoherent descriptions of a world), I have absolutely no idea what it could mean for some impossible worlds to be closer than others to the actual world. Surely, if they're really impossible, then there's an important sense in which they are all infinitely far away from the actual world?

But, to the extent that Lewis's account is interested in sets of worlds that are close to the actual one, or close to the world as it is believed to be, then we're going to have to be able to isolate the *close* impossible worlds from the impossible worlds that are further away.

At this point, I lose any sense of what closeness means. Impossibilities are all infinitely distant. There is no number of changes to this world that could make it identical to an impossible world. No such changes would be possible!

*Tatjana:* Here's an idea: Maybe the closest impossible worlds are the ones in which all the parts of the story that *are* possible are told as known facts.

*Sam:* But some of those impossible worlds allow for known facts to be told without being true. Sure, that's impossible (how can you know something if that something isn't true) but these are impossible worlds! If we include those worlds among the close impossible worlds, I don't see how we'll get the pattern of truths and falsehoods that we need. For example, it needs to be true in the story that mathematicians proved Goldbach's conjecture. After all, that's uncontroversially true in the story. But if the closest impossible worlds are the ones in which all the parts of the story that *are* possible are told as known facts, nothing guarantees that Goldbach's conjecture was ever proven in them. After all, in an impossible world, it could be told as known fact that Goldbach's conjecture was proved without it being true that Goldbach's conjecture was ever proved. I just don't think that impossible worlds are going to admit of a definition of closeness to the actual world that will get us the patterns of truths and falsehoods that we need.

*Tatjana:* I guess what I mean is that there could be an impossible world in which everything in "The Tower of Goldbach" is true (sorry, so not just the possible things) but also people walk on their hands. That must be an impossible world that's even further away from ours.

*Sam:* Ah, now I see what you mean. Just focus on the worlds with the fewest impossibilities, in which the story is told as known fact. I get you. But still, I worry, any world in which the "facts" of the story obtain will be infinitely far away. Even the worlds in which people walk on their feet rather than their hands, because we're talking about impossible worlds, might be such that they walk on their feet rather than their hands, as well as walking on their hands rather than their feet.

Moreover, not everybody believes that impossible worlds are, so to speak, possible to begin with. In other words: not everybody believes that we can coherently talk about impossible worlds. For these reasons, Lewis's account of truth in fiction, despite its tremendous elegance and flexibility, is commonly rejected these days by philosophers of fiction.

Another problem Lewis will have to face is raised by unreliable narrators. For various reasons, Lewis talks about worlds in which a text is read as known fact. But sometimes, the story itself includes a narrator who tells lies. What will Lewis do about *those* stories?

## Two Simple Accounts

There are two more ways to explain what's going on with truth in fiction that are much simpler than either Meinong or Lewis.

The first harks back to Chapter 4 and the distinction we drew between a fictional character *having* a property and a fictional character *holding* a property.

On this view, fictional characters really do exist. We don't have to go all Meinongian and say that they don't exist but have some other sort of hold on being. Instead, we say that they exist, but they're sort of abstract entities. These sorts of moves will be familiar to readers from Chapter 3.

Accordingly, Sherlock Holmes exists but he isn't a detective. All he is is a fictional character. An invention of Conan Doyle. What makes it true in the story that Holmes is a detective is that he *holds* the property of being a detective, even though he doesn't *have* that property.

This account is similar to Zalta's Meinongianism, which has Holmes encode the property of being a detective even though he doesn't exemplify it. The only difference here is that Zalta thinks that fictional characters are non-existent beings. This more straightforward account (owed to Peter van Inwagen, 1977) claims that fictional characters *do* exist, they're just not people – at best, they are things that *hold* the property of being people relative to some story or other.

Dwayne Hoover isn't a Pontiac dealer, but he holds the property of being a Pontiac dealer in the story. Kilgore Trout isn't a science-fiction writer. But he holds that property in the story. Neither of them have a nose, but they both hold the property of having a nose in the story. And so on and so forth. You get the point. On this account, what makes it true in the story that Trout has two ears is that the real entity called Kilgore Trout, which was created by Kurt Vonnegut, holds the property, in our story, of having two ears – even though, because he has no actual body, he doesn't *have* the property of having two ears (he just holds it).

One reason for rejecting this view will directly lead us to a second simple account. The reason you might reject this view is that it doesn't seem to mesh with our experience of reading fiction. When you read a Sherlock Holmes fiction, are you thinking about some impure abstractum called a fictional object, and then pretending that this non-human object is actually a human, and actually a detective, and that he actually *has* all of the properties which, in reality he only *holds*? That seems like a strange and indirect way to go about reading a story. Accordingly, a simpler way to describe what's going on is this:

- When you read a story, you treat lots of sentences as true, for the sake of the story, even though they're false. These sentences aren't made true because of what's going on in various possible worlds. These sentences aren't made true because of the nuclear properties had (or encoded) by non-existent beings. These sentences aren't made true by the properties held but not had by abstract (or semi-abstract) objects. Rather, many of these sentences are simply false. We just pretend that they're true.

## What Lewis Got Right

What we've seen so far, in this chapter, is lots of proposals as to what makes my ten claims about *Breakfast of Champions* true. On one proposal, it's non-existent beings and their properties that make the claims true. On the next proposal, it's what's going on across a set of possible worlds that make them true. On the third proposal, the claims are made true by the properties that certain entities (such as Dwayne Hoover and Kilgore Trout) hold, even if those entities don't *have* those properties. Finally, we've seen the proposal that the ten sentences aren't true at all. They're not made true by any way that any things in this or any other world are. We just *pretend* that they're true.

In this chapter, I don't want to take sides. Instead, I want to conclude with a brief discussion of how we know which sentences are true in a fiction and which are false, even if the whole thing is just a game, like the final proposal suggests. How do we know what properties apply to our non-existent beings? Or, how do we know what's going on in the relevant possible worlds? Or, how do we know what properties are held by which characters? Or, more simply, how do we know what we're supposed to pretend?

Now, I can't offer a complete analysis of what's going on, but I can give you a sketch of some of the most important elements. When we read a fiction, we place that fiction into a genre (for more on what a genre is, see Chapter 1). As we continue to read, we are – so to speak – in constant conversation with three sources of information: (1) the text; (2) the conventions of the genre; and (3) our knowledge of the actual world.

This takes us back to my suggestion, in Chapter 1, that fiction has two main focuses, the world of the story (so to speak), and the actual world. How do these sources of information interact?

Again, I can only offer a brief sketch. But the idea is this: as we read a story, we open up, in our mind, what can be called a comparison class (see Hazlett & Uidhir, 2011). What goes into that class are all of the sentences that we take to be both true in the story *and* true in the actual world. How do we know what goes into this class, and what is its function?

Well, I can't say exactly how we know what goes into it, and what is supposed to be left out. A lot of this will depend upon very subtle conventions that surround different genres of fiction. But I can say this much: the more realistic the genre, the bigger the comparison class is supposed to be. In other words, the more realistic the genre, the more similar the world of the fiction is supposed to be to the actual world.

But what is the function of this comparison class? Why do we go to such trouble to build it (or, more accurately, find it)? Well, as we know, the text itself leaves out many details that we're supposed simply to assume. We are supposed to assume, for example, that Kilgore Trout has two ears, even though the text is silent on the matter. But, given the genre of *Breakfast of Champions*, the claim that human beings have two ears is going to be in the comparison class. And, because it's there in the comparison class, and to use the terminology of Tamar Gendler (2000) and other philosophers in her wake, we can *import* the claim that all humans have two ears into the story itself.

*Tatjana:* This sounds like a heuristic device Walton and others have called the reality principle; which I discussed in Chapter 5. Is this the same idea under a different name?

*Sam:* Yes, the reality principle is what Kendall Walton and others call the assumption that the world of the story should be as close to the actual world as the story will allow.

The reason we *import* things from the real world into the world of the fiction, so to speak, is in deference to the reality principle. But the notion of import, though justified by the reality principle, is slightly different. It is the activity of bringing facts from our world to fill in the gaps of a story, and the notion, as we'll see is juxtaposed to the notion of export, which I think is a really important notion for understanding some of the educational power that fiction holds (see Chapter 11). Import and export are licensed, in a sense, by the reality principle.

Where did we get it from? We got it from the comparison class. How did we know to find it there? Because, as experienced readers of fiction, we're sensitive to the relevant conventions.

Another function of the comparison class is to license "export". If you're reading a well-researched historical novel, and it says that there was a war in North America in 1812, then – given the relevant conventions for this genre – you'll know that that claim should be placed into the comparison class. And because it's there in the comparison class, you can trust (if you trust that the author did her research) that there really was a war in the real world, in North America, in 1812. Just as you import things from the real world, into the world of the story, via the comparison class, you also export things from the story, into the real world, through the comparison class.

Even genres that invite us to have very selective and small comparison classes – stories about magical worlds, for example – still have a lot to teach us about the real world. If, for instance, the psychology of the main characters is supposed to be sufficiently similar to the psychology of human beings, then all sorts of claims about how hobbits or elves or wizards might act in certain situations will translate straightforwardly into claims about the psychology of intelligent and emotional beings in general. Those claims will thereby find their way into the comparison class, and we will be licensed to export them to the real world. We will take the story to be teaching us something about the real world.

In this genre specific way, we use the real world to fill in relevant gaps in a story, and we use the story to learn things about the real world.

This is, I think, where David Lewis (1978) was uncontroversially right about something important. The actual world, or at least the world as we believe it to be, or at least the world as *someone* believes it to be, is *always* relevant to calibrating what goes on in a story. In this way, every story is partially about the real world. This is true even if we reject the other elements of Lewis's account.

As one of my students (Muneera Abu Rock) once put the point, very beautifully: every author, however imaginative, is always forced to plagiarize God. She said this because the actual world (i.e. the world that theists claim to have been created by God) always creeps into the world of a story, however imaginative that story may be. The actual world is always there in the background, filling in the story's gaps in ways that the conventions of the relevant genre dictate.

Moreover, whatever a story might be about, since its interpretation requires a comparison class, it will always also be about the actual world. This is why I claimed, back in Chapter 1, that fiction is twofolded – it always focuses on two things at once: the world of the story, *and* the world in which the story is being read.

## Works Cited

Gendler, T. S. (2000) The Puzzle of Imaginative Resistance. *The Journal of Philosophy*, 97(2): 55–81.

Hazlett, A. & Mag Uidhir, C. (2011) Unrealistic Fictions. *American Philosophical Quarterly*, 48(1): 33–46.

Lewis, D. (1978) Truth in Fiction. *American Philosophical Quarterly*, 15(1): 37–46.

Lewis, D. (1986) *On the Plurality of Worlds*. Oxford: Blackwell.

Parsons, T. (1975) A Meinongian Analysis of Fictional Objects. *Grazer Philosophische Studien*, 1: 73–86.

Parsons, T. (1980) *Nonexistent Objects*. New Haven, CT: Yale University Press.

van Inwagen, P. (1977) Creatures of Fiction. *American Philosophical Quarterly*, 14(4): 299–308.

Vonnegut, K. (1999) *Breakfast of Champions*. New York: Dial Press Trade Paperback.

Zalta, E. (1983) *Abstract Objects: An Introduction to Axiomatic Metaphysics*. Dordrecht: Reidel Publishing Company.

Zalta, E. (1988) *Intensional Logic and the Metaphysics of Intentionality*. Cambridge, MA: MIT Press.

## Further Reading

Byrne, A. (1993) Truth in Fiction: The Story Continued. *Australasian Journal of Philosophy*, 71(1): 24–35.

Friend, S. (2017) The Real Foundation of Fictional Worlds. *Australasian Journal of Philosophy*, 95(1): 29–42.

Hanley, R. (2004) As Good as it Gets: Lewis on Truth in Fiction. *Australasian Journal of Philosophy*, 82(1): 112–128.

Howard-Snyder, F. (2002) Truth in Fiction: The Whole Story. In W. Alston (ed.), *Realism and Anti-Realism*. Ithaca, NY: Cornell University Press, pp. 253–279.

Kivy, P. (1997) The Laboratory of Fictional Truth. In P. Kivy, *Philosophies of Arts: An Essay in Differences*. New York: Cambridge University Press, pp. 120–139.

Woods, J. (2018) *Truth in Fiction: Rethinking its Logic*. Dordrecht: Springer.

Woodward, R. (2011) Truth in Fiction, *Philosophy Compass*, 6(3): 158–167.

Chapter 7

# Does Every Story Have a Fictional Narrator?

*Tatjana*

When Netflix released the first season of its TV show *You* in 2018, a couple of my friends and I arranged a watch marathon, a "watchathon". My friend Alex and I have a long-standing obsession with crime stories and this one seemed somewhat unusual. When Kathi joined us, she only had a vague idea of what to expect. Popcorn ready, press "play". We see murderous bookseller Joe, hiding in the shadows, observing a woman and flicking through books. He tells us (in a voice-over) about his risky and creepy pursuit of women who he thinks are "the One" for him. A few minutes into the first episode, Kathi exclaims: "Ugh, I *hate* it when movies have a narrator!" Alex and I sharply disagree, and after passionately sharing our reasons for loving, hating, or being indifferent to narrators in films, Kathi reluctantly agrees to give the show a chance.

But I later wondered about the role narrators, such as Joe, play in fiction films and TV shows. Joe tells the story from his perspective, and it's one that significantly downplays the evilness of his acts. How do we know he's downplaying things? Because we see him stalking, breaking in, stealing, manipulating, and killing people. While the people Joe harms may not be the kindest, most upright, or innocent people, we don't see them engage in truly morally problematic behaviour either. Joe is an unreliable narrator. He tells us one story but we learn another story by watching and listening to the film material. Is there, maybe, another hidden or invisible narrator, or presenter, who reveals to us that Joe is unreliable as a narrator? If there is such an implicit narrator in the TV show, then they must be narrating the *true* story (i.e. true in the fictional world of *You*) through moving pictures and sound recordings.

If it's accurate to describe *You* as featuring an implicit narrator, it's natural to wonder whether every fiction film or TV show has an implicit narrator who shows the fictional world to us. Could it be that implicit narrators are ubiquitous in fiction films? As we will see, this leads to a broader question: does every work of narrative fiction have an implicit narrator?

DOI: 10.4324/9781003126102-8

## The Analytic Argument

Some thinkers have arrived at a positive answer to this question. Seymour Chatman, a renowned American film and literary critic, argues that "every narrative is by definition narrated – that is, narratively presented – and that narration, narrative presentation, entails an agent even when the agent bears no signs of human personality" (Chatman, 1990, p. 115).

Chatman's argument applies to all narratives, whether fictional or non-fictional. But the argument becomes truly interesting only when we focus on fictional narratives. So, here is Chatman's modified analytic argument for the idea that every narrative fiction has a narrator.

1 A work of narrative fiction is something that is narrated.
2 All narrations need an agent who does the narration, call them "the narrator".
3 Therefore, all works of narrative fiction have a narrator.

Chatman's argument is valid. This means anyone who accepts its two premises (1 and 2) but refuses to accept the argument's conclusion (3) would be contradicting themselves. So, now the question is whether we should accept the premises of the argument. It certainly seems that we should. Works of narrative fiction are works that tell stories. The *telling* of a story, or narration, is an act, and all acts require an agent. We call this agent the storyteller or the narrator. Storytellers often use words to convey their story, but they don't need to. Stories can also be told through moving pictures and sounds, such is the case in fiction films. We should then conclude with Chatman that narrative fiction, which includes novels and narrative fiction films, need a narrator.

The argument doesn't establish any controversial conclusion or contain controversial premises. No one seriously objects to the idea that narratives require someone who's doing the narrating. After all, every novel has an author, someone who wrote the story. Every film has filmmakers, the people who create the fiction. And, in writing or in producing and editing film material, they are telling us the stories they've created.

## Doubting the Fictional Narrator

So, what *is* the controversy? Let's start with narrators in novels and then turn to narrators in films. To see what philosophers of fiction disagree about, let's talk about *explicit* narrators first.

Some novels explicitly acknowledge a narrator. That narrator will often take a first-person point of view. You'll frequently find that the narrator uses first-person pronouns, such as "I", to insert themselves into the story. This is the case with Herman Melville's *Moby-Dick* (1851), which for the most part is narrated by the seasoned sailor Ishmael, who accompanies the vengeful and obsessive Ahab in his hunt for the namesake whale. Ishmael is a storyteller. But he is not ontologically on a par with Melville. Melville tells a fictional story of which Ishmael is a part. Thus, Ishmael is a *fictional* narrator in *Moby-Dick*. What philosophers of fiction disagree about is whether all novels have a *fictional* narrator. Let's call this the *ubiquity hypothesis about written (narrative) fiction*:

> All works of written (narrative) fiction are narrated by fictional narrators.

Where the narration cannot be attributed to an explicit fictional narrator, proponents of the ubiquity of narrators in literary fiction postulate an implicit fictional narrator.

Let's return to Chatman's analytic argument. I hope you can now see that the term "narration" is ambiguous. Someone might be talking about *actual* narration, which requires a real agent, such as the author. For instance, the actual narrator of *Moby-Dick* is Herman Melville. Or someone could have in mind *fictional* narration, which is only something a fictional narrator can do. To avoid what's called the "fallacy of equivocation", we need to understand "narrator" and "narration" in the same way throughout the argument. There are now two ways to interpret premise (1). We can either interpret it as claiming, first, that narrative fiction is something that is *actually* narrated or, second, that narrative fiction is something that is *fictionally* narrated.

The first interpretive option renders premise (1) true, and we can know this truth *a priori* (i.e., just by thinking about it). But on the second interpretation, it's not clear at all that the premise expresses a truth. Narrative fiction entails an actual narrator. But it's not obvious that it entails a fictional narrator as well. The proponent of the ubiquity thesis needs an additional argument to establish that all novels necessarily involve fictional narration and, hence, a fictional narrator.

## Film and the Analytic Argument

Literary fiction is not the only narrative medium, of course, audio-visual works of fiction can also tell stories. It's natural to wonder whether we can craft an argument for the ubiquity of narrators in fiction films as well. Even though, as we have seen, the analytic argument cannot establish the ubiquity of fictional narrators in written fiction, it might be able to convince us that all fiction films have fictional narrators.

Now, films are not mainly composed of assertive sentences. This certainly sets them apart from written narrative fiction. Rather, the director, the editors, the camera operators, the screenwriters, and whoever else is involved in the making of a film tell stories through a mixture of images, sounds, and dialogue, often edited in ways that further shape the story. These filmmakers are the actual storytellers. Explicit fictional narrators are common in fiction films as well. Some films feature a voice-over by a character who is narrating the story. Both novels and films can feature explicit fictional narrators who are involved in the events, as is the murderous Joe in Netflix's *You*. But the identity of the explicit narrator can also remain obscure to us. This is the case with the explicit narrator in Jean-Pierre Jeunet's *Amélie* (2001), of whom we learn little more than the sound of his voice. Although you might forget about the film's narrator if you listed the fictional characters in *Amélie*, you probably wouldn't protest if the film's closing credits listed *Amélie*'s narrator as one of the characters. The voice actor's name, after all, is acknowledged in the credits under "cast".

Films can also feature fictional storytellers whose voices we never hear and faces we never see. The mockumentary *The Office* (Ricky Gervais' and Stephen Merchant's original version ran from 2001–2002) has us make-believe that a film team is documenting life in an average office. Clearly, *in the fictional world of the TV series*, there are reporters, camera operators and sound engineers, and editors, who together narrate office life in a medium-sized company. These fictional documentary makers engage in, what is from our point of view, fictional narration. They are fictional narrators in *The Office*. The fictional documentary makers are explicit fictional narrators because they exist in the fictional world of the TV show. But for the most part, they don't talk. All they do is present.

Now, what philosophers disagree about is not whether there are sometimes explicit fictional narrators in fiction films. They agree that there are. Neither do they disagree about whether there are actual narrators of films. Sure there are! The actual narrators are the very real filmmakers, the ones that engage in actual narration through moving pictures, sounds, and edits. What is debated is whether all fiction films feature a *fictional* narrator – if not an explicit narrator, then an implicit one. Let's call this the *ubiquity hypothesis about fiction film*: All fiction films are narrated by fictional narrators. I imagine that some of the readers of this chapter will flinch at my use of the term 'narrator' in the context of audio-visual media. They might prefer the term 'presenter' or 'show-er'. However, the way I understand the term 'narrator', it refers to anyone who is telling a story. The means by which the story is told can vary. Conversely, not everyone presenting or showing something is telling a story. Suppose I set up my smartphone camera to livestream what is happening outside my front door. While I'm presenting or showing events, I'm not necessarily telling a story. This is why, when discussing films, I prefer to keep the term 'narrator'.

The concept of narration entails that there must be an actual narrator whenever there is actual narration, and a fictional narrator whenever there is fictional narration. While it's clear that fiction films are instances of actual narration, it's far from obvious that all fiction films contain fictional narration. Some do. TV shows such as *Parks and Recreation* and *This Is Spinal Tap* feature fictional narration done by their fictional documentary filmmakers. However, there is no indication that the worlds of Boog Joon-ho's *Parasite* (2019) or Tate Taylor's *The Help* (2011) include a fictional narration of the events that we witness during viewing. So, once again, the defender of the ubiquity hypothesis about fiction film needs another argument to establish the conclusion that all fiction films feature fictional narrators. The analytical argument only establishes that all works of narrative fiction have *actual* narrators, as well as that some works of narrative fiction – namely, those that contain fictional narration – have fictional narrators.

## The Argument from Imagined Seeing

The analytic argument establishes the conclusion that all actual narrations require actual narrators. However, I hope you can see that it doesn't lead to the conclusion that there are fictional narrators in every work of fiction. We need a further argument to establish this claim. And the next argument digs deep into the way we engage with works of fiction. Parsley Levinson presents a reason for postulating fictional narrators in every fiction film, and I think it's a compelling one.

> [T]he posit, however unvoiced, of an agency that is offering us sights and [sounds] – an agency with certain powers, motivations, and limitations – seems inescapable if we are to justify our taking anything to be fictional in the film world, on the basis of the moving images that are the only thing we are literally confronted with… Reason – albeit reason operating in service of the imaginative understanding of fiction – demands an answer to how it is that a world is being made visible to us, and that demand, it appears, is only satisfied by the assumption of an agency responsible for that.
>
> (Levinson, 1996, p. 256)

Remember that we engage with works of fiction properly by imagining various propositions. And what these propositions are is dependent on what is going on in the fictional world of a novel or a film. How do we know what is true in the world of a fiction film? A film is a limited representation of the fictional world it represents. We look at the moving images and listen to the sounds emitting from the screen, and the sound system, and aided by various heuristic devices, such as the reality principle (introduced in Chapter 5). When we watch moving images (and hear recorded sounds) we are encouraged to imagine seeing (and hearing) fictional stuff. And maybe imagining seeing (and hearing) fictional stuff requires the help of an unshown, unheard (i.e., implicit), fictional agent of some kind. That's why I call the argument in this section the *argument from imagined seeing*. But before we can wonder about the narrating implicit agent, we need to ask a crucial question: When we see moving images of people and events on the screen, what is it the filmmakers are encouraging us to *imagine we are seeing*?

## Imagined Direct Seeing

Some philosophers, most notably Kendall Walton, embrace what I will call the *transparency hypothesis* when it comes to pictures:

> Rather than merely imagining seeing a mill, as a result of actually seeing the canvas ... one imagines one's seeing of the canvas to be a seeing of a mill, and this imagining is an integral part of one's visual experience of the canvas.
>
> (Walton 1990: p. 301)

When we look at a picture, a painting, or a photograph, we imagine that we are literally and directly seeing the objects or scenes depicted. Even if the objects no longer exist, or the events have passed, or never have existed or happened, they were causally responsible for what the picture depicts now as you look at it. We can extend the transparency thesis to include moving images. Thus, when we are watching a film, we are seeing the people and hearing the sounds directly.

When the film we are watching is a non-fictional narrative film, what we are seeing are real people and real events. But when it comes to fiction film, it seems there are two options. One option is that we see the actors, the film sets, and the staged scenes. The other option is that what we see are the fictional characters and fictional events themselves. Do you see Louise shooting Thelma's assailant in Ridley Scott's *Thelma and Louise* (1991)? Or is what you see Susan Sarandon pointing and releasing the trigger of an unloaded gun at Timothy Carhart? The plausible answer is that you *see* Sarandon and Carhart and their enactment of a shooting. Simultaneously, you *make-believe* of the actors that they are Louise and Harlan and of the staged killing that it is a real killing. To put it differently, you imagine of Sarandon, whom you see thanks to the transparency of (moving) photographs, that she is Louise. And now, *this* seems to entail that you would or should imagine *seeing* Louise killing Harlan.

**Imagined Direct Seeing**

When we watch a fiction film, what we see are the actors and their staged interactions. And what we imagine of these real people and events is that they are the *characters* and *events in the fictional world* presented by the film. We thus imagine seeing the fictional character and fictional events directly.

Such imaginings are personal because they are imaginings about you – it's you who sees the characters and events. And to have personal imaginings related to a fictional world, you need to imagine yourself as part of that fictional world.

This isn't as strange an idea as it may sound. Walton, for example, thinks that when we consume fiction, we regularly engage in games of make-believe that extend beyond what is true according to the fictional world. These games of make-believe include us as participants in our own make-believe game. That is, we imagine various things about ourselves, and one of these imaginings will be that we perceive the characters directly.

It's important to point out that there are two different questions here: First, what is true in the world of the fiction and, second, what is true in the extended world of your own game of make-believe. It's true, in *your game of make-believe* that you are playing when watching and engaging with *Parasite,* that you directly perceive the character Oh Geun-Sae. But it's not true according to the film itself that you directly perceive him. After all, the film never mentions or shows you – and there's no indication that Oh Geun-Sae can see you looking at him. Moreover, if viewers were part of the fictional worlds of the films they watch – not just engaged in personal games of make-believe while watching – then fictional worlds would be swamped with viewers directly observing various events unfold. Anyone who is watching *Parasite* at the same time would, according to the film, be perceiving the housekeeper's hiding husband. This doesn't seem to be plausible. It makes more sense to think that when you are watching *Parasite,* you are playing your own game of make-believe in which you are a silent, passive fictional character.

*Sam:* Yes. In fact, perhaps, according to this ridiculous theory that you rightly want to reject, every person who ever watched, is watching, or will watch *Parasite* would have to be supposed to be there, in the world of the fiction, perceiving, along with you, the housekeeper's hiding husband!

*Tatjana:* Yes, can you imagine? I can't, because I have no idea where all the past, present, and future audiences would go. Well, that's assuming that everyone has a physical body that takes up space. But what else should we imagine about them? That they are just eyes and ears? Or that they are non-physical souls? That would entail much more philosophical contemplation than most people who watch *Parasite* bargained for.

You might wonder how all of this helps the philosopher who wants to argue for the ubiquity of implicit fictional narrators in films. Doesn't it suggest quite the opposite? If you are a part of the fictional world, with direct experiential access to the fictional characters and fictional events that unfold, then, presumably, there is no need for an implicit fictional narrator. The only storytellers are the filmmakers who, through the moving images, sounds, and edits, tell you what to make-believe. This is good news for those who disbelieve in implicit fictional narrators in films. Or is it?

Now, even if you and I play different games of make-believe when watching *Parasite*, our imaginings, for the most part, overlap. We both imagine the Park family, their employees, and the events unfolding in the Parks' house. These people and events are set in a rich fictional world. So, what explains, within your and my game of make-believe, that we both focus on this narrow viewpoint? Why didn't we end up watching pensioners practising Qi Gong in the fictional world of *Parasite* for 2 hours and 12 minutes instead, and miss the whole drama? Put differently, how do we know what to pay attention to? Well, here's an answer: *someone* is showing us what part of the *fictional world* to pay attention to. The filmmakers aren't able to show us the *fictional* people and events. All they can do is show us the actors and staged events of which we then make-believe that they are fictional. This is why every fiction film requires a fictional narrator, even if they remain unacknowledged and are, hence, implicit. If imagined direct seeing in fiction films entails an implicit fictional storyteller, then we may have a good reason for accepting the ubiquity hypothesis of fictional narrators in fiction films.

It sounds promising, doesn't it? However, the idea that you yourself are a fictional character in a game of make-believe authorized by a film raises some truly awkward questions.

Recall the *reality principle*, a heuristic device we have already encountered in earlier chapters. To describe films such as *Parasite* as "realistic" just means that the stories they tell are not dominated by supernatural, science fictional, or logically impossible story lines. The reality principle allows, indeed advises, us to import facts about the real world into the fictional world. A work of fiction is a very limited description of a fictional world. After all, not much can fit on 300 book pages, or 1.5 hours of film material. We are left to construct our own rich representation of the fictional world with the help of the work, heuristic devices such as the reality principle, and our imagination. Think of a film scene in which you are first introduced to a character and all you see is the character's head. Are you to conclude that, in the world of the film, the character has no body? Most likely not. You assume that he has a body because, in reality, people's heads come attached to their bodies. And if nothing in or around the film so far indicated to you that the fictional world it presents differs from the real one in this particular regard, your conclusion is very much warranted.

Now, the imagined direct seeing hypothesis, coupled with the use of the reality principle, leads to some mind-boggling questions.

## Awkward Questions

### *Ignorant Audience*

If, within your game of make-believe, you are a fictional character, you are presumably still very much like the real you, possessing the same properties and qualities you have in the real world. Let's suppose that you can vocalize sentences or sounds and/or that you can move your body in various ways, and also that you are a kind and compassionate person. Why do you sit around doing absolutely nothing when people nearby are being bullied or killed? What is it about your imagined persona that explains your passivity and silence? After all, you surely would do something in a similar situation in the real world – even if it's just running away. What is it that renders you merely a passive bystander to people and other creatures in distress?

### *Oblivious Characters*

Perhaps a more fundamental question is why no one in the fictional worlds is bothered by, or at the very least acknowledges, your presence. After all, it would be a pretty big thing if a stranger stood in your living room observing your every move. It would be weird and creepy! Presumably, there must be some explanation within your game of make-believe that accounts for why no one else in the fictional world perceives you.

Here's one possible answer: within your make-believe, you are very different from who you actually are. Maybe you are invisible and that's why no one perceives your presence in the fictional world. Moreover, you must be causally impotent, possibly disembodied, because you cannot save, help, or even distract another character. Maybe it's just your consciousness or your soul that is a fictional entity in the make-believe with which you are engaging. Well, it's an interesting idea, but it really only raises more awkward questions. What properties do your consciousness or your soul have? Why are you so different in your games of make-believe, in response to a film, from how you are in reality? Also, it's questionable whether a game of make-believe in which you are invisible and disembodied is authorized by any film. The genre of your make-believe (if it makes sense to talk of genres here) would appear to be the supernatural or maybe science fiction. But *Parasite* is neither.

Let us pause for a moment and ask why I call the aforementioned questions and the forthcoming ones awkward. It's because our engagement with fiction simply does not require us to have answers for them. In fact, we could even view them as detrimental to a proper engagement. These questions seem to distract us from properly enjoying and appreciating a work of fiction. It would be silly of me to insist on an answer to the question of why, in your game of make-believe, you didn't help Louise recover her money when J.D. (Brad Pitt) steals it in *Thelma and Louise*. It would be equally silly of me to push you to tell me your imagined reason for why the Park's employees are not concerned that you know about their con. Now, don't get me wrong, it's fun to ask such questions anyway. It's fun to think about possible answers too. I know I have both asked and answered questions of this kind. But did I *need* to ask and answer them in order to properly engage with a film or a novel? No! Now, what would render these silly questions awkward, is if I were to insist on an answer to them. Surely, any such insistence would make you wonder whether I understand how fiction works in the first place.

### *Impotent Events*

Think of that one very intense war scene in Oliver Stone's *Platoon* (1986). A crucial part of what makes the scene so emotionally intense is the visual perspective. We see the soldiers from a very close distance, as if we were lying or standing next to them. A hailstorm of bullets flies over their heads. Many of the soldiers are killed by bullets. In one scene, it appears as if several bullets are shot directly at us, the audience. As Noël Carroll points out (Carroll & Choi, 2009, p. 199), if we imagine directly seeing such a scene, should we not also imagine being hurt by the bullets? Yet, the vast majority of people won't make-believe that they are getting injured or killed, when watching *Platoon*. And if we don't imagine getting hurt by the bullets, should we conjure a reason why we evade the fate of so many of the soldiers that are on the battlefield with us?

It wouldn't be too challenging to come up with a story of why you are not killed by the bullets flying towards you in your make-believe of the war scene. You can, for example, imagine that you are invincible. Yet, there's nothing about the film that indicates that the filmmakers wanted you to imagine that you are invincible. Indeed, it would seem that there is nothing about the film that indicates that you are encouraged to imagine *any* explanation of why the bullets aren't affecting you physically.

A film may feature shots from within a house seemingly engulfed by a fire, such as Ron Howard's *Backdraft* (1991). If the shots prescribe you to imagine that you are in the house on fire, how is it that you are not harmed by the fire? Are you wearing a fireproof suit? If so, who gave it to you? James Cameron's *The Abyss* (1989) is mostly filmed underwater. While some scenes depict the events taking place inside of the submarine, other scenes show the characters diving in open water. If what Cameron prescribes us to imagine is that we see the divers directly, are we also to imagine how we are able to remain underwater for long stretches of time? If what we ought to imagine is that we are wearing a diving suit to help us breathe, how come our view is not obstructed by the mask? And why is it that we don't hear ourselves breathing as we would in real life while diving? To be clear, we can come up with plausible answers that make sense within our imaginative engagement with the film. But the question is whether we *should* imagine any of it to get the most out of watching *The Abyss*. And given that imagining answers about our own abilities and involvement in a fictional world is something people rarely, if ever, do when they enjoy a film, the theory of imagined direct seeing seems dubious.

### *Unusual Angles*

The awkward questions do not end there. Here's another weird consequence of injecting yourself into a fictional world. Some scenes in films are shot from high angles. There's a scene at the beginning of *Titanic* (dir. James Cameron, 1997) in which the main character Rose contemplates whether she should jump off the ship (and to her death). The scene is filmed from above. What allows you within your imaginative game to perceive Rose directly from such a high angle? Are you a fly? Are you hanging from a suspension above her head? How did you get up there? Note that the question is not how the filmmakers were able to film this scene. The question is how you, as part of the fictional world, were able to see Rose from such an unusual viewpoint.

### *No Witnesses*

Sometimes it is essential for a story that there are no witnesses to an event. In one of the first scenes of Peter Jackson's *The Lovely Bones* (2009), Susie Salmon is lured into an underground room and subsequently murdered by neighbour George Harvey. We aren't shown Susie's murder, but it is crucial to the story that no one sees Mr Harvey capture Susie. To put it differently, within the film's fictional world, it is a fact that no one witnesses the horrible events unfold. So, how can it be consistent with the narrative that, within your imaginative game as you watch the film, you do observe the process of luring and capturing? Something doesn't quite add up.

Or consider a film in which one of the main premises is the complete absence of conscious and intelligent creatures inhabiting its fictional world. This could be because the film shows a time before there was intelligent life or because all conscious and intelligent beings have died. A filmic version of Ray Bradbury's utterly depressing dystopian short story, *There Will Come Soft Rains* (1950), would feature only inanimate objects and an eventually dying dog. Of course, the dog counts as intelligent life, but she dies before the story ends. It's clear that later in the story we are prescribed to imagine that no creature is alive anymore. But if you accept the imagined direct seeing hypothesis for fiction film, and apply the reality principle to interpret the story, then you ought to imagine that you – an intelligent and conscious being – are directly witnessing the hopelessly tragic events. In other words, it seems that *There Will Come Soft Rains* prescribes you to imagine that no living beings exist, yet you are present to witness this fact. It amounts to a prescription to imagine contradictory things. Now, there are stories that require you to imagine propositions that contradict each other. But such stories reveal themselves as being impossible through their content. Nothing about *There Will Come Soft Rains* indicates that impossible events are being described.

## Novels and the Argument from Imagined Seeing

Maybe the imagined direct seeing thesis fares better when it comes to written fictions. Just as proper engagement with films, true engagement with novels calls for us to imagine various propositions. But unlike films, novels don't provide us with images and sounds. It's easy to visually and auditorily imagine Chung-Sook, the mother of the Kim family in *Parasite*, because we see and hear the actor who portrays her on the screen. As I said in Chapter 5, I am not convinced that we need to sensorily imagine at all when we read a novel. But we still engage in propositional make-believe about the events in the world of Gabriel García Márquez's *100 Years of Solitude* (1967) when we read the book.

How do we know what is true in the world of a novel? A novel is a limited description of a fictional world. We read and understand the sentences that make up the novel and fill in gaps in the description by using the same heuristic devices available to us when engaging with films. We construct a less gappy presentation of the fictional world. This implies that we also use the reality principle to interpret written fiction as well. Even though the novel never explicitly reveals to you that the Buendías are human beings instead of, say, chihuahua dogs, it's reasonable to believe that in the world of *100 Years of Solitude* the Buendías are human. In the real world, only humans use complex human language. And since nothing in *100 Years of Solitude* indicates that the biological laws of its fictional world are very different from our biological laws, we're safe to conclude that it is true in the fictional world that the Buendías are humans.

Engaging with a novel entails imagining what the author mandates us to imagine and filling any gaps using heuristic devices typically employed by those literate in fiction. Thus, when you make-believe that the Buendías founded Macondo, you are imagining a fact – a fact that you didn't know before but know now. How did you learn about this fact? The novel itself does not specify the source of this piece of knowledge. So, let's search for a real-world fact that we can import into the fictional world. I think this one works well.

**Fact-Learning Fact**

We learn (empirical) facts either through witnessing these events directly or through testimony from others who witnessed the events directly.

How did you learn that things look smaller than they are when you look at them from a distance? You probably experienced the visual effect yourself when you were a child. How did I learn that manta rays don't kill people? A marine biologist revealed this fact to me. And the marine biologist knows about manta rays and whether they are dangerous to humans through direct experience as well as testimony.

Now, importing *Fact-Learning Fact* into the story enriches our imaginative engagement with *100 Years of Solitude*. Let us look at it in terms of games of make-believe. If, within your game of make-believe, you learn the fact that the Buendías founded Macondo, then presumably you learned it either by witnessing the founding directly, or you learned it through the testimony of someone else. If we are supposed to imagine witnessing the founding of Macondo directly, then we encounter many of the same silly questions that arise when we assume we're directly observing fictional events in films. Why, within your imagining, do you not warn Amaranta Úrsula and her nephew Aureliano about their incestuous relationship? Why is no one in Macondo surprised by your presence?

Earlier in this chapter, I mentioned the short story *There Will Come Soft Rains*. In the fictional world of the story, all creatures are eventually dead. You cannot directly witness a world that contains no intelligent life. *You* are intelligent life. So, if this is what you ought to imagine when reading the story, then you are asked to imagine a contradiction. Did Ray Bradbury prescribe us to imagine impossible events? I find that hard to accept.

Perhaps it's more plausible that we are asked to make-believe we've learned about the founding of Macondo through some form of testimony. But whose testimony? It cannot be the testimony of the novel's author Márquez. He cannot testify to the founding of Macondo. For Macondo is not even a real place; it's fictional. And that the Buendías founded Macondo is not a real fact, it's a fictional fact. At best, Márquez could provide a *fictional* testimony. But this would entail that Márquez is part of the fictional world of his novel. To truthfully testify to Macondo's founding, the witness must *know* that the Buendías founded Macondo. And one can only know a proposition if that proposition is true. Thus, the witness must be someone for whom the proposition is true – and this can only be the case if the witness is part of the fictional world.

It seems that the only intelligent being from which we can obtain knowledge about the fictional world of the novel is an implicit fictional narrator. How does the implicit fictional narrator know the various facts about the Buendías? Well, maybe they live in Macondo and know the Buendías personally. Or maybe they know someone who knows the doomed family. How does the information get passed on to you? Perhaps the narrator is speaking to you directly or through a voice-recording or maybe you are reading their testimony. There are options here, but the novel does not prescribe to you any particular one of these scenarios. Yet they all seem to be compatible with what the novel *does* mandate us to imagine. One of them will be true in the world of *100 Years of Solitude*. We just don't know which one it is.

But it does not seem unreasonable to me to assume that the novel prescribes us to imagine *that we learn facts about the Buendías through testimony*. Just how exactly this learning of the facts happens remains underspecified. And, of course, this is not an unusual phenomenon when engaging with fiction. We do not know whether adult Celie in *The Color Purple* wears shoe size 6 or 8 or any number in between. But we do know that there is some shoe size that she wears. This sort of reasoning applies to fiction film as well. We don't know what brand of hair dye Franka Potente's character Lola uses in the fictional world of Tom Tykwer's *Run Lola Run* (1998), but we know there is some brand that she uses. We are not prescribed to imagine that Lola dyes her hair with Directions – a brand of hair dye – but we are told to imagine that she has dyed hair. Observations like these make me inclined to conclude that the ubiquity of the implicit fictional narrator hypothesis for written fiction is somewhat plausible.

*Sam:* Right. Somebody is telling us all of this stuff. And, unless the author has inserted herself into the world of the fiction (as Kurt Vonnegut and Milan Kundera often do), it isn't the author. So, there must be a fictional somebody telling it to us, even if the fiction doesn't specify anything about them, or how they came to know the things that they're telling us.

*Tatjana:* Yes, there's some plausibility to that. Or, at least, I find it much harder to resist the ubiquity of the implicit fictional narrator hypothesis when it comes to novels.

But if written narrative fiction features implicit fictional narrators, shouldn't the same apply to all other forms of narrative fiction? We've seen that the imagined direct seeing thesis faces many awkward questions, both when it comes to written fiction and fiction film. If the imagined direct seeing hypothesis is implausible, then we cannot use it to establish the ubiquity of the implicit fictional narrator. But we have also seen that if we make-believe we're learning about the fictional world through testimony, it may very well support the idea of the implicit fictional narrator in *written* fiction. So, let's revisit fiction film to see whether we can apply similar thoughts to the audio-visual medium.

## Imagined Mediated Seeing

At this point, you might be convinced that the imagined direct seeing thesis about fiction films is unacceptable. However, there is an alternative view for you to consider. Perhaps what we are mandated to make-believe, when engaging with fiction films, is that our seeing is not direct, but *mediated.* We might imagine that we are watching recordings of the events that unfold in a fictional world, or we might imagine that we are watching a live-stream. A recording shows events that happened in the past, while a live-stream presents events as they occur in real time. I invite you to consider whether, when watching *Parasite*, *Platoon*, or *Thelma and Louise*, it's more plausible that we are asked to envision ourselves viewing a recording or a live-stream. For the rest of this section, I will assume that our imagined seeing is mediated through recordings.

**Imagined Mediated Seeing**

In viewing a fiction film we see recordings of actors and their staged interactions. And what we *imagine* of these recordings is that they are *recordings of the fictional world* the film presents.

Thus, when you watch *Thelma and Louise*, what you ought to imagine is that you're being shown recorded material of the two protagonists' final trip. You are prescribed to imagine that the moving images and sounds comprising *Parasite* are recordings of the Parks and their employees. We watch video and sound material of actors, film sets, and staged scenes, and pretend that we are watching audio-visual recordings of detectives, supervillains, and housekeepers who solve cases, commit murders, or hide spouses. What this means is that we are asked to imagine that our access to the fictional world is not direct but rather mediated.

*Sam:* This sounds plausible to me. I think we can even make some inferences about this implicit show-er, who has recorded, or put the film together; this implicit fictional character (or team of them) whose perspective we're almost forced to adopt, since we can only look at the stuff that they show us.

When my wife was younger, she took a course of film studies. One concept that really engaged her was the notion of the "male gaze". Think of how, in a film, the camera will often focus on the legs of a female character, as she enters the scene, and then move up her body, before allowing her face to come into view. It's as if we're looking at the scene from the perspective of a somewhat stereotypical heterosexual man. You or I might not choose to look at the character that way, as she enters the scene, but we're being shown her entrance from a perspective which isn't really ours to frame. This gives us another reason, I think, to adopt the view according to which there really is an implicit fictional narrator, mediating our access to what's going on in the fictional world of the film. What's more, I'm inclined to think, in cases like the one I've described, that he's a heterosexual male.

*Tatjana:* That's a really good point. And whenever I see such a body-scanning scene, I automatically roll my eyes. Who am I rolling my eyes at? One answer would be that I am rolling my eyes at the filmmakers for creating a scene that I consider both unnecessary and objectifying. Another answer would be that I am imaginarily rolling my eyes, that is, that I am staying within my make-believe and expressing disapproval. Here, the disapproval must be directed at someone who is part of the fictional world. And that must be the individual who is showing me the fictional character (perhaps they are gesturing with their hand, starting at the character's legs and slowly moving it upwards towards the character's face). Yet, my own experience is a sense of disengagement from the film when it shows body-scanning scenes. So, this type of argument doesn't persuade me to acknowledge an implicit fictional narrator who is indulging in the "male gaze".

The idea that our access is mediated through recordings makes a lot of sense. Films are heavily edited. They feature soundtracks that are clearly not being played in the fictional world. They switch perspectives from one character to another. Films sometimes contain written information for the viewer, such as the year in which an important event takes place. Obviously, these annotations are not floating around in the sky.

At other times, films may not recount events in chronological order. If we were observing these events directly, it would seem as though we were jumping back and forth in time, it seems. Yet, engaging properly with Christopher Nolan's *Memento* (2000) surely doesn't require you to grapple with time-travel. Not only would jumping in time be required, but also jumping in space. In Jordan Peele's psychological horror film *Get Out* (2017), we see protagonist Chris Washington at his girlfriend's family's estate before the film cuts to Chris's best friend who is becoming increasingly concerned about his friend's safety. At this point in time, Chris and his friend are located nowhere near each other. If you're supposed to imagine, while watching the scenes, that you see Chris first and his friend seconds later, then how did you move so quickly from one place to another? For proponents of the imagined direct seeing thesis about fiction films, the silly questions just keep coming. But if what we imagine is seeing (and hearing) recordings of real characters and events, it's unsurprising that we notice editorial moves likes annotations, scene switches, or reverse time order.

The argument for the ubiquity of the implicit fictional narrator in fiction film is straightforward at this point. If what we imagine seeing are moving imagines, then there must be someone who is presenting us these images. It cannot be the filmmakers. All *they* can show us are recordings of the actors, the filmsets, or the staged events. Only someone from within the fictional world of *Get Out* can show us Chris Washington being hypnotised by his girlfriend's mother. Thus, we are mandated to imagine that there's an implicit fictional narrator who shows us recordings of Chris, his girlfriend, his girlfriend's family and the bizarre events that unfold. And what applies to *Get Out* applies to all film: we need an implicit fictional storyteller who gives us mediated access to the fictional worlds through their recordings. Presumably, the fictional narrator is really a bunch of people that includes camera operators, a sound technician, and potentially a director as well. So, we might more appropriately speak of an implicit fictional storytelling team.

The imagined mediated seeing hypothesis frees us from some of the awkward questions we encountered earlier. It's not surprising that you don't try to help Chris, when he's strapped to a chair so that his hypnosis can be activated. After all, you are not present at the scene, you only see things happening through a recording. Naturally, the characters cannot see you and acknowledge your presence because, well, you are not present at the scene and the cameras don't go both ways. The bullets seemingly flying towards you, when you make-believe the war scene in *Platoon,* cannot harm you because they don't even come close to you. Alas, imagining that we are seeing recordings does not help us dodge *all* awkward questions, and it raises some new ones.

## Different Questions, Same Awkwardness

*You* cannot help Chris in the world of *Get Out* because you are not within reach of the character. But the storytelling team recording the event is. Why did they not bother helping Chris? As Carroll puts it (Carroll & Choi, 2009, p. 179), "if there was a camera team present, why didn't they lend a helping hand?" Now, it's arguably not that surprising that the camera team chooses not to interfere. Documentary filmmakers often aim to stay uninvolved in the events they capture, ensuring an unbiased and highly authentic record. We could imagine that the fictional storytelling team might have similar motivations (though their code of ethics certainly seems worrisome).

In your imagining, you're not at risk of being harmed by the bullets in *Platoon*'s war scene. Yet, it seems rather unlikely that all of these bullets would miss a narration team if they were present in the scene. Are we supposed to imagine that some bullets hit members of the team? Interpreting the film in this way seems rather far-fetched. And when it comes to *Get Out*, why doesn't Chris signal the team for help? It seems improbable that his reason would merely be to maintain an unbiased and maximally authentic documentation of his distressing experiences. It seems more likely that if there is indeed a storytelling team witnessing and recording Chris's ordeal, then he cannot see them. How do they manage to remain concealed? More puzzling still, in a filmic version of *There Will Come Soft Rains,* where all human life has been wiped out by a nuclear disaster, imagining that there are people present to document the aftermath of the nuclear disaster would drastically alter the narrative, and, completely undermine the emotional impact of the dystopian vision.

But the observation that, for me, is the nail in the coffin for the implicit fictional storytelling team comes from Gregory Currie (1995, p. 267). Documentary teams such as, presumably, these fictional narration teams, use cameras and microphones. But some films and TV shows are set in a time before such technological equipment existed. Surely, there were no cameras in the 14th century Italy of Jean-Jacques Annaud's *The Name of the Rose* (1986)! Much of the drama in David Benioff's and D. B. Weiss's *Game of Thrones* (2011–2019) could have been resolved with fewer murders if people could have videotaped crucial events to show to their allies and enemies. If the imagined mediated seeing hypothesis holds true, then *The Name of the Rose* and *Game of Thrones* invite us to imagine worlds where only narration teams own technologies like cameras and microphones, as no one else is even aware that such advanced equipment exists. This doesn't make sense to me.

All these newly arising and revisited awkward questions and observations render the imagined mediated seeing hypothesis equally, if not more, unattractive than the imagined direct seeing thesis. I hope you agree that the hypothesis that we imagine that our seeing the fictional characters and fictional events, mediated by a narration team, is highly questionable. Gregory Currie isn't convinced by this hypothesis either:

> [T]he only candidate [for an alternative to the imagined direct seeing hypothesis] seems to be this: that we imagine someone to be filming the action as a documentary, and that we are seeing the visually restricted result … [b]ut to imagine this (something I have never been aware of imagining) would be to imagine that the fiction contains as a part the assumption that the action is being filmed by a camera crew and that we are watching the result. Occasionally, as with *Culloden* (Peter Weir, 1964) this would be an appropriate piece of imagining, but it certainly would not be for most fiction films.
>
> (Currie 1995, p. 173)

But is postulating a storytelling team the only way to make sense of the Imagined *Mediated* Seeing Hypothesis? George Wilson thinks that there is an alternative.

## Naturally Iconic Shots

What gives rise to the awkward questions is not so much the claim that we imagine seeing recordings, but rather the idea that these recordings are being made and shown to us by a bunch of conscious people. People can intervene, be acknowledged, be burned by fire, or killed by bullets. It's conscious beings whose imagined presence leads to contradictions for an audience of a filmic version of *There Will Come Soft Rains*. People, as so often, cause all sorts of problems. Wilson denies that we imagine, or ought to imagine, a team of persons presenting us with recordings of fictional events as though they were real. In fact, he denies that we imagine *any* particular way through which we come to see the recordings. Wilson writes:

> Viewers imagine themselves looking into the movie's dramatized universe, but, as a rule, they are imaginatively oblivious about how their fictional seeing into the narrative world might have been causally produced. The question just doesn't arise for them… they imagine that they are seeing [the fictional characters and events] indirectly, i.e., seeing them through the mediation of suitable moving images…
>
> (Wilson, 2011, p. 91)

So, according to Wilson, while we do imagine seeing the fictional characters and events mediated through an edited series of moving images, we don't imagine how exactly these images come about. For Wilson, it's one of these things that just remain indeterminate in the story, and we are comfortable not questioning it. While this idea might seem *ad hoc*, it actually captures rather frequent behaviour that we display when we engage with a novel or a film. While watching science-fiction films, you probably don't ponder much about the underlying physics of UFOs or time-travel. You don't wonder about a character's shoe size, blood type, or Google password, when you are enjoying a drama. When a character confides to another that their father died in a car crash when they were a child, you typically don't question whether other people died in the crash. And the entire genre of crime comedies rely on the audience not imagining too much about the victims of the murderous main character.

The fact that we're prompted to envision ourselves watching video footage of fictional events doesn't necessarily mean that we should also imagine an additional fictional character who presents this footage. However, according to Wilson, it *does* entail that there is at least a minimal agent who presents the recording according to the film. This agent is plausibly a non-personified entity. Maybe the recordings are just what Wilson calls "naturally iconic shots" (Wilson, 1997, p. 196). And we simply do not know, nor are we prescribed to imagine, what this minimal agent is, how the shots come about, or why we get to see them. Does this mean that there is an implicit fictional narrator in fiction films? Well, yes. But given just how minimal that storytelling entity is, we shouldn't make a big fuss about it, so Wilson thinks.

Wilson's claim that we typically don't imagine how we see in fiction aligns with my own experience of viewing fictional films. But I'm not so sure about Wilson's second claim, that we imagine seeing the characters and events through moving images. At least in my case, when I watch a film, I don't find myself imagining anything about my access to the fictional world. Neither do I imagine that I am watching a documentation in black and white, when I watch Orson Welles's *Citizen Kane* (1941), nor that I am watching annotated recordings when the screen displays information such as the date of an event. But there are circumstances in which both you and I probably imagine watching shots.

## Mockumentaries

In the earlier cited quote from Currie, he mentions *Culloden,* which is a docudrama and thus, it seems to me, not a (clear) case of fiction. But there is a popular film genre that acknowledges camera crews, and that's mockumentary. A mockumentary *fictionally* documents fictional events. It represents fictional events through moving images and sounds in a documentary-style format. This makes films such as Rob Reiner's *This Is Spinal Tap* (1984) and Larry Charles's *Borat* (2006), as well as TV shows such as Matt Lucas and David Walliams's *Come Fly with Me* (2010–2011) and Ricky Gervais and Stephen Merchant's *The Office* (2001–2003), such mock documentaries.

Filmmakers of mockumentaries ask audiences to make-believe that a *documentary* team is filming the fictional characters and events. But this is not all the audience is to imagine. We are also to imagine that we learn about the fictional world through the documentary team, that is, through their recordings. For the most part, the fictional documentary team remains invisible. Yet, the fictional characters frequently acknowledge them. They might, for example, share a knowing glance towards the camera, or a fictional character might interact with a member of the documentary team during an interview scene. Undoubtedly, the documentary team is some sort of *explicit* fictional narrator.

Now, the defender of the ubiquity of the implicit narrator will hold that there must be an implicit narrator who shows us the fictional documentary team recording the office scenes. But I think there is no need to postulate an implicit narrator. My first introduction to the mockumentary genre was through the UK's version of *The Office*, which first aired in 2001. This first viewing was memorable for me, not because Ricky Gervais was funny, or because the topic of office life was strangely mundane, but because I did not quite know how to engage with the format. I recall that some of the questions that popped into my mind were: Who are these people filming? Do they film everywhere? Do the office workers not mind? Do the employees sometimes forget that they are being filmed? Did everyone consent to being filmed?

Now, I am not suggesting that these questions have definite answers. I don't think that there's anything particular that we are prescribed to imagine in response to them. But these aren't awkward questions. We *can* come up with plausible answers that are consistent with what the show mandates us to make-believe. And, importantly, including these answers in our imagining does not really detract from our engagement with the TV show. I might imagine that there are five members of the documentary team, that they are granted access to almost every location, that they have a special camera lens (and microphone) that allows them to record events from a great distance, and so on. This is important to note: while some aspects related to the fictional documentary filming are left indeterminate in *The Office*, they don't raise bizarre, silly, awkward questions that viewers typically wouldn't consider while watching the TV show.

## A Suggestion

Greg Currie describes an impersonal imagining of the fictional characters and events in fiction films that matches my own phenomenological experience of fiction film-watching (and maybe yours as well):

> What I imagine while watching a movie concerns the events in fiction it presents, not any perceptual relations between myself and those events. My imagining is not that I see the characters and the events of the movie; it is

> simply that I imagine that these events *occur* – the same sort of impersonal imagining I engage in when I read a novel.
>
> (Currie, 1995, p. 179)

So, here's what I think is going on. There's no mandate for us to make-believe that we look at the fictional characters and events directly or indirectly. Films that lack explicit fictional narrators do not prescribe us to imagine any particular way that we access the fictional worlds. We are only asked to imagine that we *have* that access. It doesn't seem right to say that we imagine watching edited shots. Such edited shots are necessarily presented later than the event. After all, the event happens first, and, with some delay, the showing of these events. But when I watch *Thelma and Louise,* I imagine that I am witnessing the events as they unfold, not some time later. There are exceptions, of course, like Daniel Myrick and Eduardo Sánchez's *The Blair Witch Project* (1999), but in these exceptional cases it is made clear, in the film, that we are watching a recording.

Here's a possible reason why we don't engage in imaginings of how we access the fictional world. A proper engagement with fiction requires us to follow the story without getting lost in minor story lines. If we get lost in minor story lines, we often lose the narrative flow. You are losing the plot – quite literally. Thus, anything that might prevent us from properly following the narrative should be treated with much caution.

*Sam:* That's nice. Yes. Perhaps there really is a literal losing of the plot when we allow our imaginations to run too freely from the central storyline. When we do that, we're no longer consuming fiction so much as making up our own, sometimes very strange, fan-fiction!

*Tatjana:* Well, we're both using the word "literally" here a little loosely! We cannot *literally* lose things like plots, but it is literally the (story) plot that is in danger. And don't get me wrong, taking a minor storyline from fictional works, and imaginarily running with it, is intriguing. But I think that is more like daydreaming prompted by a work, than meaningful engagement with the work. And, yes, this might lead to some crazy but occasionally very enjoyable fan-fiction.

Not only should we be careful not to get distracted by imaginings about our access to a fictional world in narratives, but this also applies to real-world narratives. If your friends tell you about their travels to Cambodia and you indulge in imaginings about the couple they met *en route* (whom they mention only *once* in their story), then you are not appreciating your friend's narrative. To meaningfully engage with and appreciate a work of narrative fiction (or non-fictional narrative, for that matter) we need to avoid over-imagining scenarios that could disrupt the story, distract from the plot, and potentially even change the narrative. This includes not wasting mental effort on unnecessary imaginings, such as our perceptual relationship with the characters and events in *Parasite*, why we aren't harmed by bullets during our engagement with *Platoon*, or conjuring up reasons for why Thelma and Louise aren't bothered by a documentary crew filming Louise's confrontation with Harlan in *Thelma and Louise*.

This particular convention can be disabled. And it is disabled when we are watching mockumentaries. When you watch *The Office* you ought to make-believe that a documentary team is showing you recordings of the office employees. Ignoring the team means that you are not engaging with the narrative of the TV show.

If this is true, then there is no need to postulate an implicit fictional narrator, not even a minimal one.

*Sam:* I like what you're saying. On your suggestion, we're simply not supposed to imagine anything about how or by whom we're being shown what we're being shown when we watch a fiction film. But, you're also allowing that this constraint can be suspended in certain genres, like mockumentaries. Great. But, when reading this chapter, I thought of another potential theory.

I guess it was inspired by Wilson's theory, but I think (and hope) that it's more intuitive. Here it is: When watching a fiction film, we pretend that we're seeing what we would have seen had there been cameras there to capture what we see, and somebody to show us what those cameras captured. Does that make sense? Why should we prefer your suggestion (which I also like)? Also, I'm left wondering where my observation about the male gaze is left, when processing your suggestion (and my own suggestion, for that matter).

*Tatjana:* Your suggestion seems to be this: I make-believe the following: I'm seeing what I would have seen had a storytelling team captured it (i.e. what I am seeing) and shown it to me. Did the team capture and show to you the same thing? The fictional event? Or the recording? Also, is this really our experience? I don't think I have such imaginings when watching films. Or is your suggestion this: I make-believe that I am seeing *F* (and here the make-believe ends), where *F* is what I would have seen had there been a team filming and presenting things to me? Could you please say more about your suggestion?

The point about the male gaze is really interesting, and I am still unsure what to say about it. My own experience suggests to me that I am imaginatively resisting. But if I am resisting, I am presumably resisting imagining something that the film prescribes me to imagine. My hunch is that the film is prescribing me to imagine that I am body-scanning the woman. And I simply don't want to imagine that.

*Sam:* My suggestion is the second of the two options you sketch. I think that I am pretending that I'm seeing *F* (and that's where the pretending stops). I'm not pretending that *F* was filmed by anyone. Nevertheless, I'm saying that *F* is what I would be seeing if cameras had been placed in certain locations, etc. The male gaze, on my suggestion, would be explained by the fact that I'm seeing what I would be seeing if there had been a narration team that objectifies women.

Is there a similar convention when it comes to written fiction? I am unsure. There *is* a convention not to imagine anything that makes us lose the narrative flow. But is there a more specific convention not to question how we access and find out about the fictional events of a novel? The format – sentences written in a declarative form – seems to compel us to conclude that someone is narrating the events to us, someone we imagine being part of the novel's fictional world. Specific genres of novels, like epistolary novels, just seem to replace the omniscient third person narrator with a less knowledgeable and more personal narrator. I will leave it up to you, the reader, to decide if there is a convention regarding our access to the fictional world in written literature that parallels the one in fiction film.

*Sam:* It sounds to me like your suggestion should apply equally to film and written fiction. After all, when there isn't an explicit fictional narrator, we treat the sentences of the novel as fictional testimony.

That implies that there's a fictional character testifying; telling us what happened, even if we know next to nothing about this character and how they know what they know. Moreover, if fixating about these questions is going to detract from the plot, then your suggestion automatically comes into force. No?

*Tatjana:* Here's something peculiar about written fiction, as opposed to audio-visual. Recall the fact that we learn facts either by witnessing events or through testimony, a fact that I believe we standardly import into fictional worlds. Now, consider two examples. Suppose that I ask you how you found out that Harlan tried to sexually assault Thelma in *Thelma and Louise*. You might point me to the exact time when the film scene starts and ask me to see it for myself. Now suppose I ask you how you know that the dog dies in *There Will Come Soft Rains*. This time, you might underline a passage from the short story and exclaim "it says so there". This leads me to infer that, while engaging with fiction films, we are more inclined to consider ourselves as witnesses to the events for learning facts. Conversely, when interacting with written fiction, we are more prone to perceive that we are obtaining facts via testimony.

Now, when we engage with written fiction, we conventionally don't question who is providing the testimony and how. At least not when there is no explicit narrator. But a testimony implies that there is someone giving the testimony, so we should be prepared to, at least tentatively, imagine that there is a witness. Similarly, the question of how we see fictional events when watching fiction films is one that, by convention, we don't ask. But that we see fictional events does not by itself imply that there is a narrator or a storytelling team, nor does it imply that we are seeing the events directly.

## Works Cited


Carroll, N. & Choi, J. (eds) (2009) *Philosophy of Film and Motion Pictures: An Anthology*. Chichester: Wiley-Blackwell.

Chatman, S. (1990) *Coming to Terms: The Rhetoric of Narrative in Fiction and Film*. Ithaca, NY: Cornell University Press.

Currie, G. (1995) *Image and Mind*: Film. *Philosophy and Cognitive Science*. Cambridge: Cambridge University Press.

Levinson, J. (1996) Film Music and Narrative Agency. In D. Bordwell & N. Carroll (eds), *Post-Theory: Reconstructing Film*. Madison, WI: University of Wisconsin Press, pp. 248–282.

Walton, K. L. (1990). *Mimesis as Make-Believe: On the Foundations of the Representational Arts*. Cambridge, MA: Harvard University Press.

Wilson, G. M. (1997). Le Grand Imagier Steps Out: The Primitive Basis of Film Narration. *Philosophical Topics*, 25(1): 295–318.

Wilson, G. M. (2011) *Seeing Fictions in Film: The Epistemology of Movies*. Oxford: Oxford University Press.


## Further Reading


Curran, A. (2019) Silly Questions and Arguments for the Implicit, Cinematic Narrator. In N. Carroll, L. T. Di Summa, & S. Loht (eds), *The Palgrave Handbook of the Philosophy of Film and Motion Pictures*. London: Springer, pp. 97–118.

Gaut, B. (2004) The Philosophy of the Movies: Cinematic Narration. In P. Kivy (ed.), *The Blackwell Guide to Aesthetics*. Oxford: Blackwell, pp. 230–253.

Kania, A. (2005) Against the Ubiquity of Fictional Narrators. *Journal of Aesthetics and Art Criticism*, 63(1): 47–54.

Thomson-Jones, K. (2007) The Literary Origins of the Cinematic Narrator. *British Journal of Aesthetics*, 47(1): 76–94.

Thomson-Jones, K. (2009) Cinematic Narrators. *Philosophy Compass*, 4(2): 296–311. *This is a very helpful overview of questions about the narrator or presenter in film.*
Thomson-Jones, K. (2012) Narration in Motion. *British Journal of Aesthetics*, 52(1): 33–43.
Wilson, G. M. (2007). Elusive Narrators in Literature and Film. *Philosophical Studies*, 135(1): 73–88.

# Chapter 8

# Why Are You Crying?

*Sam*

Fiction can make us laugh, and it can make us cry. In fact, fiction can make us feel all sorts of things. In the next chapter, Tatjana will address what philosophers call "the paradox of tragedy", which – in a nutshell – asks us why we willingly choose to consume fiction that we know will make us feel unpleasant sensations. But in *this* chapter, I address a different philosophical question; one which *also* emerges from our emotional engagement with fiction. The novelist and philosopher, Umberto Eco, put the question beautifully:

> What does it mean when people are only slightly disturbed by the death from starvation of millions of real individuals – including many children – but they feel great personal anguish at the death of Anna Karenina? What does it mean when we deeply share the sorrow of a person who we know has never existed?
>
> (Eco, 2011, p. 75)

Now, in fact, we *do* feel really bad about the death and starvation of millions – but, still, when we hear of such things on the news, we rarely burst into tears. Reading Anna Karenina, by contrast, can have us sobbing, even though she never existed. There seems to be something somehow *irrational* about crying for a person you know never existed. So, the question of this chapter could be put as follows: is it rational to cry for a fictional person, or about a fictional event? And, if so, why?

Back in the 1970s, this question was the subject of a very engaging dialogue between two philosophers, Colin Radford and Michael Weston (Radford & Weston, 1975). Radford argued that there really is something somehow irrational about our emotional engagement with fiction. It might be a *harmless* form of irrationality, and it might be a very *human* form of irrationality, and the benefits we get from engaging with fiction might be *worth* the irrationality of it all, but it's irrational nonetheless. Weston disagreed. He argued that our emotional engagement with mere fictions makes sense. In this chapter, I want to rehearse both sides of their argument, and let you decide (although my own personal bias won't be too hard to discover).

DOI: 10.4324/9781003125102-9

Before we jump into the debate between Radford and Weston, there's a distinction we should draw, and a question that it would be useful to answer, so as to make their debate easier to understand. The question we have to ask is, "what on earth does it mean for emotions to be rational or irrational?"

The philosophy of emotions is, itself, a giant field of research and literature. Some have argued that emotions are a certain sort of judgement. On that view, there's clearly room to say that an emotion can be right or wrong, appropriate or inappropriate, to the extent that the judgement at the heart of the emotion can be said to be true or false. This view is called cognitivism about emotions.

Cognitivists believe that emotions, or the judgements at their heart, are (sometimes, or always) truth-evaluable (for examples of such views, see Neu, 2000, and Nussbaum, 2001). On the other side of that debate are non-cognitivists. They believe that emotions are certain sorts of feelings which have no truth-evaluable content. If you fall on that side of the debate, it might be less clear what it means to say that an emotion is rational or irrational – it would be like saying that an *itch* is irrational or rational (perhaps the most radical non-cognitive view of emotions stretches back to William James in 1890). Itches just aren't the sort of things that can be assessed in terms of their rationality, or lack thereof. Likewise, you might think, if you're a non-cognitivist about emotions, emotions cannot be assessed in terms of their rationality, or lack thereof.

In addition to the debate between cognitivists and non-cognitivists, there are debates as to what role emotions play in the process of human reasoning. If you're a cognitivist, it's clear that emotions, like other judgements, will be subject to the governance of reason. But, even if you're a non-cognitivist, you might think that emotions play an important role in the process of reasoning.

For example, the so-called "search hypothesis of emotions" suggests that emotions can shine either a positive or negative light on certain hypothetical options, which serves as a short-cut, at least for *dismissing* some of them (see Evans, 2002). Indeed, you might think that certain decisions, where there's no finite limit on the number of possible options and variations, would be impossible for humans to process without short-cuts; short-cuts made possible by an emotional filter. Emotions might play this role in human reasoning, even if you're a non-cognitivist.

Accordingly, to the extent that emotions can be either beneficial to our patterns of reasoning (helping us to come more often to true conclusions, and to make good decisions), or harmful to our patterns of reasoning (causing us to rule out good options, to come to false conclusions, or to make bad decisions), to *that* extent can any given emotion be criticized as either constructive or detrimental to your exercise of reason. Accordingly, emotions could be assessed, in this sort of indirect way, for their rationality or irrationality (even if you're a non-cognitivist).

So, without delving too deeply into the philosophy of emotion, my hope is that you'll be able to make some sense out of the claim that a given emotion can be rational or irrational. If you don't like that claim, how about the claim

rule that governs our emotions: it is irrational to feel emotions in response to people or events that are not real.

In the light of these thought-experiments, and the finding that they yield, Radford could rest his case. He could conclude that our emotional responses to fiction violate this clear and obvious rule, and so our emotional engagement with fiction is irrational. But of course, that would be too hasty.

Perhaps the context of fiction constitutes a principled exception to the rule. Or, perhaps we're not really crying for Anna Karenina, when we engage with Tolstoy's novel, but for something else. Radford's strategy is to conduct a process of elimination. He seeks to examine every half-plausible way in which it could be argued that our emotional engagement with fiction is somehow different. He then tries to show how each suggestion fails. Once every other option has been dismissed, he thinks we're forced to conclude that our engagement with fiction really is a violation of our rule, and so our engagement with fiction is irrational (even if the irrationality in question is benign).

In what follows, I change the numbering of Radford's suggestions, and I miss a couple of suggestions out entirely for the sake of maintaining clarity and brevity. Interested readers should consult the original (Radford & Weston, 1975) for more detail.

- Suggestion 1: What we feel for Anna Karenina (and other fictional characters) aren't real emotions.

What makes this suggestion tempting, Radford tells us, is the observation of the philosopher, Oets Kolk Bouwsma (1965, p. 29), that, when we watch Mercutio die, on stage, and the tears run down our cheeks, chocolates continue to go in our mouth. We might even mutter to ourselves, or to our neighbour, "'How marvellous! How sublime!' and even 'How moving!'" (Radford & Weston, 1975, p. 79). This seems to prove that the emotions we feel, in our engagement with fiction, are not quite authentic. If the grief were real grief, the chocolates would stop going in. We wouldn't be able to mutter, "How marvellous!"

And yet, Radford rejects suggestion 1. It might be true that emotions don't behave in quite their standard way when we know that we're consuming a fiction. But that doesn't mean the emotion itself isn't there. It evidently is. Something about our knowledge that it's a fiction allows the emotion to run, somehow, offline. Our fear of what transpires on stage doesn't cause us to run (although it might cause us to hide behind our hands). Our tears don't stop us from enjoying the chocolate. But the fear and the tears are real. As Radford puts it:

> We shed real tears for Mercutio. They are not crocodile tears, they are dragged from us and they are not the sort of tears that are produced by cigarette smoke in the theatre. There is a lump in our throats, and it's

> not the sort of lump that is produced by swallowing a fishbone. We are appalled when we realise what may happen, and are horrified when it does.
>
> (Radford & Weston, 1975, p. 79)

The fact that these emotions are somehow offline in no way entails that they're not real. They manifestly *are* real. The problem is, of course, that these emotions seem to violate our rule about the rationality of emotions. The solution to this problem isn't to pretend that the emotions aren't real.

- Suggestion 2: We get so caught up in the fiction that we momentarily forget that it *is* just a fiction.

If this suggestion were true, it would solve the puzzle. It's only irrational to feel emotions for fictional people and events if you know that they're fictional. If, however, you've temporarily *forgotten* that they're merely fictional, then there's a sense in which, temporarily, you don't *know* (at least not consciously) that they're fictional, and thus, your emotions don't violate our rule.

The problem with suggestion 2, of course, is that's it's patently false. There is such a thing as getting caught up in a fiction, but neurotypical adults, even as they're caught up in the fiction, don't ever forget, at any time, that it *is* a fiction. When you're caught up in the drama of *Romeo and Juliet*, you give it your undivided attention. But as Tybalt is about to kill Mercutio, you don't – even temporarily – consider jumping up on the stage to defend Mercutio, or think about calling the police to apprehend Tybalt.

> *Tatjana:* It's true, I wouldn't jump up in my chair and shout "is there a doctor here who can help?" when I see Tybalt stab Mercutio. But what I will frequently do is shout at the TV or quietly mumble warnings at the screen or stage "why are you doing this", "No, that's the wrong decision" – as if my warnings could make any difference.
>
> But I guess the sheer fact that I only quietly whisper my warnings shows that I am fully aware that I am watching fiction – I don't want to disturb my fellow viewers.

- Suggestion 3: When engaged in a fiction, we suspend our disbelief.

Suggestion 3 is undoubtedly true. We *do* suspend our disbelief when engaging with fiction. As Radford points out (Radford & Weston, 1975, pp. 71–72), when in the theatre, the production company connive to help us suspend our disbelief. The stagehands wear black so that we shouldn't see them, as they move the furniture around, for example. But even so, it's not at all obvious that the truth of suggestion 3 solves our puzzle. Even as we suspend our disbelief, it never gets to a stage at which we're no longer *aware* that we're consuming a fiction. Our rule for rational emotions dictates that an emotion for people or events is irrational all the while that you know that those people or events are fictional. The fact that you suspend your disbelief doesn't rob you, even temporarily, of that knowledge.

To think that suggestion 3 should solve our puzzle is almost like saying that our emotions about fiction, unlike our emotions for the sister of the man in the bar and our emotions about Swazbeckizta, are rational because we've *chosen* to allow ourselves to feel them. We chose to suspend our disbelief. But how does choosing to feel something irrational suddenly make it rational? Surely that just makes it all the more *irrational*?

*Tatjana:* I'm not so sure. What is irrational is to have certain emotions for something we believe doesn't exist. But if we suspend the disbelief in Anna Karenina's existence while reading the novel, then the basis for the irrationality is gone. It may be less rational to feel sad for someone we neither believe nor disbelieve to exist than to feel sad for someone we firmly believe to exist. But I don't see that it would be wholly irrational.

*Sam:* That might be a good way to respond on behalf of suggestion 3. That is to say, it's odd to feel emotions for someone if you don't have any opinion as to whether they exist. It's not odd to have an emotion for someone you believe to exist. But it might also not be all that odd, or wholly irrational, to have an emotion for somebody you believe to be fictional, because – well – you've decided to engage with a piece of fiction; and while you do that, you're bracketing any belief you have about their non-existence. As we'll see, this way of strengthening suggestion 3 moves in the direction of Weston's response to Radford.

- Suggestion 4: We don't *really* feel emotions towards fictional characters and events. Instead, what happens in fictions, and what happens to fictional characters, can cause us to feel emotions for the real people who experience similar events in the actual world.

Sometimes, if I see my wife is particularly disturbed by something occurring in a fiction, I have this annoying habit of leaning over to her and reminding her that it's just a fiction. I do it, not intentionally to annoy her, but to soothe the emotional response – forgetting each time, I suppose, that she finds it annoying!

Sometimes she simply shushes me because the interruption ruins her engagement with the fiction. Other times, when she really is very upset by what's going on, on screen, she says that it doesn't help her to think that it's just a fiction, since she knows that there are real people going through very similar things in their real lives. She is, her response would seem to imply, crying for *them*. And, if that's the case, of course, then her emotions do not violate our rule for emotional rationality.

I think suggestion 4 is very compelling. In fact, I think it's about as close to the truth as any of the suggestions that Radford considers. I think suggestion 4 is in the background of Weston's ultimate argument that our emotional responses to fiction *are* rational. The way in which our emotional responses to fictions stay on the right side of rationality has something to do with the relationship between fiction and reality.

But, having said that, suggestion 4 can't be quite right. It can't be right to say that we're not crying for Anna Karenina, even if, somehow, our tears are *justified* by the relationship in which Anna Karenina stands to the world. If my wife told Radford that she wasn't crying for Anna Karenina, but *only* for people like her, he would either accuse her of lying, of not being sufficiently aware of what she's really feeling, or – at the very least – he'd tell her that her response is not standard. And I think he's right, since, standardly, when reading *Anna Karenina*:

> We weep for *her*. We are moved by what happens to her, by the situation she gets into, and which is a pitiful one, but we do not feel pity for her state or fate, or her history or her situation, or even for others, *i.e.*, for real persons who might have or even have had such a history [although we might feel for them *as well*. But, most centrally, here, we] … pity her, feel for her and our tears are shed for her.
>
> (Radford & Weston, 1975, p. 75)

*Tatjana:* And in any case, the idea that you're feeling emotions, not for the fictional character, but for people in the real world, wouldn't quite make sense when it comes to other arguably irrational emotions towards fictional characters (e.g. fear of fictional monsters). Three-headed aliens, spiders the size of a house, green slimy blobs with red eyes – who are the people like them that we fear?

*Sam:* Yes. That's a great point. I hadn't thought of that. Another good reason to reject suggestion 4, or at least to think that its answer is incomplete.

- Suggestion 5: Even though the emotions we feel for fictional characters are real, we feel them in a different way. Emotions only rationally require belief when they're felt in the non-fiction way. There is no such requirement for emotions when they're felt in the fiction-way.

If this suggestion is true, then words like "feeling" and "being moved" are actually ambiguous. There are two ways in which you could feel the feeling of happiness or sadness; two ways in which you could be moved. There's the way that's characteristic of normal life (which we could call feeling-type-1), and then there's a way that's characteristic of our engagement with fiction (which we could call feeling-type-2).

When we say that it's irrational to feel an emotion for a being that we know to be unreal, we actually say something ambiguous. Are we speaking about feeling-type-1 or feeling-type-2? Thought experiments regarding the sister of the man in the bar, and the country of Swazbeckizta, only go to show that it's irrational to feel sadness in the feeling-type-1 sense of the word, for fictional beings. But no such rule applies to the feeling-type-2 of sadness.

Again, the suggestion isn't that the sadness itself is a different emotion when felt for a fictional character (that suggestion will likely succumb to the pitfalls of suggestion 1 – that the sadness we feel for Mercutio isn't real sadness). Rather, the suggestion is that the relation we have to the emotion is different. No doubt there's some truth to the suggestion. We've already discussed how fear and sadness in response to fiction is felt in an offline way. The fear doesn't trigger an instinct to run away. The sadness doesn't get in the way of the enjoyment of our chocolate. But Radford has two responses.

His first response is that the words, "feeling" and "being moved", don't appear to be ambiguous, like the word "bank" which could refer to a financial institution, or to the side of a river. This response could be backed up with certain tests that linguists use to discover ambiguity, which all seem to undermine the essential thesis of suggestion 5.

Radford's second response is to wonder whether the distinction between feeling-type-1 and feeling-type-2 – even if true – would really resolve our puzzle. After all, suggestion 5 accepts that it really is sadness we're feeling for Anna Karenina, even if we're feeling it in a different way.

*Tatjana:* What is this "different way"? What is the special relation we have to our emotions in fiction?

Are we talking about feeling-in-the-fiction? Or feeling-while-engaging-with-fiction?

*Sam:* I think feeling-type-2 would be feeling while engaging with the fiction. The feeling isn't in the fiction itself. That's to say, the feeling is non-fictional. It's your feeling and it's real. Rather, according to this suggestion, the feeling is caused by your engagement with a fiction, and for that reason, it is felt somehow differently.

But if we accept that much, then we can still ask, what are we sad *about*? Our rule for rational emotions should apply equally to feeling them in the type-2 way.

Having eliminated what he takes to be all of the alternatives, Radford is left to conclude that our emotional engagement with fiction really is irrational. But don't worry! Some forms of irrationality are largely harmless. We support one football team over another, and if you scrutinize this fact too much, you'll come to recognize how arbitrary it is. But, so long as our fandom doesn't descend into hooliganism, it can be pretty much harmless. In fact, it can be quite fun to have a team to root for (my friend and colleague Saul Smilansky calls it benign irrationality). Similarly, there's a lot that we can get from engaging with fiction. The fact that it causes us to have all sorts of irrational emotions might be offset by those benefits. Sometimes, in fact, it's very human of us to experience irrational emotions. Radford's (somewhat controversial) example is the human fear of death.

As Epicurus argued, the fear of death cannot be rational. For all the time that we're alive, we're not dead – and when we're dead, we no longer exist. Accordingly, at no point is our own death a bad thing *for us*. And yet we fear it. Radford writes:

> Some may say that this fear is not incoherent, for what appals such men is not their also thinking of death as an unpleasant state, but the prospect of their non-existence. But how can this appal? There is, literally, nothing to fear. The incoherence of fearing the sleep of death for all that it will cause one to miss is even clearer. We do not participate in life when we are dead, but we are not then endlessly wishing to do so. Nonetheless, men fear the endless, dreamless sleep of death and fear it for all that they will miss.
>
> (Radford & Weston, 1975, p. 79)

I don't think that Epicurus's argument works to render the fear of death irrational (for an excellent discussion of this point, see Shelly Kagan's book on the philosophy of death – neatly titled, *Death* – Kagan 2012). Accordingly, I'm not convinced that Radford's example of a naturally human irrational emotion is a good one. Football fandom is perhaps a better example. Not all of our feelings can be rationally justified. And yet, I'm far from convinced that our emotional engagement with fiction falls into that category. And thus, we'll move on now to Weston's response to Radford.

*Tatjana:* There is another argument against the rationality of our fear of eternal sleep, a.k.a. death. For a fear to be rational, the person feeling the emotion has to have the potential to avoid the feared object. But none of us can avoid our own deaths. So, our fear of death isn't rational.

*Sam:* Shelly Kagan agrees with you. He thinks that argument is better than Epicurus's. Personally, I go back and forward on the issue. Sometimes I think that fear of the inevitable can't be rational, for the reason you say. Other times, I think the inevitably itself is what makes some things so scary!

## Weston's Response (or: Why My Wife Is Right)

According to Weston, Radford came to his conclusion only because he fails to recognize something about the context of our emotional engagement with fictional characters. As I understand his argument, Weston doesn't deny that we feel sad for Anna Karenina herself. Rather, his point is that these feelings for Anna are embedded in an emotional response to the work of art in which she features. Moreover, our emotional response to a work of art is embedded in a larger network of emotional attitudes that we hold towards the real world. Only when our feelings for Anna Karenina are examined from this perspective can we make sense of their coherence or rationality.

When we open a book or enter a theatre, we agree to take part in something imaginative. No such agreement is present with the man in the bar or the fake news report. Radford tries to address this difference by considering whether the suspension of disbelief can justify our emotions, but did he go far enough to distinguish the difference between these very different contexts (the contexts of the bar and the news report, on the one hand, and the contexts of reading a novel and watching a movie, on the other hand)? You can't hope to understand our feelings for a fictional character, Weston would urge, if you isolate those feelings and abstract them away from the broader context of engaging with a *work* of fiction.

In fact, Weston has a proof that to be moved by a fictional character is, at least in part, to be moved by an entire work of fiction. When we're *not* consuming a fiction, we can be moved by isolated statements of facts. Somebody you don't know could tell you that their young son was just killed by a drunk driver, and you could be moved immediately. But, saying that "Mercutio is dead", if you already know that Mercutio isn't real, but if you're not watching the play, or, at least, if you don't know the story of the play, is not prone to move a person at all. What explains this difference?

According to Weston, the difference is this: an event, in the real world – for example – of a young boy being killed by a drunk driver, can, in some sense or other, be separated from the lives of the people involved. We feel very strongly, for example, that it didn't have to happen that way. Things could have been different. But Mercutio *must* die in the way that he dies. As Weston rightly observes, "if a character in a performance of a play does not die in that way, then either he is not Mercutio, or it is not a performance of Shakespeare's *Romeo and Juliet*" (Radford & Weston, 1975, p. 85).

Indeed, legend has it that Tolstoy cried when he wrote of Anna Karenina's death. You might think that Tolstoy could have written her a happy ending, to save himself the tears, but there's also a sense in which, had he done that, he'd have written a very different novel. What Tolstoy understood was that, in order to create the work of fiction that he wanted to create, Anna Karenina *had* to die – even if to do so would make him cry.

But it follows that, if Mercutio's death is somehow inseparable from the play, unlike real tragedies which *are* separable from the other events in life, then, "if we are moved by Mercutio's death, we are being moved by an episode within the context of a play" (Radford & Weston, 1975, p. 85). It isn't just Mercutio that moves us. It's the play. It isn't just Anna Karenina that moves us. It's the novel. Does this mean that my wife is right that we're not really crying for Anna herself? I don't think so. We *are* crying for Anna, but our crying for her cannot be understood in isolation from our emotional response to the novel as a whole.

The notion that a novel or a play can move us is no more bizarre than the notion that an idea can move us. But ideas *can* move us, and no rule about rationality outlaws such feelings.

*Tatjana:* Abstract art, a certain combination of colours on a canvas, can move us to tears, even if there is no sentient being we recognize in the painting. What happens in these cases? The structured paint on the canvas just triggers a certain emotion.

*Sam:* That's a great question. I have felt powerfully moved by Rothko paintings, which are just – as you say – combinations of colour on a canvas. I have to admit that I have no clue how to make sense of what's going on in a case like that. I think we'll have to write another book together!

We can be upset by the idea that all human relationships, however rich and intimate, must all be ripped asunder by death. That isn't to be moved by a non-existent event or person. It's to be moved by an idea. If ideas can move us, then why can't novels? And it's only in the context of our being moved by a novel that we can, truly, say that we're crying for Anna Karenina.

Moreover, when we're moved by an idea, Weston would say, we're moved not by any particular event, but by a particular "conception of life". By a *conception of life*, Weston is thinking about a quite wide-framed view of the world in which we live. If we want to examine a conception of life, we sometimes need to take a step back from the particularities of given events.

> I can be saddened or angered by reading accounts of war where the object of my feeling is not the death and suffering of the particular individuals concerned, but, for example, the terrible things men can do to others in pursuit of their interests and the terrible blindness on the part of those others which enables such things to occur. What I am responding to here is, we can say, a possibility of human life perceived through a certain conception of that life.
>
> (Radford & Weston, 1975, p. 85, p. 86)

It is precisely because works of art tend to express a certain conception of life that we can find them moving. And this, I think, is where my wife is right. This is the kernel of truth at the heart of suggestion 4. What makes a conception of life moving is that it really is a conception of *this* life. It is an expression of what's possible for beings like us in a world like ours. We've already spoken in Chapters 1, 5, and 6, about the complex ways in which fiction interacts with the real world – even if the fictions are fantastical or magical, or what have you, the work of fiction itself will always draw, in complex ways, from the world in which we live, and a work of fiction will almost inevitably have things to say about the real world too. In fact, I went so far as to suggest that a definition of fiction would appeal to the fact that fictions are always about the real world in addition to the world of the story. Crying for Anna Karenina can't be easily divorced from crying for certain facts about the real world.

Were it not for these complex interactions with the real world, a fiction wouldn't be able to express a conception of the life that we human beings are living. And thus, there really is a palpable sense in which the plight of real and possible women like Anna Karenina are relevant to the tears we cry for her. That's to say: (1) we only cry for *her* because we're moved by the fiction in which she features; (2) we're only moved by the fiction in which she features because of the conception of life that it expresses (at least in its treatment of the character for whom we're crying); and (3) we can only be moved by a conception of life if we care about the real possibilities that it makes salient.

Putting things into context, in this way, explains how our emotional engagement with fiction isn't at all divorced from our emotional engagement with reality. When a man tells a lie in a bar, we're not engaging with a work of fiction. If we chose to relate to his lies as a work of fiction, our emotional responses would likely be different, and they wouldn't be impacted by the discovery that his sister doesn't exist. The same could be said about the false news report. When we don't feel aggrieved for having been lied to, and choose to engage with something as a work of fiction, we weave all of the events that the fiction reports together into a web that expresses a conception of life.

As far as Weston is concerned, Radford goes wrong because he doesn't do justice to the extent to which our engagement with fictional characters is bound up with our engagement with the works of fiction in which they feature, nor to the extent to which our engagement with works of fiction is bound up with our appreciation of conceptions of this life that we're living. Radford's thought-experiments don't really demonstrate that emotions are irrational for people and events if we don't believe that those people or events are real. Why? Because the thought-experiments draw from too narrow a set of examples. They don't take into consideration what we might be doing when, instead of being lied to, we engage with a work of fiction.

On the other hand, perhaps Radford's thought-experiments reveal more than Weston recognizes. At the very least, they illustrate the fact that emotions are irrational to the extent that they're not really responding to the world in which we live. Where Radford goes wrong is to ignore the ways in which our emotional engagement with a fictional character *can* be an expression of an underlying emotional engagement with life itself.

So there we have it. Is our emotional engagement with mere fictions irrational? Radford says yes, and Weston says no. I haven't tried to hide that my sympathies here lie with Weston. But if you disagree with Weston and me, that's great – that's what philosophy's all about; argument and debate. But what you'll have to do, I think, to rehabilitate Redford's conclusion, in the wake of Weston's response, is to find examples (either drawn from our real life engagement with fiction, or drawn from inventive thought-experiments of your own) that demonstrate how our engagement with fictional characters really *can* be detached from our emotional engagement with works of fiction, and therefore with emotional attitudes towards conceptions of this life. Weston thinks that no such examples can be found. If you want to prove him wrong, you'll have to get thinking.

## Works Cited

Bouwsma, O. K. (1965) The Expression Theory of Art. In O. K. Bouwsma, *Philosophical Essays*. Lincoln, NE: University of Nebraska Press, pp. 21–50.

Eco, U. (2011) *Confessions of a Young Novelist*. Cambridge, MA: Harvard University Press.

Evans, D. (2002) The Search Hypothesis of Emotion. *The British Journal for the Philosophy of Science*, 53(4): 497–509.

James, W. (1890) *The Principles of Psychology*. New York: Holt.

Kagan, S. (2012) *Death*. New Haven, CT: Yale University Press.

Neu, J. (2000) *A Tear is an Intellectual Thing: The Meanings of Emotion*. Oxford: Oxford University Press.

Nussbaum, M. (2001) *Upheavals of Thought: The Intelligence of Emotions*. Cambridge: Cambridge University Press.

Radford, C., & Weston, M. (1975) How Can We Be Moved by the Fate of Anna Karenina? *Proceedings of the Aristotelian Society, Supplementary Volumes*, 49: 67–93.

## Further Reading

Dadlez, E. M. (1996) Fiction, Emotion, and Rationality. *British Journal of Aesthetics*, 36(3): 290–304.

Gendler, T. S. & Kovakovich, K. (2006) Genuine Rational Fictional Emotions. In M. Kieran (ed.), *Contemporary Debates in Aesthetics and the Philosophy of Art*. Oxford: Blackwell, pp. 241–253.

Goldie, P. (2007) Emotion. *Philosophy Compass*, 2(6): 928–938. *A good introduction to the philosophy of emotion.*

Walton, K. (1978) Fearing Fictions. *Journal of Philosophy*, 75(1): 5–27.

Chapter 9

# The Paradox of Tragedy

*Tatjana*

On a warm Sunday evening in Berlin, my friend and I zapped through the TV schedule and landed on a film with the cheesy title *Never Let Me Go*. Now, I'm not a fan of romcoms, which I expected the film to be, but the ensemble of Carey Mulligan and Keira Knightly intrigued us. After one hour and forty-five minutes filled with tears, fury, hopefulness, anxiety, and desperation I declared *Never Let Me Go* to be one of the best dramas I've ever watched. I also doubted I could ever endure watching it again. For me, Mark Romanek's 2010 sci-fi drama *Never Let Me Go* is a tragic fiction film *par excellence*. The story's heroes are caught in a system that delivers one horrific blow after the other and, with few exceptions, causes them to suffer from the beginning to the end of their lives. Despite the distress that watching the film caused me, I decided to read the novel by Kazuo Ishiguro (2005), from which the film was adapted, in preparation for this chapter. As I anticipated, I experienced the same kind of heartbreak and devastation while reading the book that I felt when I watched the film.

My immediate reaction to a heartbreaking fictional story is neither incomprehensible nor is it unheard of. Fictional works have the potential to cause the full spectrum of human emotions in us. We feel happy when the novel's heroine makes a friend, and delighted when, fictionally, the cruel prison guard is punished for their actions. Watching a fictional vulnerable person experience injustice makes us angry, and we feel hopeless when we realize that no one will step up to help a bullying victim. Tragic fictions, perhaps more than any other genre, evoke a variety of unpleasant feelings in us.

Have you found yourself screaming at the screen in response to the death of a character you were rooting for? Well, you're not alone. Many of us react emotionally to events depicted in fictions. And some of these emotions, quite clearly, don't feel good; they feel uncomfortable. There are some uncomfortable emotions we readily acknowledge as outright painful: deep sadness, heartbreak, fear, distress, discouragement, hopelessness, desperation, disappointment, and helplessness. Other uncomfortable emotions lack the sting of pain that feeling heartbroken brings with it but nevertheless feel far from good: frustration, fury, anger, tension, irritation, worry, feeling annoyed, repulsion, feeling

DOI: 10.4324/9781003126102-10

overwhelmed, and anxiety. All these emotions feel uncomfortable, regardless of whether they are triggered by fictional or real events. Frustration over the injustice a fictional heroine has to suffer can be just as uncomfortable as frustration over the injustice our friend is suffering. Frustration feels bad, no matter what causes it. And it makes sense that we would react emotionally to emotionally charged scenarios – fictional or real. The depictions of suffering and joy can touch us regardless of whether the characters involved are part of our or a fictional world – just as Sam discussed in the previous chapter. This ability to empathize is kind of our superpower as humans, and it's one of the main reasons we are drawn towards fictional stories.

Quite plausibly, most fictional works trigger some unpleasant feelings, however mild. David Brent's behaviour in the original version of *The Office* constantly irritates me, yet I take no issue with the classification of the British TV show as comedy. Tragedy, however, doesn't stop at mild discomfort. The emotions it triggers, and that we expect it to trigger, are downright painful. It's these emotions that we'll be considering in this chapter.

Why do we voluntarily engage with fiction that makes us feel sad, hopeless, or devastated? Think about it. If I suggested that you burn your favourite dress or sweater, the one with all those memories attached to it, you'd politely decline. You know it would make you feel sad (and probably angry at me), and you generally aim to avoid feeling sad in real life. So why would anyone consume fictional works that trigger sadness? When I watched and read *Never Let Me Go*, I felt an array of emotions I would consider to be unpleasant. Some of these emotions were only uncomfortable, others downright painful. I don't want to spend my evenings feeling desperate. Yet, I picked up a book that I knew would make me feel just that way. Where is the logic behind that?

## Formulating the Paradox

The puzzle I describe in the above section has been named the *Paradox of Tragedy*. Logically speaking, paradoxes consist of a set of sentences that strike us as plausible when we look at each sentence individually but that cannot all be true when considered together. Here is an example of a well-known paradox, the *Sorites Paradox*:

1. One grain of sand is not a heap.
2. If one grain of sand is not a heap, then one grain of sand plus one grain of sand, that is, two grains of sand, are not a heap.
3. If two grains of sand are not a heap, then two grains of sand plus one grain of sand, that is, three grains of sand, are not a heap.
4. If three grains of sand are not a heap, then four grains of sand are not a heap.
5. If $n$ number of grains of sand are not a heap, then $n + 1$ grains of sand are not a heap.

Each of the five statements seems true when considered individually. But taken together, they imply that nothing is ever a heap, which is clearly false. That's what makes these reflections on heaps paradoxical.

Now, let's see what is paradoxical about our consumption of fictional tragedy:

1 We don't want to experience situations that make us feel painful emotions.
2 We choose to consume fictional tragedies, even though we anticipate that they will cause us painful emotions.
3 Tragedies frequently make us feel painful emotions.

Each sentence, on its own, seems plausible. All they do is describe the observable behaviour of viewers and readers. Yet, when considered together, these statements appear to be inconsistent. After all, if we know that tragedies trigger painful emotions like sadness, distress, or hopelessness, and we still choose to engage with them, then it would seem that we *do* seek out situations that elicit unpleasant emotions.

Since not all of the statements can be true, we are left with three options. If statements 2 and 3 are true, statement 1 must be false, and we *do* want to experience situations that make us feel painful emotions. That can't be right. But if statements 1 and 2 are true, then we don't seek painful emotions, yet we volunarily choose to watch tragedies; this would imply that tragedies do not, in fact, provoke feelings of sadness, distress, and other negative emotions. Finally, if statements 1 and 3 are true, this would imply that either we are being forced to engage with tragic fictions or we must be oblivious to the emotional impact they are likely to have, rendering statement 2 false.

Now, of course we sometimes stumble into a movie theatre or start reading a book not expecting a tragic fictional story. This was my experience when I first watched *Never Let Me Go*. But in most cases, we are at least aware of the genre. We get a sense of the mood when we see the movie poster or book cover or when we read or hear a summary of the story. Generally, we won't be surprised if a film or a book classified as a tragedy evokes emotions such as sadness, devastation, anger, or frustration.

Here's a confession, I'm not particularly fond of the genre of fictional tragedy. I don't ever like to feel painful emotions; or so it seems to me. And yet, I've watched and read many fictional tragedies over the years, not by accident, but by choice. I chose them knowing very well that some set of painful emotions will inevitably arise for me. And indeed, it almost seems as if triggering painful emotions is an essential feature of a compelling work of tragic fiction. Viewers or readers frequently criticise fictional tragedies for their failure to trigger some degree of sadness, anxiousness, frustration, or devastation, for failure to move the audience. I think this is what happened to Tommy Wiseau's semi-autographical melodrama *The Room* (2003), widely considered one of the worst films ever made. The film has been widely criticised for its plot inconsistencies and bad acting, ultimately leading to its inability to move the audience. So, I hope you agree that statement 2 of the paradox is beyond dispute.

This leaves us with statements 1 and 3. As it turns out, we should be cautious about accepting those two statements. It's far from obvious that we don't seek to feel distressed at times. And the precise manner in which tragedies evoke feelings of distress is crucial to understanding the paradox.

## A Question of Motivation

If people consume fictional tragedies knowing that they will cause them distress, there must be some good reason for them to do so. Of course, humans can sometimes be irrational. Suppose you're uncertain about your career path – whether to study medicine or delve into philosophy – so you let your lucky coin decide and go with whatever result. That's not very rational. Or consider the act of texting while driving. We all know that it's dangerous, yet it's a risk many of us have taken. It seems irrational that you would text while driving, knowing very well that it could end in a crash. But watching or reading tragic stories, knowing very well that they will likely cause you painful emotions, doesn't seem irrational. We don't feel bad or guilty about consuming tragedy. And we're not just a few who choose tragic fictional works; it's a very popular fiction genre! Before we brand a large part of the human population as irrational, let's see whether we can find something that is worth the pain of engaging with tragic fiction.

What, then, could potentially motivate us to engage with tragic narratives? One straightforward reason might be an external mandate. For example, your professor might have assigned a tragic novel such as Françoise Sagan's *Bonjour Tristesse* (1954) for class reading. In such a case, your motivation for reading the book could be that you desire a good grade, or you believe you should do what your professor asks you to do, or you want to be able to discuss the book with your peers. To be sure, your choice to read the book is a voluntary one. But the reward does not stem from your engagement with the novel itself. Rather, your reward is the good grade your professor will give you, or perhaps it is the inspiring discussion of the novel you will have with your friends.

Here is a related, yet different reason for choosing a tragic story. If you are a film or literature student or critic, you will occasionally be picking up a book or film whose content doesn't really excite you. Rather than on the fictional events, your main focus is on the depiction of those events – how the story is told, the prose, the lightning, the editing work, and so on. You might not even feel distress at the tragic events that unfold because you are not nearly as much engaged with the content of the fiction as you are engaged with its representation. Your motivation for reading *Bonjour Tristesse* or watching a heart-wrenching film such as Michael Haeneke's *Amour* (2012) lies in gaining a deeper understanding of the artistic or technical features of narrative representation.

Another compelling motive behind people's actions can be their sense of obligation or their desire to uphold what they consider morally right. And in some instances consuming tragedy may be justified by a sense of duty or moral obligation. If I had chosen the last three films to watch with my friends, it would seem fair to let someone else choose the next film. I opt to watch the tragedy my friends have picked because it seems to me the right and fair thing to do, even if I'm not a fan of the tragedy genre. Or you might choose to read a book that evokes feelings of despair and hopelessness because you have promised your partner that you'd read a book that addresses a social cause they are passionate about. In cases like these, we choose to consume the tragic fiction because we judge that doing so is morally required of us. Wanting to do the right thing is a powerful motivator. If it's the only, or at least main motivator, for watching or reading tragic fiction, then the question of how engaging with the tragedy might personally benefit us has slid into the background.

When it comes to making moral decisions, we *do* sometimes seek out real situations that make us feel sad, distressed, or hopeless. Consider an animal rights activist who decides that the right thing to do is to help, knowing full well that facing the horrific circumstances they will encounter will cause them great distress. If we can have a morally valid reason for confronting real situations that cause us pain, then it is plausible that we can have morally valid reasons for confronting tragic situations that are only fictional.

*Sam:* I've been in situations like this too, so I know that they happen. But it seems like this is an answer that just dodges the question.

The real question now is why does your friend, whose choice you're morally obliged to follow, or your teacher, or what have you, choose to watch a tragedy? *They're* not doing it because they have a moral obligation. So, the underlying question hasn't gone away.

*Tatjana:* Absolutely! *Your* reason may be moral in nature; you're watching the tragedy because it's your friend's turn to pick a movie. But their reason is ... well ... that's what we are still trying to figure out.

When you are picking up or turning on tragic fiction for your academic grades, to study depiction techniques, or for moral reasons, you are not facing the paradox of tragedy. You have reasons for consuming a particular tragedy which are not directly tied to the fictional content that might distress you. But there seems to be a much more common reason for people to consume tragic fiction: they hope to "get something out" of engaging with the fictional narrative. And it's here that things truly become fascinating. For what is the benefit that people expect and reliably gain from engaging with tragic stories?

## It's All about Pleasure

The great Scottish philosopher David Hume begins his essay "Of Tragedy" (originally published in 1757) with the following insight:

> It seems an unaccountable pleasure, which the spectators of a well-written tragedy receive from sorrow, terror, anxiety, and other passions, which are in themselves disagreeable and uneasy. The more they are touched and affected, the more are they delighted with the spectacle, and as soon as the uneasy passions cease to operate, the piece is at an end.
>
> (Hume 1965, p. 29)

Hume suggests that when we emotionally engage with tragedy, what arises is pleasure. Pleasure views, as responses to the paradox of fiction, hold that the fundamental reason why we engage with tragic fiction is the promise of pleasure. The suggestion is not that all human behaviour is ultimately motivated by and only by pleasurable feelings. This would be blatantly false as we've already seen in the previous section. People sometimes do things they don't find pleasurable (e.g. because it's the right thing to do). But according to pleasure views, what mainly motivates us to read or watch fictional tragedy is the pleasure we gain from doing so.

Just as pain feels bad, pleasure feels good. We'll use the term "pleasure" as an umbrella term for a whole family of comfortable emotions. This family includes ecstasy, enthusiasm, excitement, fun, delight, amazement, amusement, and joy, which are all emotions that are felt rather intensely. But it also includes satisfaction, gratification, hopefulness, contentment, peacefulness, which we feel less intensely, yet still possess a positive hedonic tone.

It's easy to see that comedic elements in fiction produce pleasurable emotions. We are amused by Ron's attempts to undermine the government in the TV show *Parks and Recreation,* and humoured when we learn that the answer to life and the universe in Douglas Adams's novel *The Hitchhiker's Guide to the Galaxy* is … 42.

Happy endings, too, can change the tone of a fictional work and influence our emotions. A fictional story that provides us with a happy ending can be uplifting even if it's been a series of devastating events for the most part – or perhaps because of the devastation right up till the end? I feel delighted when Olive's family finally unites and joins her on stage in *Little Miss Sunshine* (Jonathan Dayton and Valerie Faris, 2006), and content when Jane Eyre marries for love in Charlotte Brontë's novel of the same name. A happy ending can compensate for the hours spent watching or reading about injustice, heartbreak, loss, and missed opportunities.

Conversely, we feel empty, forlorn, shocked, and devastated if a story has a very tragic ending after bouts and bouts of love, happiness, successes, and joy. Would you agree with my observations on how the conclusion of a film or novel influences our feelings as the credits roll or as we close the book? If I'm right, then the amount of pain or pleasure we feel when engaging with a fiction does not fully determine whether we judge the experience to be painful or pleasurable overall. Whether the ending is happy or tragic matters too and can outweigh experiences we had along the way. So, perhaps it's not puzzling that people watch tragic stories that have happy endings. The pleasure we feel at a happy end, after much drama, makes up for the previous pain. We love a good "rags to riches" story, or one from heartbreak to soulmate.

But these works, though containing plenty of drama, are not tragedies. A prototypical tragedy will have a tragic ending. We might view Anne's death at the end of *Amour* as a blessing, but it does not make up for the heartbreak of seeing Anne and Georges's relationship deteriorate to the point of despair. When it comes to truly tragic fiction, the positive feelings we might experience from any uplifting moments within a deeply tragic and devastating narrative are heavily overshadowed by the negative emotions sparked by the catastrophic events.

I feel joyful when Kathy and Tommy's love begins to blossom in *Never Let Me Go*, and hopeful when they learn about a rumour that, if true, might prolong their time together. But during most of the viewing or reading, I feel utterly desperate and sad. Worse still, the few moments of hope and joy cause me to feel even more desperation and sadness when tragedy strikes. In tragic fiction, pleasant emotions caused by happy fictional events are vastly outweighed by the painful feelings evoked by the devastating events depicted in them. If watching or reading tragedy is pleasurable, this pleasure must be caused by something other than just the fictional events in a tragic story. And if the reason we seek out tragic fiction is to feel pleasure, then the pleasure must significantly outweigh any distress caused by the fictional events.

*Sam:* You're now talking about prototypical tragedies, where the ending is tragic too, right?

The pleasant emotions that crop up along the way are not enough to compensate for the tragedy. But in non-prototypical tragic fiction, where there is a surprisingly happy end, you're willing to accept that the happiness (when it comes in the form of a happy ending) can compensate for much sadness, right?

*Tatjana:* I am hesitant to call a story with a happy end "tragic". Moreover, we might still find it somewhat strange that the good feelings about a happy ending can compensate for all the unpleasant ones along the way. It makes for a good story but it's not clear whether, for example, the individual in question found life as a whole enjoyable! So something of the puzzle can remain.

## A Matter of Conversion?

Or so it seems to me. You might disagree and you wouldn't be alone in that. Some philosophers argue that the painful emotions that we feel when confronted with fictional tragic events, unlike in the case of real-life devastating events, are converted into pleasure. Pain is converted into pleasure? Yes, that sounds quite a bit like masochism. But Hume argued that the distress and hopelessness we feel when reading a tragic novel, like *Bonjour Tristesse*, is transformed into pleasure; pleasure that is derived from the beauty of the story. We admire the eloquence with which Sagan depicts the dangers of a hedonistic lifestyle. We revel in the artistry of her descriptions of the fictional world. We appreciate the narrative structure of the novel, and its inner consistency; something that depictions of real-life tragedy often lack. It is this beauty of the tragedy, so Hume argues, that transforms pain into pleasure.

If Hume is right, then the paradox of tragedy doesn't really get off the ground in the first place. After all, any painful feelings we might have are overwritten by pleasant ones that derive from artistic beauty. When we engage with tragic fiction, we might feel sad, distressed, or hopeless, but these emotions are converted into pleasant emotions. If our delight, excitement, and joy hinge on us first feeling heartbroken, devastated and frustrated, then it suggests that these painful emotions are not always unwelcome.

To be sure, feeling sad or heartbroken is still uncomfortable, and it feels bad. But we can want to experience uncomfortable feelings in particular situations. In these situations, the painful emotions are instrumental to obtaining something we truly desire. Consider the act of eating spicy food. The physical pain you feel from devouring a tasty, hot Thai curry is quickly transformed into gustatory pleasure. This suggests that we sometimes seek out painful sensations if they are converted into pleasurable ones. Now, what holds true of sensations can also apply to emotions. Think of the sadness and distress you feel when you miss your partner while you are away on a weekend trip. Yet, the yearning you feel can be sweet and pleasantly intermingled with strong feelings of love, emotions you wouldn't experience with such intensity if you didn't experience the unpleasant ones. There is nothing paradoxical about seeking out unpleasant emotions if they are converted into pleasant ones.

Now, for Hume, the pleasure we experience when consuming tragic fiction comes from the stories' artistic beauty. But do we need to feel devastated, heartbroken, or sad to derive pleasure from the artistic beauty of the fictional work? This doesn't seem quite right. I don't see why it shouldn't be possible to derive pleasure from the work's beauty without necessarily feeling distressed. Surely, we could appreciate the portrayal of Ilsa and Rick's love story in *Casablanca* (directed by Michael Curtiz, 1942), or the cinematography of *Amour*, without even a smidge of sadness. If we can gain pleasure from a work's artistry without pain, then we're back to our original question. Why do we endure the painful emotions that tragic fictions stir up? What's in it for us?

Perhaps Hume got something right and something wrong with his suggestion that we are compensated through artistic beauty. Perhaps painful emotions are converted into pleasure when we consume tragedy, it's just that the source of this pleasure isn't artistic beauty.

*Sam:* I agree. I think that the conversion theory would be more compelling if it said we actually enjoy the pain itself, but only in certain settings. I sound like a masochist.

*Tatjana:* Conversion, to me, means that the pain isn't really painful, so you never actually enjoy the pain. It never gets to be experienced as pain. But masochists find pleasure in the painful sensation.

*Sam:* I wonder. I've read about experienced meditators who, in the midst of their meditation, were able to concentrate on a bodily pain, and to experience a certain pleasure associated with experiencing the pain. I'm not sure I understand the nature of the experience they report, but I wonder if the possibility of such experience might present an alternative to conversion theory.

*Tatjana:* Perhaps it's a pleasure that comes from realizing they're the kind of person who perseveres through pain. I'll get to a suggestion along those lines shortly.

I think there is a more damning objection to the conversion theory. The conversion theory claims that the painful emotions we experience while reading or watching tragedy are transformed into pleasure. But this is not, or at least not usually, how I experience my emotions when consuming fictional tragedy. Let us refer to objections that highlight a discrepancy between real-life experience and what a theory predicts as appeals to a *phenomenological gap*. The heavy heartedness I feel after having read Françoise Sagan's *Bonjour Tristesse* does not go away because I enjoyed the novel. I am disgusted by Raymond's betrayal of his fiancée Anne, and angry at Cecile's selfish behaviour. When their carelessness cumulates into a tragedy, I feel sorrow for Anne. It doesn't seem to me that my feelings of disgust, anger, and sorrow have been transformed into pleasure by the time I read the last sentence of the book. I don't feel happy, I just feel sad. My sadness transforms only into desperation when I watch *Amour*. And I find it hard to imagine that someone who truly engages with the film can feel anything but desolate by the time the closing film credits roll.

What shall we conclude? Although Hume's conversion theory points to an interesting fact – that the artistry of the writer or filmmaker contributes to our enjoyment of a fictional work – it doesn't align well with our experience with tragedy. It creates a phenomenological gap. The theory fails to correspond with our usual experience where feelings of sadness, frustration, and despair evoked by tragedy rarely transmute into a sense of pleasure.

## Compensating the Audience

The painful emotions we experience when we engage with tragedy don't seem to be converted into pleasure, but perhaps we are *compensated* for our experience with pleasure. According to the conversion theory, our painful emotions are transformed into pleasure so that by the time we reach the end of the book or film, the dominant emotions are pleasant ones. But a compensation theorist does not argue that our distress is magically replaced by joy. Instead, the idea is that we are compensated for our pain with pleasure. I hope you can see that the compensation theory is less threatened by the phenomenological gap objection than the conversion theory. We still experience and judge tragic films and novels as sad, frustrating, devastating or disheartening but we are repaid for our pains with delight, amazement, satisfaction, or hopefulness. So, what is the source of this compensatory pleasure?

### *Artistic Beauty Revisited*

If we are compensated for engaging with tragic fiction, the source of our pleasure doesn't have to be our painful emotions either. One source of delight, enjoyment, or satisfaction could certainly be the artistic features of the narrative or its representation, just as Hume suggested. A beautiful shot, an intriguing description, the way in which the artist chooses to depict the fictional events can strike us as particularly artful, effective, or moving, and we take pleasure in such aspects of a fictional work. The telling of a tragic story in a particularly beautiful way can compensate for the painful emotions its content elicited in us. Although we feel heartbroken when star-crossed lovers Ilsa and Rick say their final goodbyes in *Casablanca*, our sadness, triggered by the fictional events, may well be outweighed by our enjoyment of the eloquence and technical ability of the times (it's the 1940s, after all) with which the story is being told.

You won't be surprised to hear that there is a challenge to the suggestion that pleasure gained by artistry usually compensates us for our pain. I'll call it the *not-enough objection*. Granted, the pleasure derived from appreciating the artistry might partly offset the distress that watching a tragic film causes us, but it's not clear that this pleasure is substantial *enough* compensation for consuming tragic works. After all, painful feelings don't feel great. It is natural that we would only willingly endure such emotions if, in turn, we were promised a repayment equal to, or better yet larger than, our pain. The costs should not outweigh the benefits. After all, would you repaint a stranger's house with the promise that they will compensate you for your labour by humming a song for you? Probably not. It simply isn't enough compensation for your effort. However, if they proposed to help you with moving house in return, you might well consider the offer.

To be sure, sometimes the pleasure derived from the artistic features may well be enough compensation. *Casablanca* might be worth watching simply for the pleasure gained from its artistic beauty. But can the compensation theorist who appeals only to artistic beauty as compensation say the same about the neo-Western film *Brokeback Mountain* (Ang Lee, 2005)? While the story is certainly beautifully told and expertly crafted, our delight in the artistic features does not outweigh the sadness and hopelessness we feel as the tragic events unfold.

### *Catharsis*

Some people enjoy watching tearjerkers or reading dramatic novels because they appreciate a good cry. Crying can be cathartic. It can improve our overall well-being by releasing stuck emotions. We might even feel cleansed and renewed after a heavy sob. I, for one, enjoy the sense of relief after a purge of strong emotions. If tragedy facilitates catharsis, then experiencing the unpleasant emotions that tragic fiction often incites might indeed be a worthwhile trade-off. In such cases, the benefits of cleansing of our emotional household outweigh the costs of experiencing desperation and sorrow from the harrowing events that befall the fictional characters in tragedies.

*Sam:* This is interesting. As you're presenting it, catharsis is a pleasant feeling that we get, to compensate for the painful feelings of, say, crying in the film.

I think I'm thinking of catharsis, by contrast, as more intimately bound up with the crying (or other painful emotion) itself. The catharsis is the pleasure of actually crying, when deep down, something in you needed a cry. Is this a substantive disagreement between us, or is it a relatively superficial difference?

*Tatjana:* Strictly speaking, I am thinking of catharsis as the process of releasing strong emotions that ends in a sense of relief. So, I don't mean a pleasure that lies in crying itself. My personal experience aligns more with a sense of relief either during or after a bout of crying than pleasure coming from crying itself. Could you describe the pleasure more for me? It doesn't primarily involve relief, does it?

*Sam:* I suppose that when I've been feeling a bit down, I have sometimes resisted the attempt of loved ones to cheer me up. Perhaps that's an example of a negative feeling that, in some sense, I'm enjoying, in the very midst of feeling it. Of course, I wouldn't say that I'm enjoying it. That's not the language that I'd use at the time. But my refusal to be cheered up indicates that perhaps there's something that I want about that melancholy state.

Yet, even if catharsis does occur for some fiction consumers, it doesn't always happen for every viewer or reader. Some people engage with tragic fiction and never cry to release their pent-up emotions. And some works of tragic fiction are so gut-wrenching that the suffering we experience as we engage with them is too profound to render our crying cleansing. We may even feel down in the dumps for days after. This happened to me when I watched *Never Let Me Go*.

Now, you might wonder whether someone who does not find catharsis in consuming tragedy is not engaging enough with the fiction. Or perhaps they are not engaging with it in the right way. Maybe they don't make-believe what the fictional work prescribes them to make-believe. Perhaps catharsis is the whole point of our engagement with tragic fiction. However, I doubt that catharsis is necessary for meaningful engagement with tragic fiction. We are not supposed to feel better than we did before entering the theatre after watching *Brokeback Mountain* or *Amour*. If you left the screening of *Amour* exclaiming "I feel better now, I really needed a good cry!" you'd probably get a number of disapproving looks. "How inappropriate!", someone might counter. Some viewers might argue that you have missed the point of the film; catharsis does not seem to be it.

To be sure, consuming tragic fiction *can* be very cathartic. If a recent break-up has left you catatonic, then a heartbreaking film may help you release those emotions of anger, sadness, fury, and desperation, and support you in your quest to move through your grief. These benefits of experiencing catharsis explain why *some* people in *some* situations choose to read or watch tragedy – it is for the benefit of purging their unwanted emotions. However, we still need an explanation for why many other people, or the same people in different situations, engage with tragedy without experiencing or expecting catharsis. And, ideally, we'll find a unified account: a view that explains why *all* people in *all* situations choose to consume tragedy (when they do), well knowing it will cause them distress.

### ***Meta-emotions***

Have you ever revelled in your own ability to deeply empathize with another person? Maybe you comforted a friend who recently experienced a loss, and you felt a slight sense of pride in being such a supportive friend who could empathize with their pain. Or perhaps you read about mass animal farming and took some solace in the fact that you are the kind of person who feels deeply distressed and desperate about the cruelty inflicted on other animals. The delight and solace you felt in these situations are meta-emotions; they are emotional responses to your emotional responses. Your emotional response to your friend's suffering was feeling pain, and the resulting meta-response was a sense of satisfaction or delight derived from your capacity for empathy.

Susan Feagin (1983) argues that we experience such responses when engaging with tragic fiction. Her theory suggests that we don't merely react to the events and characters within the story, but we also have a strong emotional response to our own reactions. When we feel furious and devastated while watching *Precious* (directed by Lee Daniels, 2009), Feagin proposes that we don't just react to the horror of the titular character's situation. We also experience a secondary emotional response – a sense of satisfaction. Satisfaction that we are the kind of people who react appropriately with sadness, desperation, or anger to portrayals of sad, hopeless, or unjust situations. This satisfaction is not derived from the tragic events in the story. Instead, it comes from our ability to react appropriately to these events with painful feelings. Our response affirms our empathy and also our humanity. Our pleasant meta-emotions are our benefit; these emotions are what we gain from tragedy. While we might not derive any pleasure from a tragic narrative itself, we do find the experience of having appropriate, empathetic, and universally human emotions pleasurable. In Feagin's view, it is the pleasantness of our meta-responses to our own unpleasant emotions that motivates us to engage with tragic fiction.

I believe the meta-emotions theory points to an interesting observation: we can notice and emotionally process our own emotions while reading or watching a fictional story. That's pretty awesome! And complex! But, I think, as a general account of why people engage with tragedy it falls short. It encounters a phenomenological gap. While it is plausible that we *sometimes* reflect on our unpleasant emotions, when reading or watching tragic stories, and revel in our ability to feel deeply towards the characters, this doesn't seem to happen frequently. It didn't happen to me when I watched and later read *Never Let Me Go*. Perhaps my emotional reaction wasn't as intense because I wasn't in dire need of a cathartic release. A significant critique of the meta-emotions theory is that we don't typically seem to bother with the cognitively demanding task of reflecting on our own emotional responses. Experiencing meta-emotions seems to be the exception rather than the rule. Yet, this doesn't deter us from watching a tragic film or reading a heartbreaking novel.

The view that we derive pleasure from our meta-responses also faces the not-enough objection. Feagin's approach seems to require that when it comes to fiction, our uncomfortable feelings never reach the threshold to make them truly painful. Imagine your emotional intensity being measured on a scale from 1 to 10, with 10 representing the most intense level of pain. Seeing a friend suffer the loss of a loved one is, say, an 8. But when you watch the fictional heroine of a film fictionally lose their loved one, the intensity of the pain you feel isn't typically an 8. Perhaps the emotional scale only rises to a 6 or even a 4, at which point we might no longer describe the feeling as pain but rather just as discomfort. Well, I don't know about you, but I've certainly watched films and read novels that caused me to feel intensely painful emotions. Even though the fictional nature of a story can sometimes keep the intensity of our emotions at bay, it doesn't always have this effect and we are well aware of this. It doesn't appear as if the painful emotions we experience in response to the fictional events depicted in a tragedy are reliably outweighed by our pleasant meta-emotions. Even if we derive satisfaction at our empathy towards Precious's circumstances, the positive feelings generated don't surpass the negative ones, neither in their intensity nor in their volume. After watching the film, I felt drained and shocked, and no pleasant meta-emotion would have compensated for it. I hope you agree that if pleasant meta-emotions were our primary motivator for engaging with tragic fiction, we would likely consume it far less often. After all, the repayment would not be adequate.

## It's Not All about Pleasure

Pleasure views of the paradox of tragedy hold that the benefits we reap when engaging with tragic stories are pleasurable emotions. It's the overall experience of pleasure that motivates us to pick up Khaled Hosseini's *The Kite Runner* (2003), attend a theatre performance of Shakespeare's *Romeo and Juliet,* or watch *Atonement* (directed by Joe Wright, 2007). But is pleasure the sole driving force for people to engage with tragic fiction? Recall that the fact that my anger at Cecile's selfishness in *Bonjour Tristesse* feels unpleasant to me does not mean that I wish I didn't feel this emotion. It's an appropriate emotion to have when presented with selfish behaviour that leads to tragic events. So, even though my feelings of anger, disgust, and sorrow are unpleasant to me, they are not unwanted.

My favourite example of a painful but wanted emotion is the devastation people feel as part of a grieving process. Devastation is painful, no doubt, but it is also an appropriate reaction to the loss of someone we deeply cared about. Our intense emotional reaction reminds us, maybe even proves to us, that we truly valued the lost relationship, that the relationship was meaningful. This makes devastation a painful yet wanted experiential part of the grieving process. Of course, we did not want to experience the loss in the first place. We do not value the loss. Rather, given that the loss has occurred, we value our painful emotional response to it.

If emotions can be unpleasant but wanted, then maybe the payoff for reading or watching fictional tragedy lies less in pleasant emotions but more so in creating situations that are valuable to us in some other way. Consuming tragic fiction might enrich our lives, even if the pleasure we derive from the experience isn't sufficient to outweigh the pain we feel. To see what value fictional tragedy brings, let's first consider the difference between fictional and real tragedy.

## Why We Prefer Fictional Tragedy to Real Tragedy

Why is it that we enjoy or appreciate fictional tragedy while avoiding real-life tragedy? Aaron Smuts offers an answer:

> I propose that the reason we usually seek out these experiences from art rather than real life is prudence and sometimes cowardice. Art provides a certain degree of safety not present in situations that arouse extreme distress, disgust, anger, fear, horror, misery, paranoia, and a host of other responses. Simply put, most of these reactions cannot be had in real life without incurring significant risks to ourselves and our loved ones, risks that we typically do not take because they far outweigh the rewards.
>
> (Smuts, 2007, p. 72)

When real-life tragedy strikes, it causes harm to us or our loved ones. It does not just hurt if you lose your partner, it has wide-reaching consequences for your life. But when you watch *Brokeback Mountain* or read *Bonjour Tristesse*, you engage with tragic events that are contained. Since they are fictional, these events have no direct consequences for your life or the lives of the people you love. Moreover, there is nothing you can do to directly influence the events. You cannot write a heartfelt letter to Ennis, and you cannot talk Cecile out of her selfish plans. That fictional tragedies are contained reduces your role to that of a necessarily passive bystander to the fictional events, but it also makes engaging with tragic fiction safe since none of the tragic events can harm you.

Unlike with real-life tragic events, you can frequently control your exposure to fictional events. Guillermo del Toro's *Nightmare Alley* (2021), Danny Boyle's *127 Hours* (2010), and Jennifer Fox's *The Tale* (2018) are just three recent films that allegedly sparked mass exoduses during their screenings. Why did people leave? The intensity and amount of distress and disgust must have surpassed their threshold. Audiences employ various methods to control their exposure to fictional events and, hence, to regulate the intensity of their emotional responses. They leave the cinema, cover their eyes (and ears), play with their phones to distract themselves or close the book. My preferred method is to read summaries of films and books, as well as emotional spoiler alerts, on Wikipedia and on doesthedogdie.com. These summaries spare me much of the distressing details and leave little space and time to bond with a character. They also make less use of emotional communication through words, images, or music. This way, my unpleasant emotions stay within the boundaries of what I can endure.

## Values Beyond Pleasure

Because tragic fiction is both contained and controllable, we prefer experiencing fictional tragic events to real distressing situations. But we still need to explain why we engage with fictional tragic events in the first place rather than just stick with lighthearted works of fiction.

### *Rich Experience*

Aaron Smuts (2007) thinks that we sometimes choose to feel unpleasant feelings not because we are masochists, but because we value the experience itself. The pleasure or pain we derive from an experience is not always the sole factor that motivates us to seek it out or avoid it. We value *experiencing*. Smuts describes a skit from a *Saturday Night Live* episode from 1998:

> A family sits down to dinner around a large table. A boy at the end of the table takes a sip of milk from his glass and spits it out, saying "Ugh! This is rotten." The person to his left replies, "Let me try," and has the same response. This is repeated until everyone at the table has confirmed first-hand how bad the sour milk tastes.
>
> (Smuts, 2007, p. 71)

"The skit is funny", Smuts explains, "not because it shows a particularly stupid family that would not take someone's word about the state of a glass of milk and thereby avoid a disgusting experience, but for exposing our desire for firsthand, experiential knowledge of the world." (Smuts 2007, p. 72) Experiences relate our inner world to the outside world. To experience the birth of your child is not merely to witness the event; it's to live through it. It means to undergo a whole bunch of private events, such as thoughts, emotions, sensations, in response to the birth. Accidentally drinking from a can of fruit flies drowned in lemonade invokes thoughts like, "What is this? Flies!" It also involves emotions such as disgust, and sensations, such as small morsels touching one's tongue and feeling nauseated.

Some people actively seek experiences they expect to be mostly unpleasant. These may include climbing Mount Everest, traveling to Chernobyl, or visiting McKamey Manor, which some call the scariest haunted house in the world. And now, recall claim (1) of the paradox of tragedy: we don't seek out situations (in real life) that make us feel painful emotions. This doesn't seem entirely accurate, given what I've just pointed out. We sometimes not merely accept, but bring about experiences that we expect to trigger unpleasant, even downright painful emotions.

If we agree that we sometimes opt for unpleasant and distressing experiences in real life, possibly due to the depth and meaningfulness they offer, then it becomes easier to see why we also choose to experience tragic fictional events that will evoke distress. Now, fictional events are only fictional. Since neither Raymond, Cecile, nor Anne exist in reality, Anne's tragic accident resulting from Raymond's lifestyle and Cecile's manipulation does not actually occur. It does not make much sense to wish this fictional situation had never happened. Well, that conclusion may be a bit hasty. It is reasonable to wish that a fictional dramatic event hadn't happened *while we are immersed in the fiction*. We wish Harry Potter hadn't lost his parents. We feel hopeless when Lady Sybil Crawley dies following the birth of her child in *Downton Abbey* (created by Julian Fellowes, 2010–2015). And we are devastated when Rick and Ilsa say their final goodbyes in *Casablanca*. We don't want a true love to shatter, an innocent person to die, or a vulnerable person to be wronged – whether it's within a fictional world or in reality. This is precisely why fiction has the power to evoke intense emotions, often causing us to slump back in our seats, overwhelmed by a profound sense of despair.

Yet, when it comes to fiction, we often find ourselves desiring the heroine to endure harrowing and heartbreaking events. *Casablanca* would likely not be a classic if Ilsa hadn't boarded the plane. A happy childhood would not explain why it's Harry's destiny to fight the One-Who-Cannot-Be-Named. And without Sybil's death, the storyline of former driver Tom would not have developed the way it has. More generally, a story set in a fictional world that's all sunshine and rainbows rarely makes for very entertaining content. We want to see the heroine experience joy and heartbreak, success and failure, master tough challenges, and learn from grave mistakes. And we desire to emotionally accompany the heroine on her journey. We are willing to do this, even if it's painful. Fiction offers us the opportunity to sample from a rich smorgasbord of experiences – experiences of varying kinds and intensity. We often feel the emotions associated with tragedy more intensely than those linked with comedy or other more lighthearted fiction. Unlike real life, fiction provides a contained environment where our exposure to these events is within our control. As a result, we can willingly immerse ourselves in tragic situations that we might actively avoid in reality.

It's easy to see the allure of the rich experience theory. And yet, I think the idea that we consume works of tragic fiction for the deep and varied experiences they offer is merely part of the answer to the paradox of tragedy. That's because there appears to be a myriad of reasons why people engage with tragic fiction. I'll elaborate more in the final section of this chapter. For now, here are three more reasons why people might engage with fictional tragedy which have nothing to do with pleasure.

### Shared Humanity

Depictions of human misery in fictional stories can bring our shared humanity to the fore; we all lose someone we love, we all experience disappointments in life, we all die. In the movie adaptation of *Never Let Me Go*, Kathy's final words connect the destiny of clones to that of every human being:

> What I'm not sure about is if our lives have been so different from the lives of the people we save. We all complete. Maybe none of us really understand what we've lived through, or feel we've had enough time.

Note that "completing" is a euphemism for "dying" in the world of the story. Kathy's words remind us that we are not alone in our suffering. As the band REM sings in one of their songs, "everybody hurts sometimes". It's plausible that part of the reason we particularly enjoy watching sad movies, reading devastating novels, or listening to heartbreaking songs when we are sad, devastated, or heartbroken ourselves is that doing so makes us feel less lonely in our misery. Arguably, feeling less lonely is not really a pleasant feeling, even though it does alleviate the painful sensations. So, if a sense of shared humanity is what we gain from engaging with tragedy, it's not necessarily a gain of pleasure but rather a reduction of our pain.

### *Exposure "Therapy"*

Fictional tragedies frequently portray harrowing situations, and quite often these are situations that are unfamiliar to us. But while we have not encountered these situations in real life, we may well encounter them in the future. We learn about the devastating impact of dementia on a couple through Anne and Georges in *Amour,* and it prompts us to ponder how we would handle such a tragedy if it were to befall our own relationship. When the depicted tragic events are events that could likely occur in our lives, the exposure to these situations in a controlled environment, like fiction, can prepare us to better cope with our emotions should they happen in real life. We know that we can walk out of the cinema, or close the book, when our emotions are getting too much for us.

Moreover, we know that the depicted events are fictional. In a way, exposure to fictional heartbreaks, losses, and deaths is similar to the exposure to the picture of a spider. Exposure therapy is a popular therapeutic approach that allows people to face distressing situations in a controlled and safe environment. This approach can be helpful for people who suffer from particular fears, for example, a fear of spiders. If you are terrified of spiders, then the picture of a spider will still scare or disgust you. But you also know that you don't need to run away or scream for help because a picture of the spider is not an actual spider. You don't need to take action and can instead fully focus on your own emotions. Now, perhaps when we dive into stories that stir up intense and sometimes distressing emotions, we are giving ourselves some sort of emotional exposure therapy. We are confronting challenging emotions within a safe space. When we feel heartbroken for Ennis and Jack in *Brokeback Mountain*, we don't need to intervene for these star-crossed lovers. After all, the love story is not only fictional, but it also isn't *our* doomed relationship. Just as exposure therapy can help the arachnophobe face their fear of spiders, engaging with tragic fiction helps us to face those human emotions that are rather painful. So, when we read or watch tragic fiction, we are preparing ourselves to face real-life hardships with more strength and resilience.

### *Learning about Life and Ourselves*

Tragedies can also teach us about different ways of coping with difficult situations, some of which may be more effective than others. Take, for instance, *Bonjour Tristesse*, where we learn of the heart-wrenching consequences of manipulation, leading us to recognize the risks involved in interfering with others' love lives. Tragic stories like these can serve as inspiration, prompting us to find our own solutions to life's challenges. Or consider the iconic dilemma faced by Rick in *Casablanca*, as he contemplates whether to ask Ilsa to board the plane. What would *you* do if the person you love, and who loves you, were already married to someone else? Such scenarios prompt us to confront our own moral values and to consider the complexities of loyalty, sacrifice, and the pursuit of personal happiness amidst challenging circumstances. By delving into these fictional lives, we gain intimate access to the characters' thoughts and emotions. Doing so offers us a perspective that is rarely accessible to us in real life.

Engaging with tragic fiction is often valuable even if the overall experience isn't pleasant. Although doing so may evoke uncomfortable emotions, the value of works of tragic fiction transcends mere entertainment. It's through witnessing the tribulations and triumphs of fictional characters that we gain profound insights into how tragic events impact people's lives and discover strategies for resilience and growth. These are pretty good reasons for watching a tragic movie or reading a saddening novel.

## There's Something about Depiction

David Hume didn't limit his attention to fictional tragedy alone. He also considered non-fictional tragic literature such as great speeches. There is something important that fictional tragic novels or films have in common with their non-fictional counterparts. Something that they don't share with the real-life events that befall us. They are *depictions*. When engaging with depictions, we are not directly confronted with tragic situations; instead our experience is mediated through a writer's, filmmaker's, storyteller's, or journalist's representation of a tragedy. If you perceive your friend getting their heart broken, that is a tragic event you experience directly – it's a confrontation. If your aunt tells you about her neighbour's broken heart, that's a tragic event you experience only mediated through your aunt – it's a depiction. The distinction between direct experience and mediated depiction is crucial in understanding the unique nature of engaging with tragic novels and films. When we encounter real-life tragic events, we are directly confronted with the raw emotions and immediate consequences of those events.

But when we engage with tragic depiction, whether fictional or not, we get to keep an emotional distance between us and the events that unfold. Depiction also typically grants us a level of control that the witnessing of real-life events doesn't. Confrontations often cause harm to ourselves, or to our relationships; they threaten us, our future, or that of our loved ones. And when they do, we experience sadness, hopelessness, or devastation. These are painful emotions that we cannot avoid because life will naturally throw challenging situations at us. While we cannot escape these painful feelings, we have the power to control the pain triggered by depictions. We can simply choose to turn off the TV, close the book, or interrupt our conversational partner when things are getting too much for us.

And there seems to be a common feature to the *depictions* of tragedy discussed in this chapter that makes them particularly apt at creating a satisfying emotional experience. It's the fact that novels, newspaper articles, movies and documentaries all have *narratives*.

Real life tragic events are seldom presented to us in a particularly pleasing form; real life is chaotic and often seemingly incoherent and random. But narrative depictions can be well-crafted. A tragic story, whether it's fictional or based on real events, can be more or less coherent, gripping, informative, aesthetically pleasing and so on. The way the story is told can give us a sense of order and closure, even if there is no discernible order, or any closure, to the tragic event that is depicted. All of these features of, and experiences with, a tragic story contribute to our attraction.

*Sam:* Does this take us back to Hume's suggestion that we derive pleasure from the artistic beauty of well-crafted tragedies; or is this a slightly different point?

*Tatjana:* Oh, I do think that Hume is right that artistic beauty *contributes* to the pleasure we gain from engaging with tragic fiction – at least sometimes for some people. But I don't think our painful feelings are *converted into pleasure* because of the artistic beauty of a work of fiction.

More importantly, I don't think that the crucial difference between real-life tragic events and their depictions lies in artistic properties. Good narratives are coherent. They offer their audience meaningful interpretations of life's events. (Even if the interpretation is that life is incoherent and random.) Good narratives satisfy our craving for certainty and closure, not merely for beauty.

Even a sad ending is an ending – perhaps this is why Netflix's *The Watcher* (2022) left so many viewers, including myself, profoundly unsatisfied. Good novels, newspaper articles, films, or documentaries offer what real life cannot. As Josh Groban sings in the brilliant TV show *Crazy Ex-Girlfriend* (created by Rachel Bloom and Aline Brosh McKenna, 2015–2019), "life doesn't make narrative sense".

Now, it might be tempting to assume that fans of tragedy enjoy immersing themselves in tragic depictions, whether they are in the form of books, films, or real-life accounts. However, this doesn't always seem to be the case. Suppose I told you a fictional story that revolves around you. In my story, you encounter various tragic events. My guess is that you wouldn't enjoy the story very much. And it wouldn't matter whether you're a fan of tragedy, or that the story is fictional rather than non-fictional. Well, I know I wouldn't appreciate it if someone were to construct a tragic story about me and my future, even if it were entirely made up. Even though the tragic events that befall fictional Me would be mediated through someone else's depiction, it would likely create all kinds of unpleasant and, importantly, unwanted feelings in me. The feelings would be unwanted regardless of the fact that the tragic events have not happened. My guess is that I am not alone in feeling uneasy with the idea that someone might turn Me into a tragic figure in an otherwise fictional story. Perhaps it's because we desire to avoid any kind of tragedy that involves *us*. Only when a story *doesn't* involve us (or our dearest) can we afford an emotional level of detachment that appears to make our painful emotions more bearable.

Of course, we'd still rather hear a fictional tragedy that features us as the main character than experience tragic events ourselves. What we aim to avoid when we wish not to feel sad, distressed, and hopeless are the events that trigger these painful feelings. Such events usually harm ourselves, or our relationships; they threaten us, our future, or our loved ones. Our emotions are responses to real threats. Fictional events are not real threats. We are not required to act. But that does not mean that we derive (enough) pleasure, or other kinds of direct benefits, from engaging with fictional tragedy that revolves around ourselves or our loved ones.

## Curiosity

It seems that some people seek out the direct experience of tragic events but only when it happens to others. For example, traffic jams frequently occur after car crashes due to curious onlookers, who choose to take a good look at a gruesome scene. Does the scene arouse uncomfortable, even painful emotions in them? I would say so. Seeing the consequences of a severe car crash will likely cause a great amount of emotional distress for those who empathize with the victims. And yet, something must motivate the onlookers to drive by slowly and stare. We may be disgusted by rubberneckers, but it's hard to deny that we all experience a sense of curiosity when tragedy befalls other people. And to satisfy our curiosity, we sometimes seek out situations that we know will upset us.

And it may well be that curiosity is also the reason we engage with tragic fiction. When a friend recommended Isao Takahata's animated film *Grave of the Fireflies* (1988), which he described as "utterly heart wrenching", I knew I would find it too distressing to watch. Instead, I headed over to Wikipedia. As expected, even the concise plot summary of fewer than 500 words left me feeling sad, hopeless, and in distress. It was evident that I didn't derive any pleasure from this experience, and I wouldn't consider it a profoundly enriching one either. I read the summary because I was curious about what all the fuss was about, and because my curiosity was stronger than my reluctance to experience unpleasant emotions. Moreover, I expected those unpleasant emotions to stay within the boundaries of what I can endure.

Both fiction films and novels, as well as their summaries, present fictional narratives. Yet, the narrative style of a summary is less prone to trigger intensely painful emotions than the narrative style typical of a film or a novel. The same narrative style that fiction movie makers and authors use is also often employed in great documentaries or newspaper articles.

*Sam:* I relate to this particular power of narrative prose over other sorts of prose later on, in Chapter 11.

There, I argue that this power explains one of the ways in which narrative helps us learn about the world. It has a certain vividness that non-narrative prose lacks.

I'm a fan of true crime shows, but I'd abhor any direct encounter with a crime. But why do I watch these shows? I find no pleasure in looking at gruesome pictures, or listening to gross descriptions, or hearing about the lives that have been destroyed. I don't feel a sense of shared humanity or meaning, and the knowledge I gain from watching true crime is barely applicable to my own life. What drives me to watch true crime shows, it seems to me, is sheer curiosity.

Curiosity can be a strong motivator for people. We seem to be wired for curiosity. A strong sense of curiosity has greatly contributed to the survival of our species. Without curiosity, there would have been no discovery of how to make fire, and nor would our species have invented the smallpox vaccination. But curiosity needs to be counterbalanced by prudence. Without prudence, if we didn't exercise caution and careful judgment, the ability to make fire would have have resulted in the destruction of the planet, and we would have engaged in reckless behavior like injecting every substance into each other's veins.

You might choose not to gawk at the site of a car crash because you judge it to be morally wrong. Perhaps you feel curious, but you want to avoid feeling guilty. When we engage with tragic fiction, we don't need to feel guilty about our voyeurism. After all, fictional events and fictional beings are not real events, people, and animals. In real life, we also might choose to act against our curiosity because doing so would potentially bring harm to us or our loved ones. Cheating on your partner might destroy your relationship, so even if you are curious about it, it's prudent to refrain from cheating. But since fictional tragedy is contained, our voyeuristic tendencies can easily outweigh our desire not to be harmed by watching the film or reading the novel. And where we fear harm to ourselves, or our loved ones, we can control our exposure to the tragic fictional events. For instance, we could read a summary of a tragic fiction film instead of watching it, or we could leave the cinema.

## What Now?

Curiosity motivates us to read Jodi Picoult's *My Sister's Keeper* (2004), or watch Darren Aronofsky's *Requiem for a Dream* (2000). But not everyone will consume tragic fiction to satisfy their curiosity. And perhaps no one loves the tragic fiction genre solely out of curiosity. Some people may sometimes be looking for aesthetic pleasure, or to feel good about themselves or humankind. We might be hoping for catharsis on one occasion or seeking to learn more about ourselves and life from a safe distance. On another occasion, our weekend might have been pretty "meh," and we might need some emotional stimulation; we might need to experience the fictional dilemma that *Amour* depicts. Sometimes, people consume tragic fiction *despite* the painful emotions it makes them feel, and other times, people watch or read tragic stories precisely *because* they trigger sadness, despair, or hopelessness.

Perhaps the majority of people are, most of the time, at least partly motivated by a desire for a life rich in experiences. Or by curiosity. Most likely, motivations differ between persons as well as situations. You might choose to watch *Casablanca* because you are heartbroken and need a good cry, while I might engage with the film because I'm celebrating Ingrid Bergman–week. Another time, you might rewatch *Casablanca* not for its cathartic potential but because you want to revel in its aesthetics.

This might seem like a dissatisfying outcome. Weren't we looking for a unified theory that explains why anyone would choose to engage with a tragic fictional work? Well, I don't think such a theory can be given. In the end, I believe, we will have to give up on the idea that a unique feature of tragic fiction can explain audience behaviour. But that's ok. We've still identified and discussed various motivations for engaging with fictional tragic stories; each of which unravel the paradox. While a unified theory might be the icing on the cake, the real reward is gaining a better understanding of our engagement with tragic fiction.

## Works Cited

Feagin, S. L. (1983) The Pleasures of Tragedy. *American Philosophical Quarterly*, 20(1): 95–104.

Hume, D. (1757) *Four Dissertations*. New York: St. Augustine's Press.

Hume, D. (1965) *Of the Standard of Taste, and Other Essays. Edited, with an Introd., by John W. Lenz*. Indianapolis, IN: Bobbs-Merrill. Edited by John W. Lenz.

Smuts, A. (2007) The Paradox of Painful Art. *Journal of Aesthetic Education*, 41(3): 59–77.

## Further Reading

Aristotle (1934) *Poetics*. Oxford: Oxford University Press. *Here you learn more about Aristotle's idea of catharsis.*

Friend, S. (2007) The Pleasures of Documentary Tragedy. *British Journal of Aesthetics*, 47(2): 184–198. *In this article, Stacie Friend discusses the conditions under which documentaries have the potential to produce tragic pleasure.*

Levinson, Jerrold (ed.) (2013) *Suffering Art Gladly: The Paradox of Negative Emotions in Art*. Basingstoke: Palgrave Macmillan. *This book contains several chapters devoted to the paradox of tragedy.*

Chapter 10

# The Puzzle of Imaginative Struggles

*Tatjana*

I've always been intrigued by time-travel. Wouldn't it be exciting if we could travel back to our childhood days, advise our younger selves, or even save the world? One of the reasons I love the film *12 Monkeys* (directed by Terry Gilliam, 1995) is that it highlights the logical complications of time-travel. Towards the end of the movie – spoiler alert! – the protagonist, James Cole, travels back in time. He is shot dead while his much younger self witnesses his death. Being shot on a trip to the past, or meeting oneself during time-travel, raises all sorts of logical challenges – how does time-travel really work, if it works at all? And yet, we don't struggle to imagine that James Cole travels in time. That's a good thing! It means that despite the logical issues *12 Monkeys* raises, we can meaningfully engage with the film. Similarly, in Nnedi Okorafor's 2010 novel *Who Fears Death*, the main character, Onyesonwu, shape-shifts into a dragon-like creature, a transformation that no one achieves in the real world. And yet, we don't struggle to imagine her possessing magical abilities.

As we've seen in Chapter 6, engaging properly with fiction requires us to imagine various propositions that the fictional work prescribes us to imagine. Some of these propositions are simply untrue of the real world. We know that there wasn't a skilful detective named "Sherlock Holmes" in Victorian London. We understand that, unlike in the world of *Game of Thrones*, there never were several noble families that fought over their seat on the Iron Throne. Let's refer to propositions that are true within the world of a fiction but are contrary to reality or known facts as *factually deviant*. Some of the factually deviant propositions we are prescribed to imagine could not even possibly be true.

Now, time-travel, or shape-shifting, isn't *obviously* impossible. Can you travel back in time? Can you transform yourself into another creature? Or is our species membership essential to us and, therefore, unchangeable? These are difficult metaphysical questions that we don't typically ponder when consuming fiction. But even if these scenarios are impossible, we've seen in Chapter 5 that we can imaginatively engage with impossible fictional stories. Tamar Gendler thinks so too and invented a short story, which she calls "The Tower

DOI: 10.4324/9781003126102-11

of Goldbach", introduced by Sam in Chapter 6, to illustrate her view. As a reminder, here is the shortened version:

> Long long ago, when the world was created, every even number was the sum of two primes. Although most people suspected that this was the case, no one was completely certain. So a great convocation was called, and for forty days and forty nights, all the mathematicians of the world labored together in an effort to prove this hypothesis. Their efforts were not in vain: at midnight on the fortieth day, a proof was found. "Hoorah!" they cried, "we have unlocked the secret of nature." But when God heard this display of arrogance, God was angry. From heaven roared a thundering voice: "My children, you have gone too far. You have understood too many of the universe's secrets. From this day forth, no longer shall twelve be sum of two primes." And God's word was made manifest, and twelve was no longer the sum of two primes. The mathematicians were distraught – all their efforts had been in vain ... God ... called upon Solomon to aid ... Carefully, Solomon weighed both sides of the issue ... [W]ith great fanfare, the celebrated judge announced his resolution of the dispute: From that day on, twelve both was and was not the sum of five and seven ...
>
> (Gendler, 2000, pp. 67–68)

Now, we all know what it means to compromise, and Solomon's solution looks like a good one. The mathematicians need to accept that twelve is not the sum of five and seven, but they also get what they wanted, namely that twelve *is* the sum of five and seven. And God compromises too: Twelve *is* the sum of five and seven, which is unfortunate for God, but God also gets what God wants; that twelve is not the sum of five and seven. You might find it a silly story – as I do – but you don't simply give up. We don't seem to struggle to engage with "The Tower of Goldbach" from the beginning to its end, despite the impossibility of its content.

## Struggling Imaginatively

Let's think of fiction as a game. Through their fictional work, authors or filmmakers invite us to make-believe various things. And, if you are prepared to play the game, you will accept the invitation.

If you were attending an author's reading of *Who Fears Death*, it would be inappropriate to tell Okorafor that you can't imagine something so patently false. Making such a statement would indicate that you either don't grasp the distinction between fiction and non-fiction or that you are an uncooperative reader or listener. It seems that creators of fictional works have almost unlimited freedom when it comes to constructing a fictional world. They can make people time-travel or shape-shift, they can make animals solve crimes, and supernatural beings kill humans. Authors and filmmakers can even break the rules of logic to create their fictional world. As a general rule, it is up to the creator to determine what is true in a fiction. And as a cooperative audience, we make-believe whatever is true in the fiction. It's an essential rule of the fiction game that we make-believe what we are asked to imagine. In fact, we can call it *the number one* rule of engagement with fiction. If we fail, or refuse, to imagine what we are prescribed to imagine, we are withdrawing from the fiction game – or at least we're not playing it properly.

Except, sometimes we break the number one rule of the fiction game. In his essay "Of the Standard of Taste", David Hume observes:

> Where speculative errors may be found in the polite writings of any age or country, they detract but little from the value of those compositions. There needs to be but a certain turn of thought or imagination to make us enter into all the opinions which then prevailed and relish the sentiments or conclusions derived from them. But a very violent effort is requisite to change our judgment of manners, and excite sentiments of approbation or blame, love or hatred, different from those to which the mind from long custom has been familiarized ... I cannot, nor is it proper that I should, enter into such [vicious] sentiments.
>
> (Hume, 1987 [1757], p. 219)

Hume seems to suggest that there is an important difference between propositions that we can easily imagine and propositions that we can only imagine with significant effort – if we can imagine them at all. The difference lies in the fact that the propositions we struggle with are not only factually deviant but also *morally* deviant.

Let's engage in a thought experiment where we imagine the existence of a fictional novel titled *Giselda's Dream*. In this hypothetical work of fiction, an omniscient implied narrator portrays the life of a fictional character named Giselda, an ambitious but initially unsuccessful actor. As the story unfolds, Giselda encounters a series of fortunate circumstances that ultimately lead to her being cast in a feature film, earning her an Oscar in the category of Best Supporting Actress. As you delve into the captivating story of fictional character Giselda, experiencing the highs and lows of her life, one particular sentence within the narrative leaves you startled: "In killing her baby, Giselda did the right thing; after all, it was a girl."

If you struggled to imagine that committing female infanticide is ever morally right, you are not alone. Kendall Walton (1994) crafted this particular sentence with a purpose in mind: to illustrate the difficulty we would encounter in accepting and engaging with it. When a fictional work asks us to imagine a proposition that we consider morally deviant, we frequently find ourselves unable or unwilling to comply. If we refuse or fail to accept the fiction's invitation to make-believe, we are essentially stepping out of the realm of the fictional game, or at least disengaging from a portion of the narrative.

You might have noticed that when grappling with the morally problematic proposition you acknowledged the role of the narrator: "Well, that's what the *narrator* claims (but he's wrong)". Gendler (2000, p. 63) calls this the "that's what you think" move. But the story doesn't tell you to imagine that *a narrator thinks* it's morally right to kill newborns based on their gender. Nor are you asked to imagine that Giselda, or the society she lives in, mistakenly believes in female infanticide. Instead, it appears that within the world of *Giselda's Dream*, female infanticide is acceptable, and thus Giselda, her society, and the narrator hold the belief that it is morally permissible.

*Sam:* Is this because the narrator, in this novel, is supposed to be omniscient?

*Tatjana:* Yes, I suppose so. Unless we have reason to believe otherwise, we assume that the narrator (a) knows what is going on in the fictional world and (b) is honest in their descriptions of the world to us.

Thus, to play by the rules of the fiction game, we are expected to make-believe that killing one's newborn because of their gender is indeed totally fine.

Now, our struggle to imagine that killing female babies is morally acceptable is odd. No one is asking you to *believe* that it's morally acceptable or even required to kill female babies. You are merely asked to make-believe this proposition. Moreover, you *are* willing and able to make-believe numerous propositions that you believe to be false. You willingly make-believe that a coke-snorting detective lived on London's Baker Street, that a rich man invented an iron suit to fight villains, or that Lizzy Bennett accepted Mr. Darcy's proposal to marry him. You even agree to imagine that some people travel through time, that Onyesonwu shifts their shape, or that the Axis powers won the Second World War (as Philip K. Dick's *The Man in the High Castle* (1962) asks us to imagine). So, why do we experience difficulties when confronted with morally deviant propositions? This is the puzzle that we will explore and attempt to unravel in this chapter.

**The Puzzle of Imaginative Struggles**

When we engage with fictional works, we make-believe the fictional world presented by the work. However, there are instances when we struggle to imagine that certain propositions, which we know to be false in reality, are true in the fictional world. This raises the question of why there is this deviation from the usual rules of engagement with fiction.

Before we address the puzzle, I should caution you: the puzzle of imaginative struggles has been widely discussed in contemporary philosophy as a puzzle of *imaginative resistance*. When we resist something, such as eating the whole bar of chocolate instead of just eating a piece of it, we voluntarily choose not to do it. It's not as if we couldn't eat the whole bar of chocolate if we wanted to. But as we'll see, not all philosophers agree that we *resist* imagining certain propositions. Some believe we are *unable* to imagine these propositions. This is why I've chosen the more neutral term "struggle" to frame the puzzle.

Moreover, when philosophers started thinking and writing about imaginative resistance, their focus was on solving the puzzle arising for *morally* deviant propositions. Yet, as many theorists have pointed out since, we also find ourselves struggling imaginatively with certain *non-morally* deviant propositions. For example, you likely struggle to make-believe that puppies, those fluffy, affectionate, dorky animals with big eyes, are disgusting. Such examples of struggles with non-morally deviant propositions are worth considering as well. However, for the sake of brevity, I will focus primarily on morally deviant propositions. Here's why I have chosen to concentrate on the moral cases: It seems to me that any struggles we have with deviant propositions are greatest and most common when it comes to morally deviant propositions. You might struggle to imagine that puppies are disgusting, but this is not the kind of proposition we are often (or ever) asked to imagine when engaging with fiction. As we shall see, however, there are plenty of invitations to make-believe morally deviant propositions.

Now, you might not feel that you struggle imaginatively when invited by *Giselda's Dream* to imagine that female infanticide is morally applaudable. So, to get a firmer grip on the phenomenon of imaginative struggles, let's look at two more examples invented by philosophers.

Richard Moran (1994, p. 95) presents a hypothetical variation of Shakespeare's *Macbeth*. In this version, the facts of the murder remain as they are in fact presented in the play, but it is prescribed in this alternate fiction that "[the murder] was unfortunate only for having interfered with Macbeth's sleep that night". You're not just being asked to imagine that Macbeth or the people around him *think* that murdering someone is morally irrelevant. You are being told to imagine that murdering someone *is indeed* morally irrelevant. And that's just a bit, well, hard to imagine. After all, the fictional world of *Macbeth 2.0* is rather different from our own, a world in which committing murder is morally wrong. So what if the world of *Macbeth 2.0* differs from our world? The world of *Doctor Strange in the Multiverse of Madness* is radically different from our world, and yet we don't struggle to make-believe that people can meet their counterparts in other parallel universes. And *that's* what is puzzling; we stumble when invited to imagine a moral falsehood, yet have no issue imagining sorcerers and parallel worlds.

The third example of imaginative struggles is Brian Weatherson's *Death on a Freeway* (2004, p. 1):

> Jack and Jill were arguing again. This was not in itself unusual, but this time they were standing in the fast lane of I-95 having their argument. This was causing traffic to bank up a bit. It wasn't significantly worse than what normally happened around Providence, not that you could have told that from the reactions of passing motorists. They were convinced that Jack and Jill, and not the volume of traffic, were the primary causes of the slowdown. They all forgot how bad traffic normally is along there. When Craig saw that the cause of the bankup had been Jack and Jill, he took his gun out of the glovebox and shot them. People then started driving over their bodies, and while the new speed hump caused some people to slow down a bit, mostly traffic returned to its normal speed. So Craig did the right thing, because Jack and Jill should have taken their argument somewhere else where they wouldn't get in anyone's way.

Did you struggle to fully engage in the make-believe when you read the short story?

*Sam:* I just imagined the story, but I imagined that the narrator was wrong in his moral evaluation of Craig's action. I deny that the narrator is right. Does that mean I was playing the "that's what you think" move?

*Tatjana:* Imagining that the narrator was wrong is your way of trying to make sense of what is going on in *Death on a Freeway*. So, yes, you are performing a "that's what you think" move. But the interesting question is: why did you make that move?

If your reaction was anything like mine, you will have been appalled at Craig's decision to shoot the couple. And when you learned that according to *Death on a Freeway*, Craig's actions were morally right, chances are that this new piece of information hardly changed your feelings towards Craig. Perhaps you attempted to justify Craig's action by pointing out that *in Craig's society*, shooting people for obstructing traffic is deemed morally right. But this move does not resolve the issue. Craig and the society in which he lives might *find* his action morally acceptable, but that does not make killing someone for stopping traffic morally acceptable.

We struggle to imagine that actions we deem immoral are actually moral. *Giselda's Dream* invited us to imagine that female infanticide is morally required. *Macbeth 2.0* prescribed us to imagine that murder is nothing more than an inconvenience for the murderer. And *Death on a Freeway* asked us to make-believe that killing people is morally permissible when they slow down traffic. Why do we struggle to imagine these morally deviant propositions?

Philosophers have proposed two main perspectives to help us understand the puzzle of imaginative struggles. There are the Wontians who say that we just don't *want* to imagine morally deviant propositions – and therefore won't. And there are the Cantians who hold that we struggle imaginatively because we *can't* imagine moral falsehoods.

## I Won't – Wontian Suggestions

In the video game *Grand Theft Auto II*, players complete missions to earn money in order to progress through the game. In the PC version of the game, there is a mission called "Hot Dog Homicide" where you, as the player, control the character Claude Speed. In this mission, you pick up civilians at a bus stop and drive them to a meat plant where they are processed into hot dogs and, now hot dogs, are delivered to a diner. Yuck!

Now, the game employs a 2D, top-down perspective, and without the textual cues, it would be hard to even identify what is happening in the game. So, the game itself is not graphically shocking. It's shocking for its content: the torture, killing, and cannibalism of innocent human animals. And it's you, the player, who enables these horrific actions; actions most of us (including you, I hope) find deeply morally wrong. It seems that the game prescribes you to imagine that those pixels on the screen are real people, who you help turn into real hot dogs against their will. I suspect that you would be appalled if someone enlisted your help for these crimes in real life. But *Grand Theft Auto II* rewards you for your assistance with fictional money. So, it appears that the game is asking you to make-believe that Claude's actions are not morally wrong enough to resist the temptation of a small amount of money and participate in the evil mission.

Unsurprisingly, some players struggle with their mission. Their difficulties don't stem from an inability to complete the mission. These players don't *want* to complete the mission. It seems that they refuse to imagine themselves being okay with such heinous actions. If you firmly believe that such a "hot dog" homicide is wrong, you will likely struggle to imagine that you approve of the atrocities.

Now, this doesn't necessarily mean that you'll avoid the mission entirely. But chances are that you will engage with the story to a lesser degree, perhaps by reassuring yourself that it's merely a game or by distancing yourself from the violence, considering the victims as pixels rather than people. This is your choice. You refuse to fully engage with the morally deviant fiction.

*Sam:* I remember playing that mission. This was before the *Grand Theft Auto* franchise became much more realistic, graphically. It's funny. I felt the tension as it arose in *Giselda's Dream*, in *Macbeth 2.0*, and in *Death on a Freeway*. I either refused to make-believe what I was asked to make-believe, or I played the "That's what you think" move, by pretending that the narrator was unreliable, and wrong.

But I don't remember having any problems whatsoever playing the "Hot Dog" mission. I wonder why! Perhaps I was just thinking of killing pixels rather than people, or perhaps I was thinking that I'm not Claude; that Claude is doing evil things, and there's a certain amount of fun to be had in controlling Claude's actions without identifying yourself with him. Or, perhaps I wasn't thinking too much. I was young!

*Tatjana:* I think these are all very useful ways to avoid any imaginative struggles. But I would question how substantial your engagement with the game was if you used these strategies.

Wontians hold that we are *unwilling* to make-believe morally deviant propositions. According to their view, we refuse to imagine that "Hot Dog" homicide is morally acceptable, or that female infanticide is a moral requirement.

*Giselda's Dream, Macbeth 2.0, Death on a Freeway,* or *Grand Theft Auto II* ask us to engage in make-believe games that we don't want to play. It's one thing to request that the audience imagine that Gisela gives birth to a female baby. It would be unusual for readers to refuse to imagine this proposition. After all, it's nothing more than a description of events unfolding in the world of *Giselda's Dream*. But requesting readers to conceive female infanticide as morally correct is a different matter entirely. This is an *evaluative* proposition. And when it comes to evaluative propositions, authors and filmmakers generally have a harder time persuading us to make-believe something we deem false. But why?

## Bad Intentions

Gendler, a Wontian pioneer, argues that we sometimes disapprove of the author's or filmmaker's *reason* for asking us to make-believe a proposition we think is false. That's when we imaginatively resist. She posits that "whether or not we are inclined to respond with imaginative resistance is going to turn out to depend on *why* we think we are being asked to imagine them" (Gendler, 2000). Let me give you an example.

Suppose you move to Austria, where you soon learn that "Edelweiss" is not the traditional Austrian song that you thought it was after watching the film *The Sound of Music* (directed by Robert Wise, 1965). You might be upset with the filmmakers for seemingly suggesting that "Edelweiss" *is* an Austrian song – not only within the realm of fiction but in the real world as well. So, upon rewatching the film, you feel some resistance to even make-believe that the song is a part of traditional Austrian culture. You perceive that the filmmakers want you to make-believe that "Edelweiss" is an Austrian song, with the expectation that you will export this proposition as a fact into the real world. In your judgment, the creators want you to make-believe *and believe* that the song is Austrian. And it's the latter motivation you don't approve of. Now, the proposition that "Edelweiss" is an Austrian song is not a morally deviant one; it's a factually deviant proposition. That's fine, as it simply means we can experience imaginative resistance towards factually deviant propositions as well. But the example highlights that we sometimes refuse to imagine falsehoods to be facts because we disapprove of the creator's motivations. What we disapprove of is the creator's suggestion that we believe a proposition we firmly believe to be false.

"But it's fiction, aren't we only required to *make-believe* what's true in the fictional world?", you might wonder. And rightly so. To see how we get from make-believing to believing, I need to add a little detour. We typically anticipate that realistic fiction will mirror the real world. Jane Austen's *Emma*, CBS's *The Big Bang Theory*, Leo Tolstoy's *Anna Karenina*, or Alice Walker's *The Color Purple*, all exemplifying (to varying degrees) realistic fiction, describe fictional worlds that are very similar to our world. We usually take it that the same laws of physics and biology, principles of psychology, geographical truths, or societal norms that apply in our real world also apply in the world of realistic fiction. To borrow terminology that Sam introduced in Chapter 6, these fictions fall into broad comparison classes. In *The Big Bang Theory*, when Leonard stares at Penny for longer than is typically considered usual you infer that he is attracted to Penny, since that's what a long stare usually suggests in our world. When Sophia is brutally beaten by the police in *The Color Purple*, you know she is feeling excruciating pain. When the traffic light turns red in a realistic fictional world, you understand that the car must stop. None of these propositions need to be made explicit in fictional works. You infer these fictional truths by applying real facts to the fictional facts of the stories. In other words, you import real-world facts into the fictional worlds.

As I had previously explained in Chapter 5 and Sam has outlined in Chapter 6, we import numerous facts when we engage with fiction. Indeed, without continuously importing real-world knowledge, we would struggle to make sense of a story. By its very nature, a novel or fiction film is a limited portrayal of a fictional world. In fact, any such portrayal is naturally limited. It cannot reveal every detail of its world, including aspects that might be relevant to the story. No one has the time and space for such exhaustive detail. When newspaper articles report on human trafficking, you rely on several implied facts: humans have rights, forced labour violates these rights, pain is generally undesirable, all living beings die, and loneliness crushes spirits. The article does not need to mention these facts, because you know, and the writer knows that you know, how to apply your knowledge about the world to make sense of the new information. You apply the same strategy when it comes to fictional works.

To fully and meaningfully engage with Park Chan-Wook's brilliant *The Handmaiden* (2016), you need to import – among many, many other facts about the real world – that rare books are highly valuable, that uncles are related to their nieces, and that discovering you have been conned feels bad. Gendler suggests that the following import rule applies to fiction: if something is a fact in the actual world, it is also a fact in the fictional world.

Now, the import rule is very permissive, but it is really only a *default* rule. There are various situations in which the rule does not apply, and one of these situations is when we are engaging with *speculative* fiction. Suppose you are watching the Daniels' *Everything Everywhere All at Once* (2022) for the first time. The biggest film enthusiast in your circle can't shut up about how much they love the film. So here you are. You know nothing about the film's content. During the first scenes of the film, you find out that Evelyn Quan Wang's life is falling apart, you meet her husband who wants to divorce her, you learn about their struggling business, and encounter their daughter, who is trying to get her mother to fully accept that she's gay. None of these fictional facts are explicitly said in the film, but you infer them. A lack of customers indicates a struggling business. A refusal to call your daughter's girlfriend her girlfriend indicates a lack of acceptance. So far, you are free to draw extensively from your knowledge of the real world. For instance, you seem to be free to import the actual fact that it is physically (and maybe conceptually?) impossible to jump to a parallel universe, until … Evelyn jumps to a different universe.

By the time Evelyn prevents a black-hole-like "everything-bagel" from destroying the multiverse, you're fairly certain that this is speculative rather than realistic fiction. What you are asked to imagine is a world rather different from the actual one where no one travels between universes, and where climate change is a much bigger threat to planet earth than human-created black holes.

When a fictional work starts talking about "verse-jumping", magic, ghosts, superheroines, Martians, elves, or proposes that Elvis is alive and kicking, there's your signal to refrain from importing actual facts into the fictional world willy-nilly. You will enjoy *12 Monkeys* most if you don't question time-travel based on your knowledge of physics. And if you enjoy supernatural horror, you better not think too hard about scientific explanations for phenomena such as ghosts killing through videotapes or young boys seeing dead people.

We usually import our laws and principles of physics, psychology, and other empirical disciplines when engaging with fiction, but there is a set of non-empirical facts we also standardly import: moral facts. So, when we learn about Celie's abuse by her father, we don't hesitate for a second to see what the novel prescribes us to make-believe about the morality of the abuse. We are immediately morally disgusted. We import the real-world fact that abuse is morally wrong into the world of *The Color Purple*. So, when Weatherson's realistic short story, *Death on a Freeway,* asks you to make-believe that Craig rightly killed the couple, that make-believe clashes with your imported truth that killing people to unblock traffic is morally wrong. No wonder you were puzzled!

To resolve the clash, you can either "unimport" the moral truth, or you can refuse to make-believe that Craig was right to kill Jake and Jill. Keep in mind, we *can* make-believe contradictions when stories prescribe us to. "The Tower of Goldbach" is one such example. But nothing in *Death on a Freeway* indicates that we should make-believe a contradiction.

However, when it comes to moral facts, it seems that we choose to import them into fictional worlds and refuse to imagine clashing propositions. That's not the case for all facts. While we standardly import historical facts into fictional worlds, we become more selective in our import when we engage with alternative history fiction. I suppose you don't hesitate to imagine that the Axis Powers won the Second World War when watching Amazon's *The Man in the High Castle* (2015–2019). But why is it that you do not feel the need to decline the series's invitation to imagine alternative historical truths? Why do we decide differently when fictional works invite us to imagine morally deviant truths?

To see why, it's important to recognize that we don't only import real facts into fictional worlds, but we also *export* facts from fictional worlds back into our real world. As Sam will discuss in much more detail in Chapter 11, by exporting facts, we *learn* from fictional works. When we export facts from fiction, we incorporate new beliefs into our belief system. *The Handmaiden* taught me, among other things, about the complicated relationship between South Korea and its historical colonial power, Japan, as well as the fact that even professional con people can be conned. James Mangold's *Girl, Interrupted* (1999) showed you that you cannot tell if a person suffers from a mental illness by whether they appear "crazy", or that you can pretend that you have taken your meds by hiding them under your tongue. *Boys Don't Cry* (directed by Kimberly Pierce, 1999) educated viewers that a trans man is not the same as a butch lesbian. Engaging with a fictional work requires us to make-believe what is true in the fictional world. And by *make-believing* a fictional world, we can come to *believe* various facts about our real world.

*Sam:* Though I agree that fictions invite us to export claims about the real world from the world of the narrative, I'm not sure that I've understood your case for that claim. Why does the requirement that we make-believe lead us to believe?

*Tatjana:* One might, for example, come to the belief that "normal" people can suffer from mental illnesses, through one's make-believe that Susanna seems like a normal woman who turns out to suffer from serious mental issues. Simply by modelling a hypothesis, through make-belief you may find the idea becoming more plausible, leading you to believe it.

Gendler suggests that the rule for exporting facts is analogous to the import rule. Generally, if something is a non-specific fact in a fictional world it is also a fact in the actual world. A fact is specific, and therefore not licensed for export, if it concerns merely fictional creatures and events, such as the fictional fact that Lady Hideko is infatuated with her handmaiden Sook-Hee. We should not export *that* much. While the export rule is wildly permissive, it too is only a *default* rule. We don't export from *12 Monkeys* that *real* people travel through time, or from Shaun David Hutchinson's novel *We Are Ants* (2016) that aliens abduct citizens. And we understand that the creators of these fictional works don't intend for us to export these propositions. In most cases that involve factually deviant propositions, it would simply be ludicrous to ascribe export intentions to the author or filmmaker. After all, we generally agree that people can't travel in time or that aliens abduct earthlings.

Not so when it comes to morally deviant propositions. It's safe to assume that for any proposition that you consider to be a moral truth, there is someone out there who considers it a falsehood. Unlike the laws of physics or biology, moral principles are contested and frequently violated. So, when a fictional work prescribes us to make-believe a morally deviant proposition, it's quite possible that the creator intends us to add that proposition to our belief system. And one thing you definitely wouldn't want when engaging with fiction is to be manipulated into believing concepts that you consider, with good reason, to be malevolent. Indeed, even the slightest attempt at being manipulated this way can provoke moral disgust in us. There is nothing subtle about *Death on the Freeway*'s attempt to persuade disbelievers that killing people to unblock traffic is a good thing. In comparison, I think that Alfred Hitchcock's *Marnie* also does a pretty good job at subtly delivering the message that it's not sexual assault when your smart, handsome, and devoted husband forces you to have sex with him. He probably knows best what's good for you, seems to be the message. But I will return to *Marnie* shortly.

A Wontian like Gendler, then, contends that you refuse to fully engage with a fictional work if you suspect that the creator of the work intends for you to export certain moral principles – principles you regard as false – into your belief system. Gendler (2000, p. 77) notes that "cases that evoke genuine imaginative resistance will be cases where the reader feels that she is being asked to export a way of looking at the actual world which she does not wish to add to her conceptual repertoire". By rejecting the work's invitation to make-believe such morally deviant propositions, you show your disapproval for the creator's perceived intentions.

Now, here's a worry. If Gendler is right, then it's our disproval of the creator's intention to export a falsehood that makes us resist imagining it in the first place. But if that's true, then we should feel resistance, regardless of the *kind* of falsehood we are encouraged to export. We should be equally unwilling to make-believe and export the physical falsehood that hydrogen cyanide can melt jaws. But perhaps that is exactly what happens to some chemical experts who watch Sam Mendes's *Skyfall* (2012). They might be willing to make-believe that hydrogen cyanide can melt body parts as long as they don't sense that the filmmakers intend for them to *believe* that proposition as well.

If we need an explanation of why we feel a stronger resistance towards moral falsehoods that creators ask us to export, here's one: exporting moral falsehoods is potentially more harmful to us or others than exporting non-moral falsehoods. This would be a reason for feeling a stronger resistance towards *Macbeth 2.0* or *Grand Theft Auto*'s hot dog homicide mission than towards *Skyfall*. After all, believing that murdering people is morally acceptable is more dangerous than believing that hydrogen cyanide can melt body parts. It looks like Gendler's Wontian can expand its explanation of why we resist imagining morally deviant propositions to all sorts of propositions that we wouldn't want to export from fiction. Moreover, there's a good reason for highlighting our resistance to moral falsehoods, since exporting such falsehoods can have dire consequences.

Except, I have doubts that the origin of our imaginative struggles to morally deviant propositions can always be traced back to the intentions of the author or filmmaker. And here is why. What we are asked to make-believe by a fiction depends on the intentions of the creator. The creator intends that various propositions be true in the fictional world of their work, and we play along by make-believing these propositions. Gendler argues that we refuse to cooperate with the author, and imagine morally deviant claims, when we feel that we are being encouraged to believe these claims about the real world. And one frequent way of encouraging export is by creating a realistic work of fiction. But sometimes, we resist even when we know that the author isn't asking us to export the deviant proposition.

Recall Weatherson's short story *Death on a Freeway*. The realistic story prescribes us to imagine that Craig's act of shooting the traffic-blocking couple is justified. If your reactions to the short story were similar to mine, then the proposition that Craig did the right thing somewhat startled you. Could it be that you felt compelled to export the proposition? Weatherson, through his story, certainly invites you to make-believe that Craig acted morally. But even though he wrote a realistic story, Weatherson certainly does not encourage you to believe that shooting people, so as not to be late to work, is morally acceptable. We know that this doesn't reflect Weatherson's personal views. So, in the case of *Death on a Freeway*, although we understand that the author does not prompt us to apply the morally deviant proposition beyond the confines of the story, we still grapple with imaginative struggles. But this seems to contradict Gendler's predictions.

Now, there is plenty of room for defending Gendler's Wontian account against my objections. If you have Wontian inclinations, the best idea might be to argue that *Death on a Freeway does* ask you to export what you don't want to export, despite Weatherson having no such intentions.

*Sam:* That's certainly what I was thinking, when reading your objection.

Brian Weatherson seems like a perfectly nice guy. He clearly doesn't believe, and doesn't want you to believe, that it's morally acceptable to kill people so as to alleviate traffic. But, it still feels as if *Death on a Freeway* (i.e. the fiction that Weatherson spun for the sake of a philosophical argument) *does* invite us to export that horrible moral falsehood. It's not Weatherson who issues this invitation so much as the fiction itself. In fact, that's the reason why Weatherson finds this fiction interesting, and worthy of our philosophical attention.

*Tatjana:* Even outside of a philosophical setting, an author can intend to play with their audience by writing a fictional work that *seems* to invite us to export an immoral proposition – a proposition the actual author strongly opposes – as truth. One way to explain this phenomenon, I think, is to distinguish between the actual author and the implied author. The actual author and the implied author are the creators of the story, but they do not need to share all qualities, personality traits, or convictions. So we might say, while Weatherson, who's the actual author, does not invite us to import immoral beliefs, the implied author does.

But before you put all of your eggs in the Wontian basket, give the Cantian a chance to argue that resistance is not the problem: we *cannot* imagine that Craig rightfully killed the traffic blockers.

## We Can't – Cantian Explanations

*Content Advisory: Please be aware that this section contains discussions and references to sexual assault. Some readers may find this content distressing. Reader discretion is advised.*

In Alfred Hitchcock's *Marnie* (1964), thief Marnie is blackmailed by handsome and wealthy business owner Mark into marrying him, with the promise of not reporting her to the police. As the film develops, he saves Marnie from drowning, reimburses Marnie's theft victims to encourage them to drop their charges against Marnie, and helps her figure out why she hates physical intimacy, thunderstorms, and the colour red.

On their wedding night, Mark insinuates that he wants to sleep with Marnie. When she screams "No!", he pulls off her robe to undress her. Seemingly conflicted, Mark apologizes to her, gently hangs her robe back over her shoulders and places a kiss on her lips which she clearly does not return. We see Marnie slowly being pushed onto the bed, her eyes staring emptily into space. We are encouraged to imagine that Mark has sex with Marnie without her consent. Now, I think that you and I agree that the scene suggests that a groom rapes his bride. But in 1964, forced marital sexual relations were not considered rape – neither by law nor by society at large.

In an interview, Hitchcock revealed that he wasn't particularly impressed with Sean Connery as *Marnie*'s lead character Mark:

> You know, if you want to reduce *Marnie* to its lowest common denominator, it is the story of the prince and the beggar girl. In a story of this kind you need a real gentleman, a more elegant man than what we had.

What a "gentleman" Mark is! Marnie did not want to be saved by Mark. She also did not want to become physically intimate with him or anyone for that matter, but Mark rapes Marnie during their wedding night. Mark is portrayed as a hero in the story, a "prince", as Hitchcock put it. The narrative is that he is committed to Marnie and determined to help her, even though she is clearly disturbed. Mark forces Marnie into sexual relations with him, and pries into her past without her consent. And, apparently, we're supposed to see these actions as justified by love and care. And because he's such a charming guy with those irresistible puppy dog eyes, it's not really that big of a deal, right? At least, that's what the story seems to want us to make-believe.

By the way, we may now recognize the invitation to imagine that Mark's actions are acceptable as morally deviant. But until recently most audiences would accept the same kind of moral indifference when the victim is male. In the romantic comedy *40 Days and 40 Nights* (directed by Michael Lehmann, 2002), the main character Matt's ex, Nicole, has sex with Matt while he is asleep. Matt did not consent to sexual intercourse with his ex, and he rejected Nicole's previous advances. So, we should conclude that Matt has been raped by Nicole. Yet, we are led to make-believe that Matt's being the victim of non-consensual sex borders on cheating. And it is common to hear or read jokes about male rape in fiction. Etan Cohen's comedy *Get Hard* (2015) is entirely built on the premise that Will Ferrell's character does not want to get raped in prison. Rape is rape. And any fiction that invites you to believe otherwise, or that downplays its moral severity, is morally deviant.

Now, I don't know about you, but it's a Herculean task for me to even begin to imagine that engaging someone in sexual acts without their consent could be morally acceptable. I just don't know what to do with such propositions! It seems that I simply *cannot* make-believe them. And Cantians agree. They argue that audiences are *unable* to imagine propositions they consider to be morally deviant.

Many philosophers uphold the idea that morally true propositions, also known as moral facts, are universally and consistently true. They could not possibly be false. They are necessarily true. Morally false propositions, on the other hand, are impossible. They could never and nowhere be true – neither in the fifteenth century nor 500 years from now, neither in Luxembourg nor in a fictional world. Morally false propositions cannot be true at *any* time or in *any* world. They are necessarily false. That's a very plausible view. What people *think* is moral or immoral can vary significantly across different times and places. But there is a clear distinction between what people think is moral and what is indeed moral.

Some communities believe that there is nothing wrong with female circumcision. But it *is* morally wrong. Slavery was thought to be morally unproblematic in many parts of the planet throughout history. And yet, slavery *is* morally reprehensible. So, people in the world of *Death on a Freeway* can believe all they want that it's morally permissible to kill someone for blocking traffic. Craig's murder is still immoral, even in the fictional world.

*Sam:* Right. If it's immoral in any world, then it's immoral in every world. So long as we're thinking about possible worlds. But, I suppose, if we introduce *impossible worlds* into the discussion, things become less clear, no?

*Tatjana:* That's a good point! I suppose a novel with impossible storylines, such as Robbe-Grillet's *La Maison de Rendez-vous*, that I mention in Chapter 4, might also include impossible moral truths. If the human companion of the inanimate and animate dog in Robbe-Grillet's novel shot (and did not shoot?) a couple for blocking traffic, and the narrator judged him to have done the right thing, then we might just treat this moral evaluative statement as another impossibility, in a sea of impossibilities described in a nouveau roman.

*Sam:* Right. And I guess that's why Gendler, as a Wontian, brings impossible storylines into her discussion of *imaginative resistance*. She resists the Cantian, because our ability to follow impossible story lines reveals to us that we *can* imagine impossible things. But I guess, you're saying that when there are no other impossibilities in a story, other than moral ones – such that the moral impossibility of the story isn't just one detail in a whole "sea of impossibilities" – it's as if we're being asked to imagine that the morally impossible is actually *possible*, and that's perhaps what the Cantian is saying: we simply *cannot* imagine such a thing.

*Tatjana:* Or, you might think, as I will discuss in a few paragraphs' time, "There must be something that distinguishes impossible moral propositions from logically impossible propositions that accounts for imaginative struggles." Perhaps we can imagine the impossible, but not the immoral.

So far, so good. But we imagine various falsehoods when engaging with fictional works. Fiction pretty standardly *is* imagining things to be a way that they aren't in reality. How do we get from the claim that moral facts are necessarily true, and moral falsehoods are necessarily false, to the conclusion that we cannot imagine morally deviant propositions? Here's a rather bad argument for it: We can imagine things that could happen but don't. We can imagine that cats talk, or that the axis won the war. But we cannot imagine impossibilities. Try imagining an all-black dress that's red all over – you'll fail. Or try to visualize a bright summer's day and a dark winter's night in the same place and the same time – you can't. So, if we struggle to imagine that killing people for obstructing traffic is morally permissible, it's because this proposition is impossible.

However, impossibility (alone) does not seem to be the source of our troubles. You might struggle to picture a round square, but what about imagining that a proposition about a round square is true? It strikes me as less clear that we cannot imagine this proposition, even though it is conceptually impossible. As Gendler demonstrates, we're capable of imagining impossible propositions when they're skillfully woven into a narrative. Recall Gendler's "The Tower of Goldbach". God made it such that twelve is and simultaneously is not the sum of five and seven. But that's a logical contradiction! Nothing can have a property (e.g., being the sum of five and seven), and at the same time not have that property. In other words, it's impossible that twelve is and isn't the sum of five and seven. Are we unable to *make-believe* that twelve is and isn't the sum of five and seven? Gendler doesn't think so and many others agree. Our make-believe around the number twelve might not be very detailed – we don't imagine exactly how this logical contradiction is possible – but we can still imagine it to be true and follow the story.

*Sam:* Gendler even talks about how we have to kind of trick ourselves into pretending that these impossibilities are true since we cannot picture them vividly, in the way that we can vividly picture fictions that are *possible.*

She discusses strategies that we have for shielding the impossibility from view. For example, you said that we can imagine that a proposition is true, without actually painting a picture of what that truth would look like. So, without painting a picture, in our minds, of a square circle, we just imagine that the words "there is a square circle" say something true!

*Tatjana:* I have argued in Chapter 5 that I don't think that we need to do more than propositionally imagine when engaging with written fiction (see Chapter 5). My main reason for thinking this is the intriguing variation in imagining called aphantasia. But I also have my doubts that readers really engage in as much visual imagining when they read novels as we seem to assume. At least I would argue, most of the time, for most people, the visual imaginings are rather vague. So, an impossible proposition in a fictional world shouldn't trip up the reader too much.

If we experience any struggle to make-believe logically impossible propositions, these struggles are light. It doesn't compare to the difficulties we experience when trying to make-believe impossible moral propositions. What should we conclude? There must be something distinguishing impossible moral propositions from logically impossible propositions, which accounts for imaginative struggles.

## The Devil's in the Detail

Suppose that your father calls you in a state of panic. Your old elementary school teacher, Mrs. Wassum, did something horribly immoral. But you can't really hear what she did over your dad's sobbing and before you can make any sense of his word scraps, his mobile phone dies. Now you panic too. Your former teacher could have done anything, really. She was never kind to you as a young student. Unless you know what exactly it is she did that warrants your dad's moral judgement, you are none the wiser. Moral facts, such as that your teacher committed an immoral act, *depend* on various other facts that describe the situation; facts that describe who did what, when, how, and why. Let us follow Weatherson in calling the kind of facts that moral facts depend upon, *lower-level facts*. That they are lower does not mean that they are less valuable. It just means that they ground the moral facts; the higher-level facts depend on them. Weatherson (2004, p. 20) observes that "we can imagine the [moral claim] only some way or another, just as we imagine a chair only as some chair or other".

Try to imagine a chair without visualising a specific type or model – you can't! Maybe you imagine an armchair, a desk chair, a cantilever chair, an egg chair, a metal chair. But you cannot visualise a chair without it having a distinct shape or form. In the same way, you cannot imagine a moral action without imagining it as some particular kind of action. An act is morally right or wrong *because* it is a killing of an innocent bystander, or *because* the now-dead person drew a gun, or *because* the agent was bored, empathetic, won the lottery the day before, or lost their job a week ago.

Now suppose you learn that a couple died on a freeway near your home. Local news outlets report their findings about the situation. The couple, the outlet reports, was arguing in the middle of the freeway. Cars had to go around them, which, naturally, caused traffic to slow down quite a bit. So, one driver shot the couple dead, you learn. Then the outlet shows a video of people driving over the dead bodies. Surely, you would be shocked! You'd think that obstructing traffic is not an offence that warrants getting killed. Killing someone because you're in a hurry is morally wrong, no matter what the murderous driver or any of the other benefitting drivers might think. If a later news segment reported that the couple had guns and had been randomly shooting at passing cars, you'd probably reconsider your moral evaluation of the situation. Therefore, given these circumstances, the driver did the *right* thing. Here, too, your moral evaluation of the driver's action depends on the lower-level facts about the situation. In fact, you don't think that this is a matter of opinion. What the driver did was *objectively* morally wrong.

The lower-level facts of the situation described above are identical to the lower-level facts of the fictional situation in *Death on a Freeway*: a couple argues while standing on the freeway and blocking traffic when a driver decides to solve the problem by shooting them dead. Since the morality of an action depends on the lower-level features of the situation, and the lower-level facts of both situations are analogous, fictional Craig's actions are also morally wrong. It doesn't matter that it all happens in a fictional world or that you're told he did the right thing. Killing someone merely for slowing down traffic is morally wrong, regardless of where it happens or what you are asked to make-believe.

Similarly, your moral judgement of the situation follows *once* you have evaluated what has happened. You can make-believe that someone kills their newborn for no other reason than the baby's sex. You can also just make-believe that you are evaluating the morality of this action. But what does this evaluative process look like by which you arrive at the conclusion that it is morally right to commit female infanticide? It seems to me that to imagine that female infanticide is morally required, you also need to imagine what makes such actions moral. We need to be convinced by the "why" – why is it morally required to commit female infanticide? Without a convincing "why", it's hard to make-believe that we are so convinced. It's like being presented with a flawed argument – for example, 'politicians are elected, therefore they are beloved by their voters' – and then being asked to imagine that this argument is a good one, even though the details of the argument remain the same. How do we imagine *that*? What does this even mean? The request seems to make no sense. I suspect the better you succeed at make-believing that you have a "why" (even if you cannot imagine what it looks like), the less resistance to imagine a morally deviant proposition you experience.

Was it morally wrong that Jamie brought peanut brittle to your birthday party? Well, it's impossible to answer this question without knowing more about the circumstances. Perhaps they bought it using money taken without their sibling's permission. Maybe you, the birthday person, are highly allergic to peanuts. Or maybe Jamie just used their hard-earned money to buy the peanut brittle, which is a favorite among everyone at the party. Any of these are essential to the morality or immorality of Jamie's action. So, when you learn that according to *Death on a Freeway*, Craig did the right thing, your mind boggles. Discussing his *Death on a Freeway*, Weatherson (2004, p. 20) suggests that

> fictions understood as invitations to imagine have a "That's all" clause ... So not only are we instructed to imagine something that seems incompatible with Craig's action's being morally acceptable; we are also instructed (tacitly) *not* to imagine anything that would make it the case that his action is morally acceptable. But we can't simply imagine moral goodness

in the abstract; to imagine it we have to imagine a particular kind of goodness.

Given the lower-level facts you are aware of about the situation, you conclude that Craig acted immorally. But, somehow, the story wants you to conclude from this very cluster of information that Craig's actions are morally permissible.

To resolve this dilemma, you might have reached for interpretations of the story that would make a moral difference. Perhaps there is something the story doesn't tell us. Maybe the couple were really mass murderers on a spree, or maybe Craig resurrected them soon after he killed them. Now, the fictional situation differs significantly from the real situation, and it might lead you to a different moral conclusion. Finally, you think to yourself, with your new interpretation in hand, there is no more tension between my moral conclusion and the morally deviant proposition that the story wants us to make-believe. But these interpretations of *Death on a Freeway* are clearly not permitted. We have no reason to assume that we are reading a supernatural story or that the story withholds information that would be relevant to our moral evaluation of the situation. Doing so would be to ignore the "that's all" clause. Rather, we have to assume that the story gave us all of the relevant information required to make it true that Craig did the right thing. The lack of any further information leaves us no option but to conclude that despite the story telling us otherwise, Craig's action was immoral. And so, we simply cannot adhere to the fictions' prescriptions to imagine that acts such as killing people for blocking traffic, engaging in female infanticide, or murdering someone are morally correct or insignificant. We cannot make-believe that these are true propositions.

We fail to imagine moral falsehoods, such as that female infanticide is morally required. But we don't struggle to imagine logical falsehoods, for example that twelve is and simultaneously is not the sum of five and seven. Can you now see what explains the difference between the two imaginative situations? Whether an action is morally right or wrong depends on various lower-level facts about a situation. But when we look at logical truths, we don't find the same kind of one-sided dependency on lower-level facts. It's a logical fact that it's false that twelve simultaneously is and isn't the sum of five and seven, and that fact does not depend on who did what, when, how, and why, or what the current state of the universe looks like. To imagine a logically deviant proposition, we don't need much more than just the invitation to make-believe that the logically false proposition is true.

Not so when the proposition is morally deviant. Moral facts depend on all kinds of lower-level facts, such as the 'what', 'when', 'how', and 'whys'. A prescription to make-believe a moral falsehood is not enough to engage you. You need to know the lower-level details. And when those details don't support the moral falsehood that you are invited to imagine, you cannot make-believe the morally deviant proposition. What you experience is imaginative failure (but it's not your fault).

## A Bit of Both Worlds

You probably guessed it: my sympathies lie with the Cantian.

I just don't know how to reconcile the proposition that it wasn't so bad for Mark to force Marnie to have sex with him, or the claim that there's nothing morally wrong with Macbeth's murdering the king. At least, I don't know what to do with such propositions short of wrongfully blaming it all on the implied narrator. I simply cannot comprehend the claim that it was right for Giselda to kill her female baby.

Now, does this mean that when I watch *Marnie,* I don't feel anything akin to what Gendler describes on her Wontian account? No, it doesn't. I *do* feel moral disgust towards Hitchcock when watching his film. I disapprove of his encouragement to export the proposition that forced sex is not rape if you're married. I do resist being manipulated into believing what I consider a moral falsehood. But I don't think that explains my *imaginative* struggles.

I would be willing to bet all of my humble savings that it is not, and could never be, morally permissive to force someone into sex. And given that I am convinced that forcing people into non-consensual sex is morally reprehensible, and based on what I've learned about Mark and Marnie's relationship, I don't know *how* to make-believe the propositions that Mark's forcing Marnie to have sex with him is acceptable. For what it is worth, even if I did know how to, I would not *want* to imagine that such a morally deviant proposition is true.

*Sam:* I think I can sometimes allow that people living in less enlightened times were not altogether evil for doing or taking part in those evils that were, at that time, thought to be morally permissible.

But, I still agree with you. I can't imagine that the evil things that they did were okay, or anything other than evil. The perpetrators of those evils may have been less blameworthy, to the extent that they were blamelessly ignorant of the moral facts, than modern-day perpetrators of the same crimes; but the evils themselves were just as evil.

## Works Cited

Gendler, T. S. (2000) The Puzzle of Imaginative Resistance. *Journal of Philosophy*, 97(2): 55–81.

Hume, D. (1987 [1757]) Of the Standard of Taste. In D. Hume, *Essays Moral, Political, and Literary*. Carmel, IN: Liberty Fund, pp. 226–249.

Moran, R. (1994) The Expression of Feeling in Imagination. *Philosophical Review*, 103(1): 75–106: 95.

Weatherson, B. (2004) Morality, Fiction, and Possibility. *Philosophers' Imprint*, 4: 1–27.

Walton, K. (1994) Morals in Fiction and Fictional Morality. *Aristotelian Society Supplementary Volume*, 68(1): 27–66.

## Further Reading

Clavel-Vazquez, A. (2018) Sugar and Spice, and Everything Nice: What Rough Heroines Tell Us about Imaginative Resistance. *Journal of Aesthetics and Art Criticism*, 76(2): 201–212. *This article explores unequal responses to male and female characters defying morality, attributing resistance to gender norms' violation.*

Gendler, T. S. (2006) Imaginative Resistance Revisited. In Shaun Nichols (ed.), *The Architecture of the Imagination*. Oxford University Press, pp. 149–173. *Gendler's seminal article from 2000 (listed under "Works Cited" above) generated extensive discussion. In "Imaginative Resistance Revisited" she refines her view in light of this discussion.*

Liao, S. (2016) Imaginative Resistance, Narrative Engagement, Genre. *Res Philosophica*, 93(2): 461–482.

Priest, G. (1997) Sylvan's Box: A Short Story and Ten Morals. *Notre Dame Journal of Formal Logic*, 38(4): 573–582. *If "The Tower of Goldbach" has given you a taste for impossible stories by philosophers, you might be interested in this one.*

Stock, K. (2005) Resisting Imaginative Resistance. *Philosophical Quarterly*, 55(221): 607–624.

Walton, K. (2006) On the (So-Called) Puzzle of Imaginative Resistance. In Shaun Nichols (ed.), *The Architecture of the Imagination*. Oxford University Press, pp. 137–148. *Is there a puzzle of imaginative resistance? Walton questions the phenomenon in this essay.*

Chapter 11

# What Can We Learn from Fiction?

*Sam*

The question of this chapter doesn't sound like a deep philosophical puzzle. It seems immediately obvious that we *can* learn all sorts of things from our engagement with fiction, and it doesn't seem like much of a challenge, for anyone who has engaged with any fiction, to list all sorts of things that we *have* learnt from it. And of course, we're not talking about the obvious fact that, in reading a story, you'll learn what happens in the story; or that you'll learn something about how the author writes. We're talking about what you can learn about *the world beyond the story*. Even so, the question doesn't seem to be all that puzzling.

More often than not, in philosophy, the questions are more interesting than most of the candidate answers. In fact, that's one of the most striking features of philosophy as a discipline. It's a discipline that seems to generate more compelling questions than it does compelling answers.

*Tatjana:* Oh, I don't think I fully agree, Sam. There always seems to be at least one answer to every philosophical question that is surprising and absolutely fascinating. Although these captivating theories also often come at the cost of not being the most persuasive answers.

*Sam:* Yeah, you're probably right. I guess a lot hangs here on what I mean by "compelling" and what you mean by "fascinating!"

Sometimes, philosophy strikes me as this exotic world of powerful questions that probe into extremely deep waters, but which – unlike questions that face natural scientists, for example – seem to have very little prospect of giving rise to convincing or persuasive answers.

When that's how philosophy strikes me, then I guess I'd say, if you're looking for convincing and persuasive answers to questions, then maybe choose another discipline. But, if you're looking for questions that will keep you up at night, wondering about the countless possibilities that they throw up, then philosophy is for you.

DOI: 10.4324/9781003126102-12

In other moods, I might feel differently and say that "no, philosophy is as much about finding, and perhaps even trying to defend, surprising and fascinating possible answers to questions as it is about finding the interesting questions to begin with".

This chapter's question will – I hope – prove to be something of an exception to that rule. Here we have a question that isn't all that puzzling, but the more we investigate the answers that philosophers have proposed, the more we realize – I hope – what an important and probing question it was all along.

Along the way, we'll even discover philosophers (whose arguments I'll try to resist) who deny that we can come to any new or significant knowledge through engaging with fiction. Philosophy can lead people to think some pretty wacky things!

## Fiction as a "Clearinghouse"

To address the question of this chapter, I first want to borrow an important distinction from Tamar Gendler (2000), for thinking about narrative. In fact, I think we can extend her distinction to cope with all sorts of fiction – including non-narrative forms. So, instead of narratives, I'll just talk about fictions. The distinction is this: a fiction can function either as a "clearinghouse" for knowledge, or it can function as a "factory" for knowledge. And, as we'll see, any given fiction can play both roles.

What does it mean for a fiction to be a clearinghouse for knowledge? In Chapter 6, I mentioned that, when we read a fiction, we're not merely invited to pretend that a certain set of propositions are true – we're also invited to construct what I called a "comparison class" (following Hazlett & Mag Uidhir, 2011).

*Tatjana:* Do you obtain the comparison class by applying what I (and some others) call the reality principle?

*Sam:* Yes. Although the application of the reality principle is sensitive to the genre of the fiction. Sometimes the genre invites us to import more from the real world, thereby applying the reality principle more extensively. Other genres invite us to import less from the real world, thereby applying the reality principle more modestly.

The comparison class of a fiction is that set of propositions which are supposed to be true both in the fiction, and in the real world. It's a subtle matter just how we go about constructing such a class. We do it in conversation with the text, but also in conversation with all sorts of conventions.

The conventions that help us to build a comparison class are genre relative. In a realistic genre, the comparison class is supposed to be quite wide, as we smuggle lots of the actual world into the fiction, and as the author herself will have made an effort to incorporate actual historical facts into her fictional world. In a more fantastical genre, we're entitled to smuggle much less, and the author will be less interested in incorporating accurate representations of real-world states of affairs into her fiction.

It's with reference to this comparison class that we can talk about the notions of *import* and *export* (see Chapters 6 and 10). The propositions we import into a fiction are those propositions that we feel entitled to bring from our background knowledge of the real world into the comparison class. The propositions that we export from a fiction are those propositions that the author seems to have placed, for our benefit, into the comparison class, even though we didn't know them to be true of the real world, until we read the fiction. It's with reference to the notion of *export* that we can understand how fiction can function as a clearinghouse for knowledge.

As I said, back there in Chapter 6, if you're reading a well-researched historical novel, and it says that there was a war in North America in 1812, then – given the relevant conventions for this genre – you'll know that that claim should be placed into the comparison class. And, because it's there in the comparison class, you can trust (if you trust that the author did her research) that there really was a war, in the real world, in North America, in 1812. This is a fact about the fiction that, because you know that the author has, given the conventions of the genre, placed it into the comparison class, and given that you trust her research, you are licenced to export into your set of beliefs about the actual world.

It is because fictions can licence this sort of export that they can serve as a clearinghouse for knowledge. Gendler tells us that, when fiction functions as a clearinghouse:

> I export things from the story that you the storyteller have intentionally and consciously imported, adding them to my stock in the way that I add knowledge gained by testimony. In this way, for instance, I might learn how women wore their hair in nineteenth-century France, or when the serfs were emancipated, or how far away a particular village is from London.
>
> (Gendler, 2000, p. 76)

In explicating how fiction plays this role, Gendler has explained something that would otherwise be something of a mystery. How is it that we're able to treat historical fictions, for example, as reliable testimony? How is it that you can say, without embarrassment, that you learnt what year the Russian serfs were emancipated, by reading a *novel* about it, even though you know that the novel is a work of fiction, and therefore may contain all sorts of *falsehoods*? It is because we appreciate the function of a comparison class.

And thus, in answer to the question of our chapter, the first category of fact that we can learn from fictions are the facts that we export when a fiction functions as a clearinghouse. The facts in question are not all that exotic – we're talking about all sorts of sundry facts about real-world states of affairs – how women wore their hair in nineteenth-century France, or how far away a particular village is from London. But, even if this category of fact is far from exotic, the ways in which we arrive at them, through a fiction, and the construction of a comparison class, are subtle. They reveal all sorts of interesting dynamics that hold between a reader, an author, and the evolving conventions that govern our consumption of a given genre of fiction.

## Fiction as a "Factory"

A second sort of fact, that we can learn from a fiction, emerges when a fiction functions not as a clearinghouse for knowledge but as a factory. Gendler explains:

> I export things from the story whose truth becomes apparent as a result of thinking about the story itself. These I add to my stock the way I add knowledge gained by modeling. In this way, for instance, I might learn that the relation between loyalty and adultery is more complicated than I had suspected, or that the deleterious effects of a rigid class structure are (un) equally distributed among the classes.
>
> (Gendler, 2000, pp. 76–77)

Gendler is referring to a very different route to knowledge, through fiction. The first route is really just using fiction as a sophisticated vehicle for testimony. The author is basically telling you that, say, the Russian serfs were emancipated in 1861, by making it clear that this claim lies in the comparison class of the story, thereby allowing you to export that knowledge, so long as you trust that the author has done the requisite research. But this second route to knowledge, through fiction, doesn't rely on the testimony or knowledge of the author at all (and if it does, it does so less directly).

Gendler's point is that by reflecting upon the fiction itself, perhaps on your emotional experience through your engagement with the fiction, or perhaps upon your running through the fictional events of the story in your head, you come to think things about the world, beyond the fiction, that you didn't think before you read the fiction. This is fiction functioning as a factory, rather than as a clearinghouse, for knowledge.

It's interesting to note that Gendler gives two quite different sorts of claims as examples of what one may learn from a fiction as a factory:

1 that the relation between loyalty and adultery is more complicated than I had suspected; and
2 that the deleterious effects of a rigid class structure are unequally distributed among the classes.

The first claim is a claim about the real world, but it doesn't necessarily require any empirical research (that's to say, it doesn't necessarily require that a person go out and look at real-world data about real people) in order for a person to reliably arrive at this claim. By thinking of *fictional* people in fictional scenarios, you can test what "loyalty" really means. You do this by seeing how the expectations we have about loyalty behave in extreme hypothetical cases. You can do the same thing with regard to "adultery". And, in running these fictional scenarios in your head, you can come to recognize that these two notions are – and always have been – related in more complicated ways than you had previously thought.

The second claim, it seems, is harder to justify from the comfort of an armchair. How do you know what the socio-economic and psychological fallout of a rigid class system really would be, without doing the empirical research (that's to say, without going out and gathering real-world data)?

But perhaps this is what Gendler has in mind. You read a realistic fiction about a real culture in which there really was/is a rigid class system. Because you trust that the author has done their research about the culture in question, and because it's clear to you that the author has intentionally placed various claims about this culture, and the observable effects of its rigid class system, into the comparison class, for you to export, you come to believe those claims. So far, the fiction has functioned as a clearinghouse for knowledge. And yet, note: the fact that the deleterious effects of this rigid class structure are unequally distributed, is not one of the claims that the author explicitly places in the comparison class. Rather, it's by thinking about the real-world facts that you've learned from the novel, and then reflecting upon those facts in the context of the fictional story, that you come to see how unequally distributed those deleterious effects must be – not just in the story, not just in the culture at hand, but in any similarly structured society. In that case, the fiction is functioning as a factory on the basis of the things it's already taught you as a clearinghouse.

## The Challenge from Logical Positivism

There's another key distinction between the two claims that Gendler presents as examples of knowledge generated by fiction as a factory. Her first claim regards a matter of fact, without any sort of value. The relationship between loyalty and adultery either does or doesn't exemplify a given degree of complexity. That's not a value judgement. But her second claim, with its reference to "deleterious effects" does seem to be making, or to be closely associated with, a value judgement.

Between the two world wars, a school of philosophy emerged that came to be known as logical positivism. One of the key beliefs of logical positivism was a doctrine known as verificationism. Verificationism is the belief that a sentence is only meaningful if there is, in principle, some way in which its truth or falsehood could be verified. Accordingly, "The moon is made of cheese" is a meaningful sentence. It's meaningful because it was always, in principle, possible that we could one day devise some sort of machine for going to the moon, sampling some of the stuff that it's made of, and checking whether or not it's cheese. But one of the surprising consequences of verificationism is that sentences that make a value judgement turn out to be meaningless.

The sentence, "Poverty is evil" isn't the sort of thing that could be verified or falsified. You *can* prove that poverty hampers education, health, longevity, and much more. But how can you prove that those things being hampered is *bad*? What sort of laboratory would you need to test the claim that these things are bad? Of course, you feel passionately that these are bad – terrible – things. These judgements seem just obviously true. But, on the other hand, these are not the sort of things that can be verified in any sort of laboratory. Accordingly, statements of value, according to logical positivists, tend to be expressions of emotion, rather than meaningful claims about the world. When we say that poverty is evil, we're really only expressing the fact that we don't like poverty.

*Tatjana:* Is it because empirical researchers do not measure badness as such, but they can only empirically measure some hard-fact consequences that we, beyond the lab, judge to be bad consequences?

*Sam:* Yes. Precisely.

When a sentence has the sort of meaning that could be called true or false, philosophers will say that the sentence in question has "cognitive content". So, if you want to get the jargon right, the logical positivists are telling us that value-statements have no cognitive content. This claim then gets to be called "non-cognitivism about statements of value".

It seems that, in a great many cases, when we say that we learnt something from our engagement with a work of art (be it a work of music, a painting, or a work of literary art, such as a work of fiction), the thing that we claim to have learnt will have something to do with value, or it will turn out to be the sort of claim that can't, in principle, be verified; the sort of claim that – for a verificationist – could have no cognitive content. Catherine Wilson (1983, pp. 489–490) notes:

> Morris Weitz claims to find in Proust the revelation that "there are no essences to our emotions": "that jealousy, love, and suffering manifest themselves in different ways and are recognized according to different criteria". For Peter Jones, *Middlemarch* contains the implication that past desires and present hopes govern our interpretation of present sensory experience. According to John Hospers, *Paradise Lost* implies that "man's state after the Fall is much better, in that he has free-will in a sense which he lacked before". And finally, Coleridge claims that in writing *Hamlet*, "Shakspeare wished to impress upon us the truth, that action is the chief end of existence."

Some of these claims might be the sort of thing that, at least one day, would be open to scientific verification.

*Tatjana:* It's not entirely clear to me why the statements in the passage are value statements.
*Sam:* I agree. And I didn't select these statements. Wilson did. But still, take each statement and see whether you could figure out a way to verify their truth by empirical experiment. Whether or not they have anything to with value, most of these statements, I guess, would be difficult if not impossible to verify empirically.

But most of them don't seem to be. This gives rise to a number of philosophers, inspired by logical positivism, who would deny that we tend to learn very much at all from fiction. If most of the claims that we arrive at, when fiction functions as a factory for knowledge, are claims that have no cognitive content, then we're not really learning anything about the world. We're just feeling certain emotions. Nothing more. As Wilson explains the position:

> Richard, Ayer, and Carnap presumably never intended to deny that novels, poetry and plays contain implicit and explicit statements. What they wished to argue was that propositions like those listed above are incapable of communicating knowledge; they make no contribution to our understanding of the world, and it is in this sense that they are to be regarded as "meaningless" or as "pseudo-statements.
>
> (Wilson, 1983, p. 490)

The sorts of propositions that we tend to claim that we've learnt from a fiction are, by the lights of a verificationist, empty of cognitive content, so they cannot be seen as making a contribution to knowledge.

To summarize: the challenge from logical positivism could be put this way: we (tend to) learn nothing from fiction, because the things we (tend to) claim to have learnt are not the sorts of things that can be verified, and therefore – since they're not the sort of things that can be verified – they are meaningless. The acquisition of meaningless claims, however emotionally engaging and satisfying the process, cannot be called *learning*, or the acquisition of *knowledge*.

*Tatjana:* I don't get the logical positivists. Why would we need to scientifically confirm everything? And why can we not verify claims such as the claim about the complicated relationship between loyalty and adultery in the lab?

Presumably, psychology researchers can design various experiments to see whether people struggle with seeing a clear relation between adultery and loyalty. Would this not suggest that the relationship is complicated? Sure, we don't have a complicatometer that measures complicatedness. But could the lack thereof possibly render the claim meaningless? Remember that my first comment was on wacky but fascinating answers to perfectly reasonable questions? This would be one such example to me.

*Sam:* Here you're asking a few different questions. Let me respond to them in a slightly different order to the order in which you raised them. First of all, I guess that the experiment that you imagine wouldn't reveal how complicated the relationship between loyalty and adultery are, so much as how complicated people *think* it to be. That's not the same thing.

Second, I guess that the logical positivists would be sceptical that complicatedness comes in empirically measurable units, especially if it's being treated as an objective feature of the relationship between loyalty and adultery, rather than as just a measure of how complicated people *find* that relation to be.

Third, I'm with you when it comes to logical positivists. I don't share their intuition at all that only the verifiable can be meaningful.

But finally, I guess I disagree. I don't think this is an example of a wacky answer to a perfectly reasonable question. What I think we're going to see is something very different, namely: a really interesting, and not at all wacky, answer to a question that I never would have thought needed to be asked! Let me explain. Since I think that logical positivism is a little bit silly, I would see no reason to ask, "how can we explain, if we assume the truth of logical positivism, the role that literature plays in learning?" I wouldn't ask it because I see no reason ever to assume the truth of logical positivism. And yet, I think that Wilson will provide us with a really brilliant and likely true theory of how fiction contributes to learning, and she provides this convincing theory primarily as an answer to that question I would never have asked!!

At first glance, this doesn't seem like a great argument. The first thing we can do, in response, is to point to all of that knowledge that we gain from fiction, not as a factory, but as a clearinghouse. Much of that knowledge tends to be eminently verifiable: that a certain village in England is a certain distance from London, that the Russian serfs were freed in 1861, or that women in France used to wear their hair in a certain style.

Unfortunately, the logical positivist could resist this response. After all, it's not really the fiction that taught us that stuff. Instead, it was the testimony of the author, whose research we trust. That research was then all dressed up in an historical novel, but we only arrived at the knowledge by stripping away all that fiction, and then finding the kernel of research that the author injected into her story. Accordingly, when fiction functions as a mere clearinghouse, there are grounds to say that it isn't really the fiction doing the work at all.

Okay. Another way to respond to this challenge from the logical positivists is to point to the non-value judgements that we acquire from fiction, even when fiction functions as a factory. For example, and as Gendler said, we might learn that the relationship between loyalty and adultery is more complex than we had originally assumed, simply by reading and then reflecting upon a novel. But here too, the positivist might resist our response.

What are we really discovering about the world when we realize, from the comfort of our armchairs, and without doing any real empirical research (i.e. without going out into the field to collect and analyse data), that loyalty and adultery are related in more complicated ways than we had initially assumed? It seems that all we've really come to learn is something about the meaning of two words: "loyalty" and "adultery". It's like coming to learn that all bachelors are unmarried men. You don't need to do any empirical research to discover that all bachelors are unmarried men. Instead, you simply need to discover the ways in which the meaning of "bachelor" is related to the meaning of "unmarried" and "man". When the truth of a claim is based upon nothing more than the meaning of the words in that claim, we philosophers say that the claim is *analytic*.

Some analytic claims are very obviously true, like the claim that all bachelors are unmarried. Other analytic claims are far from obviously true, and we need to work hard to recognize their truth. For example, the claim that "25.5 ÷ 0.2 = 127.5", is not one that most of us can immediately recognize to be true (some of you probably could – but not me!). Even so, its truth is analytic. It is true merely in virtue of the meaning of "25.5" and "÷" and "0.2" and "=" and "127.5".

When we discover things via fiction as a factory, and when those things we discover have nothing to do with value, they tend to be complicated analytic truths: things which are true just in virtue of the meaning of the concepts. For example, through reading a novel, we come to realize that *loyalty* and *adultery* are related in more complicated ways than we had recognized before.

*Tatjana:* I don't think I quite understand why this is an analytic truth. Our realization is that it's more complicated than we thought. Even if we just judge that it's complicated, it seems that "is complicated" asks for a comparison: complicated compared to what? And the resulting sentence, it seems to me, is not something that is analytic.

*Sam:* I think most logical positivists, rightly or wrongly, would think it to be analytic. Why? Because, at the end of the day, all you had to think about, to arrive at the conclusion, was what "loyalty" seems to mean, and what "adultery" seems to mean, and how the meaning of those words seem to interact as you imagine, from the comfort of your armchair, different scenarios that test and push the limits of the meanings of those words. But still, since all we're talking about is the meaning of words, and since an analytic truth is a truth that is true in virtue of nothing more than the words that you use to express it, there's a case to be made for the analyticity of this truth about the complicatedness of the relationship between loyalty and adultery.

But still, the relations between those concepts are analytic. The knowledge that we've gained is analytic. The problem here is that the logical positivists tended to think that analytic truths were somehow defective.

Think about it: an analytic truth is, when you boil it down, a tautology – a sentence that is true merely in virtue of the dictionary, and not in virtue of anything else. In fact, our example of a complicated analytic truth, "25.2 ÷ 0.2 = 127.5" is really telling us nothing more than this: the stuff on the left-hand side of the equals sign refers to the very same amount as does the stuff on the right-hand side. And thus, it's really just telling us that A = B. What's more, if A and B really are the same thing, then our equation has only really told us that A = A. True, sometimes it's harder for us, and sometimes it's easier for us, to detect that a truth is analytic. And yet, there seems to be a formal sense in which all analytic truths are trivial. So says the logical positivist.

Accordingly, if the only type of knowledge that we really gain from fiction is analytic, there's a sense in which the logical positivist will want to claim that we've learnt nothing much at all! Hence, we haven't yet succeeded in mounting a strong rebuttal of the logical positivist's claim. According to them, we learn nothing, or nothing much, or nothing non-trivial, from our engagement with fiction.

Sometimes, the best defence is to go on the offence. Instead of finding a type of knowledge, acceptable to the logical positivist, that we acquire from our engagement with fiction, why not attack logical positivism to begin with? It turns out to be pretty easy to do. After all, the whole attack on the cognitive value of fiction is grounded in the doctrine of verificationism. But is verificationism true?

Remember: verificationism is the claim that a statement is only meaningful if, in principle, we could design some sort of test or experiment that could verify or falsify it. Now, verificationism is a doctrine that certain philosophers dreamt up from the comfort of their armchairs. Worse still, it turns out that it isn't the sort of doctrine that you could test for its truthfulness in a laboratory. This immediately entails that verificationism is, by its own lights, meaningless! We shouldn't allow doctrines that are meaningless by their own lights to worry us about the cognitive value of fiction! If verificationism is false, then all of those value judgements that we come to endorse upon our engagement with fiction can once again claim to be candidates for real knowledge.

Admittedly, there may be ways to salvage verificationism from the threat of meaninglessness, by qualifying it somehow. There might also be other reasons, besides verificationism, to think that value-statements have no real cognitive value. But at least we can see that there's plenty of room to resist this attack on the cognitive value of fiction.

We can also attack the logical positivist's claim that all analytical truths are trivial. After all, when I learn that certain concepts are related in certain ways, I come to experience the world around me in new ways. When I learn that 2 + 2 = 4, I have learnt something about the concept of twoness and fourness and addition, but I've also learnt to expect, of any pair of apples, in the real world, and any other (wholly distinct) pair of apples, that if you put them together, you'll have four apples. That seems to be something eminently worth knowing.

*Tatjana:* I recently overheard a conversation between two people, one explaining to the other that a colt is an uncastrated male horse under the age of four. That's an analytic truth that was anything but trivial to me.

*Sam:* I completely agree. Anything but trivial. Especially if you're a horse!

Accordingly, if I were to defend the cognitive value of fiction against the attack of the logical positivist, I would simply attack logical positivism. I would attack verificationism, and I would insist that even the analytic truths that we discover from our engagement with fiction, are far from empty; that they are non-trivial truths that are worth knowing. But what Catherine Wilson (1983) demonstrates is that, even if we were to accept verificationism, and even were we to accept that analytical truths are somehow empty, there's still a very real sense in which we *learn* through reading fiction. I think that Wilson is right. It all depends, as we shall see, upon what it means to *learn*.

## Fiction and Learning

Is learning merely a process of expanding your knowledge of which propositions are true and which propositions are false?

In defending the claim, even against dogmatic logical positivists, that we can learn a great deal from fiction, Wilson encourages us to reassess what it means to learn. She encourages us to recognize that learning involves much more than the acquisition of knowledge of true propositions. In fact, this is how she defines *learning*:

> [T]he term "learning" applies primarily to a modification of a person's concepts, which is in turn capable of altering his thought or conduct, and not primarily to an increased disposition to utter factually correct statements or to display technical prowess.
>
> (Wilson, 1983, p. 495)

Let's break this definition down. It's certainly true that a person who's been educated about some topic will be able to say true things about it – this is what she means by having an "increased disposition to utter factually correct statements". But her point is that this is not the primary achievement of a good education. The primary achievement is that your concepts – by which, I suppose, we mean the ideas that you have that shape your very experience of the world around you – have been changed in ways that affect your conduct, and the ways in which you might act or think in a given circumstance.

Imagine a person who's finished a long course of study, in which she trained to be a civil engineer. Wilson thinks that such a person should be able to "state facts and theorems", but that we should expect much more from her than that. For one thing, we'd expect that she could "actually build" things (Wilson, 1983, p. 495). Here we're talking about *know-how*. The education in civil engineering hasn't just given the engineer knowledge of true propositions. We could call such knowledge, knowledge-that, since it's always about knowing *that* some proposition or other is true. In addition to this knowledge-that, the engineer has a newfound *know-how*; *the ability to build*.

Some philosophers have tried to argue that know-how really can be explained in terms of knowing true propositions, and thus that know-how can be reduced to knowledge-that (see, for example, Stanley & Willlamson 2001). But it's a controversial claim. To many it seems obvious that know-how is just a very different type of knowledge. You can know every true proposition about piano playing without actually knowing how to play it. And, you can know how to play it without knowing very many propositions about piano playing. So, to summarize, the engineer's education will have given her know-how in addition to knowledge-that. Moreover, and in addition to knowing how to build stuff, Wilson continues: "we should expect the engineer to be able as well to solve engineering problems of a novel sort, and to be able to evaluate and criticise novel engineering proposals" (Wilson 1983, p. 495).

It's for that reason that a medical professional, with years of training, is armed with more than just the knowledge of lots of facts. I could look those facts up on the internet, I suppose. But her training also gives her the ability to understand the significance of those facts, and their inter-relationship. This ability isn't some extra fact. It's more like another form of know-how. Likewise, she is better placed than I am to accommodate and assimilate novel medical data into her theoretical frameworks. It's as if, through her medical education, in addition to being fed all sorts of facts, there was an "alteration in the way in which the learner perceives" her environment (ibid.). She sees things differently now. That is part of what learning involves.

*Tatjana:* It sounds like she has undergone a transformative experience. I can see how some fictional works can be transformative for us as well. It doesn't seem unreasonable for me to think that *Never Let Me Go* has had some transformative influence on me.

*Sam:* I totally agree. For more about transformative experiences, by the way, readers might be interested in the work of L.A. Paul (2014).

If learning is about altering the way you process information, and gaining new forms of know-how, then it's plausible that fiction could play a role in a person learning, even if we agree with the logical positivist that we don't learn any substantive cognitive content from our engagement with fiction; that is to say, even if we learn no new true propositions from the fiction. It turns out that there's much more to learning than acquiring new true propositions.

In addition to the propositions that we take to be true, we also have to have, for pretty much any given topic, what Elizabeth Camp calls a perspective. What does she mean? Camp defines a perspective as a "holistic principle for organizing our thoughts about some topic".

> It organizes those thoughts by imposing a complex structure of relative prominence on them, so that some features stick out in our minds while others fade into the background, and by making some features especially central to explaining others. A perspective often also imposes certain evaluative attitudes and emotional valences on its constituent features.
>
> (Camp, 2009, pp. 110–111)

Having said that, Camp is quick to point out that a perspective isn't just some complex thought about how your less complex thoughts and feelings are related to one another. Even if a perspective includes such a thought, it also functions more like a tool than that. She explains:

> Being a "tool for thought" means at least two things here. First, a perspective helps us to do things with the thoughts we have: to make quick judgments based on what's most important, to grasp intuitive connections, and to respond emotionally, among other things. And second, it provides us

> with a "way to go on," incorporating new thoughts about the focal topic and often about related topics as well.
>
> (Camp, 2009, p. 111)

Had Wilson had this technical terminology, she may have said that learning is primarily about acquiring new perspectives. If that's what learning is about, then it's clear that fiction stands ready to be a very effective teacher. This is because an author or narrator does more than merely to present the facts of a fictional world. She also does it from a particular perspective, and she expects her readers to share this perspective, or at least to try. As Camp explains:

> If a reader scrupulously pretends true all of the propositions that the author explicitly makes fictional, but assigns them wildly different structures of relative importance, explanatory connection, and emotional and evaluative valence than the author intended, then she has significantly misinterpreted the fiction. A serial killer who relishes *American Psycho* as a joyful romp, for instance, or a pedophile who laments that Humbert Humbert is brought to justice in *Lolita* – or even a reader who focuses all her imaginative energy on the slaves in *Gone with the Wind* – has gotten something importantly wrong about those novels, even if they've gotten all the constituent events just right.
>
> (Camp, 2009, p. 117)

*Tatjana:* I am not sure how this example fits in the with other two. In the case of the serial killer and the paedophile, they both resist adopting a certain moral perspective that the works suggest.

But a reader who feels prompted to make the slaves in *Gone with the Wind* the focus of her attention is not necessarily adopting a different moral perspective, she is simply attentive to different aspects of the world.

*Sam:* Yes. I hear what you mean. I suppose that Camp has in mind a reader who is so distracted by the casual acceptance of slavery in *Gone with the Wind*, that they're unable to pay attention to the plot itself. She needn't accept, even for the sake of the story, that slavery is morally acceptable. But, if she fixates on the widespread acceptance, among the characters, of slavery, she's likely to miss a lot. This brings to mind your discussion in Chapter 5, about imagining things, as a reader or a consumer of fiction, that detract from the unfolding of the plot.

Recognizing that reading a fiction involves adopting a perspective can help to explain the phenomenon of imaginative resistance that Tatjana explored in Chapter 9. We might be happy to imagine all sorts of things, for the sake of argument. But there are some perspectives that we find so deeply offensive that we're uncomfortable occupying them, *even* for the sake of argument. But the fact that adopting new perspectives is part of what it means to engage with fiction is one of the reasons that we value fictions so much:

> They enable us to "get inside the head" of an alternate personality, to experience in an intimate, first-person way what it's like for someone else to meet the world around them (cf. Currie, 1997). Further, this experience may end up altering our own perspective on the real world. What begins as a temporary exercise in perspective shifting may unwittingly cause a modification of our ongoing dispositions to notice, interpret, and respond to related situations as we encounter them in reality.
>
> (Camp, 2009, p. 117)

And, according to Wilson, it is precisely the modification of dispositions to notice, interpret, and respond to situations that sits at the beating heart of what it means to learn.

Personally, I altogether reject the logical positivist argument against the cognitive value of fiction. I think that value-statements are meaningful propositions. Moreover, I think that analytical truths can be non-trivial. So, I think that there are all sorts of propositions that we learn from fiction, both as a clearinghouse and as a factory. But, I think that Wilson is right too. Her point is that learning is about much more than acquiring new propositional information. Learning is about modifying our perspectives, and it seems clear that fiction is a powerful vehicle for doing just that.

## First-Personal Knowledge

We can come to know all sorts of true propositions through our engagement with fiction. We do this when fiction functions as a clearinghouse, and when it functions as a factory. We also learn from fiction in the sense that fiction plays a role in shifting our perspective on the world. Are fictions essential for these modes of learning? Not necessarily. There are other ways to shift perspectives than to read a novel. Narrative nonfiction, for example, may be just as good. Moreover, there are plenty of ways in which to learn true propositions, both those concerning value, and those concerning dry matters of fact, than through fiction as a clearinghouse or factory. Nevertheless, fictions may be especially good vehicles for these forms of learning, even if they're not essential. Moreover, there are some forms of knowledge that perhaps *only* narrative fiction can deliver.

Neurologists have discovered that narrative writing has certain effects over our brain that are not caused by more sanitized non-narrative prose. I imagine that the distinction between narrative prose and non-narrative prose is more like a spectrum, with a big fuzzy grey area in the middle, than it is a binary distinction with a sharp cut off. But, to get a sense for the difference, imagine reading the entire novel of *War and Peace*, and then imagine reading the Cliff Notes on the book. The former presents the story in narrative prose. The latter presents the same story but in non-narrative prose.

What neurologists have found is that when we read a narrative account of some event, then the very same parts of our brains that would be active when actually witnessing such an event, are activated (see, for example, Oakley, 2008, and Tatjana's discussion of Currie in Chapter 5). This has led people to talk about how, when reading narratives, our brains perform an "offline simulation". Its being a simulation explains why we can feel so afraid, or so sad, or so happy, when reading a narrative. Its being "offline" explains why the fear doesn't cause you to throw the book on the floor and run out of the room!

That narrative gives rise to this type of offline simulation in our brains makes narrative, and narrative fiction in particular, singularly well placed to help us learn various things about ourselves. Lots of questions, such as, how might you feel, or how might you respond, if X, Y, and Z were to happen to you, are very difficult for us to answer, because it's just so hard to imagine certain situations. But a good narrative about those sorts of situations, and sometimes these narratives will *have* to be fictional because the sort of situation might be so rare or extreme, or may never yet have happened in real life, helps to unlock the parts of your brain that really would be active in situations of that kind. Accordingly, you can learn all sorts of things about yourself, and your own emotional landscape and ethical beliefs, that you'd be hard pressed to access without the aid of fiction (which is something that Tatjana already discussed in Chapter 9).

We can call what you're learning in these examples, *first-personal knowledge,* because, in engaging with the fiction, you're learning about yourself. So, perhaps there are forms of first-personal knowledge that only fiction can help you to access. The image of offline simulation feeds nicely on to the notion of *training*. When a person is learning to be a fighter pilot, they train in a simulator long before they take control of an actual plane. The simulator is much safer, and much less expensive. Moreover, in the simulator, the pilot can train for all sorts of eventualities of extreme danger that may never occur in her career going forward, and may be extremely difficult to choreograph as a training exercise in real life. And yet, despite never occurring in real life, these extreme simulated situations can train reactions and dispositions that will aid her in her career.

It is for very similar reasons that Martha Nussbaum has argued that engagement with literary fiction should be viewed as an indispensable aid to our training as ethical agents (see Nussbaum, 1992, especially chapters 4–6). Fiction allows our brains to simulate all sorts of ethical dilemmas and difficult situations, from all sorts of perspectives. Some of these situations may never arise in our everyday lives, or in anybody's life in the history of humanity, and yet the simulated experience may play a crucial role in developing our reactions and dispositions, helping to refine our behaviour in the real world.

Summarizing this role that fiction plays in our ethical, and perhaps in our emotional, training, Camp writes:

> I might, for instance, gain a more intimate appreciation for the anguish of orphanhood, or for the attractions of gambling or being a bully, by empathizing with characters who undergo those emotions... By broadening our range of experience, fiction can provoke us to notice and respond empathetically to similar people and situations as we encounter them in real life; and this awareness may in turn lead us to reconfigure our moral and psychological theories more generally. Here, art is functioning as a proxy for life, allowing us to acquire experiential knowledge without the pain, risk, and time investment – and sometimes, metaphysical impossibility – that they normally entail.
>
> (Camp 2009, p. 116)

It is the first-personal experience of fiction as a simulator that allows us both new knowledge of ourselves, and a training ground for the shaping of our ethical and emotional lives. But there's one more form of knowledge that narrative fiction seems extremely well placed to deliver, once again, because of the unique role that narrative can play in generating offline simulations in our brains.

## Second-Personal Knowledge

Part of Wilson's response to logical positivists is that not all knowledge is propositional. That's to say, not all knowledge relates a knower to a true proposition. Lots of knowledge, of course, is propositional – for example, my knowledge that Paris is the Capital of France relates me to the true proposition that Paris is the capital of France. In fact, all knowledge-that – all knowledge *that something is true* – is propositional. But Wilson had us focus on know-how, which doesn't seem to be propositional. Similarly, lots of our first-personal knowledge is not propositional. In fact, knowing what things feel like, which philosophers call *phenomenal knowledge* never seems to be propositional.

Frank Jackson devised a thought experiment about a brilliant neuroscientist, Mary, who – despite growing up in a totally black and white environment – knows every true proposition that a complete neuroscience (and, indeed, a complete physics) could furnish her about the human experience of the colour blue (Jackson, 1982). Mary knows exactly what light does when it stimulates the retina; exactly how that affects the brain, and exactly how it affects human behaviour. But, given her environment, she can't know what the colour blue looks like. She's only ever seen things in black and white.

Jackson's point isn't about the relationship between phenomenal and propositional knowledge. All he's interested to prove is that knowing everything there is to know about physics isn't to know everything there is to know about the world. There are facts that are not physical facts. She knows all the physical facts, but she still doesn't know what blue looks like. But we should ask, what sort of knowledge of the world *does* Mary gain, when she finally escapes from her prison and discovers what blue looks like?

As Eleonore Stump points out, what Mary learns upon seeing blue for the first time doesn't seem to be merely the truth of a new proposition. Admittedly, she *does* learn the truth of new propositions, such as the proposition that "blue looks like this", but "the 'this' here simply gestures toward what she [has come to know]: it does not reduce it to propositional form" (Stump, 2010, p. 51). Primarily, she's not come to learn that some proposition is true. She's simply come to learn what blue things look like.

Stump argues that there's another sort of non-propositional knowledge that often gets overlooked – it's not know-how and it's not phenomenal knowledge; it is what she calls *knowledge of persons*. To motivate the claim, she asks us to reimagine the Mary thought experiment. This time, Mary has access to colour in her prison, but what she doesn't have, is access to any interpersonal interaction. We're to imagine that she knows every true proposition about personal and social psychology, sociology, and anthropology, so that she knows every true proposition that there is to know about personal interaction. She also knows every true proposition about her poor mother, from whom she was brutally kidnapped; her mother who is desperate to see her in the flesh. When Mary escapes from the prison, and meets her mother, about whom she knew every true proposition, did she learn something new?

Sure, she may have acquired some new first-personal phenomenal knowledge, such as what it feels like to be in her mother's gaze. But it seems like she's learnt more than that. There's a gap between knowing every proposition about a person, and actually knowing *the person*. There's a gap also, between knowing every true proposition about interpersonal relationships, and the very distinctive sort of interpersonal knowledge that you acquire in virtue of actually *being* in a relationship with another person. As Stump puts the point:

> Mary will be surprised by the nature of a second-person experience, no matter how good her science textbooks have been or how rich her isolated introspective experience may have been. And her surprise makes two things clear to us: first, that Mary is learning something she did not know before the personal interaction, and, second, that it is not possible to teach her by means of the science books she has what she comes to learn through personal interaction. The thought experiment thus shows that there are things we come to know from our experience of other persons and that

> these things are difficult or impossible to formulate in terms of knowing that.
>
> (Stump, 2010, p. 53)

Let's accept what Stump says, even if only for the sake of argument, that there is a distinctive form of knowledge that can't be cashed out in terms of the propositions that you know, and that this knowledge is the knowledge of other persons. But if narrative prose is really capable of getting our brains to simulate experiences, then if – instead of science text books – Mary had had, in her prison, all sorts of novels, and perhaps a narrative and literary biography of her mother, rather than just a sanitized set of propositions – then her surprise, upon meeting another human being, upon meeting her beloved mother, for the first time, would be much less. As Stump describes matters:

> A story takes a real or imagined set of second-person experiences of one sort or another and makes it available to a wider audience to share. It does so by making it possible, to one degree or another, for a person to experience some of what she would have experienced if she had been an onlooker in the second-person experience represented in the story. That is, a story gives a person some of what she would have had if she had unmediated personal interaction with the characters in the story while they were conscious and interacting with each other, without actually making her part of the story itself.
>
> (Stump, 2010, p. 78)

Perhaps this is another reason why engagement in fiction (or at least narrative prose – be it fictional or non-fictional) is such an important, and perhaps indispensable, part of our training in ethics. Our engagement about fiction doesn't just teach us about ourselves, it teaches us about others (even if those others are just fictional people). It allows us, to a certain degree, and in an "offline" mode, to experience what it means to be in the presence of other people, to be interacting with them, and to be sensitive to their needs as other people, as second-persons (i.e. not as a *he* or a *she* or a *they*, but as a *you*).

It should go without saying that we can learn all sorts of things from engaging with fiction. That's why I said, right at the start, that the question of our chapter doesn't seem puzzling at all. I don't think it's particularly hard to face down the challenge from logical positivists on this front. But in the process of doing that, we came to recognize that the varieties of learning that fiction has to offer are much more diverse and subtle than we may have realized.

Against the logical positivists, I would say that fiction gives us new propositional knowledge, as both a clearinghouse *and* as a factory. These propositions can be about any topic under the sun, but they will also include value judgements that we come to endorse on the basis of our engagement with fiction.

Moreover, and even if the logical positivists were right, fiction can play a role in altering our perspectives – which may well be the very definition of *learning*. Finally, and through the offline simulation that it generates, narrative fiction gives rise to forms of first and second-personal knowledge that may be essential to our education as ethical agents.

## Works Cited

Camp, E. (2009) Two Varieties of Literary Imagination: Metaphor, Fiction, and Thought Experiments. *Midwest Studies in Philosophy*, 33: 107–130.

Currie, G. (1997) The Paradox of Caring: Fiction and the Philosophy of Mind. In M. Hjort & S. Laver (eds), *Emotion and the Arts*. Oxford: Oxford University Press, pp. 63–77.

Gendler, T. S. (2000) The Puzzle of Imaginative Resistance. *The Journal of Philosophy*, 97(2): 55–81.

Hazlett, A. & Mag Uidhir, C. (2011) Unrealistic Fictions. *American Philosophical Quarterly*, 48(1): 33–46.

Jackson, F. (1982) Epiphenomenal Qualia. *The Philosophical Quarterly*, 32(127): 127–136.

Nussbaum, M. (1992) *Love's Knowledge: Essays on Philosophy and Literature*. Oxford: Oxford University Press.

Oatley, K. (2008) The Mind's Flight Simulator. *The Psychologist*, 21: 1030–1032.

Paul, L. (2014) *Transformative Experience*. Oxford: Oxford University Press.

Stanley, J. & Williamson, T. (2001) Knowing How. *Journal of Philosophy*, 98(8): 411–444.

Stump, E. (2010) *Wandering in Darkness: Narrative and the Problem of Suffering*. New York: Oxford University Press.

Wilson, C. (1983) Literature and Knowledge. *Philosophy*, 58(226): 489–496.

## Further Reading

Conolly, O. & Haydar, B. (2007) Literature, Knowledge, and Value. *Philosophy and Literature*, 31(1): 111–124.

Gibson, J. (2009) Literature and Knowledge. In R. Eldridge (ed.), *Oxford Handbook of Philosophy and Literature*. Oxford: Oxford University Press.

Chapter 12

# Are You Fictional?

*Sam*

In this chapter, I'm going to make a claim that just seems to be bonkers. I'm going to argue for it in two different ways. My claim is that you are, or that you are extremely likely to be, a fictional character in a fictional story.

Given certain assumptions about what possible worlds are (assumptions that we discussed in Chapter 6), and about what fictional characters are (which we discussed in Chapter 3), it's actually not so hard to imagine that, in some sense or other, we're fictional characters in multiple stories.

Remember: David Lewis believes that for every way our universe could be, there really exists some other universe – which he calls a possible world – which really is that way (Lewis, 1986). You'll also remember that, for Lewis, a sentence is true in a fictional story if (and only if) that sentence is true in all of the closest possible worlds in which the text of that story is asserted by someone as known fact (Lewis, 1978). Given such an account, you could say that to be a fictional character is just to be a person to whom a text, asserted as known fact in his or her own world, but told as a fiction in some other possible world, refers.

Well, let's give this a little thought. Are there any texts in this world, the world in which we actually live, that refer to *you*? I imagine that there are. Your school reports, for example, refer to you. Your CV is a text that refers to you. Perhaps you've appeared in a newspaper article, or you've been written about on some social media platform. Well, let's take one of those texts – a text that's about you in the real world, and call it a YOU-text. Now, there certainly exists a possible world in which somebody just dreamed that YOU-text up, even though, in that world, you don't exist. They dreamed it up, from their own possible world, as a fiction. It might not be a very good fiction, but the person doing the dreaming might not be a very good author.

> *Tatjana:* Is this because there are so many (merely) possible worlds, one for every way that the world could have been, that there must be not only one but several, in which I am not concrete but someone dreams up my latest Instagram post?

DOI: 10.4324/9781003126102-13

*Sam:* Exactly. Yes. Even if your Instagram posts are terribly boring (which obviously isn't true). The fact that somebody possibly could dream them up means that there is a possible world (and yes, you're right, countless possible worlds) in which somebody does dream up your Instagram posts.

So there you have it, it turns out that you're a fictional character, in that you *are* referred to by a text asserting known fact, in your own world, that is told as a fictional story from some other world.

But this argument isn't very impressive. First of all, it relies on all sorts of assumptions about what fiction is, and what fictional characters are, and how they relate to possible worlds. We have good reason to reject many (if not all of) those assumptions. Moreover, in the way I defined my terms, I tried to hide the fact that all I've really done is this: I've ascertained, on the basis of some dubious assumptions, that you are, from the perspective of some *other* possible world, a fictional character. But surely all that means is something like this: you could have been a fictional character, but you're not.

Sure, there are some possible worlds, in which you're fictional. But what's actually true is what's true in *our* possible world, which we call *the actual world* (the one in which Tatjana and I are writing this book, and in which you, dear reader, are reading it). And in our possible world, you *haven't* been dreamt up as a distant possibility. In our possible world, you're actual, not fictional. So, not only is the argument based on dubious premises, but even given those premises, it doesn't really deliver the conclusion that it promised. It only really establishes that you are possibly a fictional character, but not in a way that seems to undermine at all the claim that you're actually not a fictional character!

*Tatjana:* I find that a somewhat unsatisfying consequence. It *should* be possible for us to be fictional!

*Sam:* Yeah. Your dissatisfaction may be an artefact of a wider dissatisfaction that people often feel with Lewis's account of possibility. According to him, what it means for you to have possibly been a spy is just that, in a different world altogether, you have a counterpart who *is* a spy. But that's not really all that satisfying. It still seems to entail that there's a sense in which you, yourself, the actual you, couldn't really have been a spy, because you are not your counterpart. But Lewis would reply that there is nothing more to possibly being a spy than having a spy counterpart, so stop complaining!

*My* arguments (and I'm going to present two of them in this chapter) are very different. They don't seem to rely on any particular conception of what a possible world is. They also don't seem to rely on any particular or controversial conception of what a fictional character is. The first argument, admittedly, requires belief in God. This is a belief that I endorse. This makes me something of a rarity (but certainly not an endangered species) in academic philosophy. But, even so, theism is a widely held doctrine in the world at large, and it would certainly be a surprising philosophical discovery to establish that, on the assumption of theism, we turn out to be fictional characters.

*Tatjana:* And if we don't like being fictional characters, we can use your first argument to reject theism, no? One person's *modus ponens* (i.e. a proof of a consequence) is another one's *modus tollens* (i.e. a proof against the antecedent).

*Sam:* Absolutely, yes. An atheist could accept the basic point of my argument from theism. They could accept that theism entails that we're fictional characters, and then use that fact to feel all the more confident that atheism must be true! I, on the other hand, convinced of my theism as I am, am willing to bite the bullet, and say – oh well, turns out that (in a sense), I'm fictional!

Better still, my second argument for the same conclusion doesn't rely on my theism at all, so maybe, by the end of this chapter, we'll all be in trouble!

## From Theism to Fiction

With my friend and colleague, Tyron Goldschmidt, I have developed three arguments that start from the assumption of theism, and end up with the conclusion that, from a fundamental perspective, we are fictional characters (Goldschmidt & Lebens, 2020). I won't present all three of the arguments here. I'll just present one of them. Here it goes:

1 God is necessarily perfectly rational and necessarily omniscient (i e. He knows all things).
2 If God is necessarily perfectly rational, and necessarily omniscient, He would not do what He knows to be otiose (i.e. what doesn't need to be done to achieve His goals), and He knows what is otiose.
3 It's possible (even if it strikes you as very unlikely) that you are a fictional character, in the mind of God. All of your experiences could be just as they are, even if (however unlikely it may seem) you and all of those experiences are fictional. God could have made things that way.

4 If God could have created you as a fictional character without taking any of your experiences away from you, then making you into a concrete non-fictional being of flesh and blood would have been otiose.

*Tatjana:* Ooh! I'm eager to read your defence of this one!

5 God doesn't do anything otiose. (This follows from lines 1 and 2.)
6 Making you into a concrete non-fictional being of flesh and blood would have been otiose. (This follows from lines 3 and 4.)
7 Therefore, God didn't make you into a concrete non-fictional being of flesh and blood. (This follows from lines 5 and 6.)
8 Therefore, you are a fictional being in the mind of God. (This follows from line 7.)

Before you jump at me with objections, let me be clear. I know that lots of the assumptions in this argument could be questioned. Give me a chance to defend them. The argument has four assumptions (which we philosophers call the premises of the argument). Those are the first four statements. The argument also has four conclusions, which are statements 5–8. If all four of the assumptions are true, then so are the conclusions. Accordingly, if you want to resist this argument, you'll have to reject at least one of its four premises.

Of course, if you're an atheist you'll just reject the first premise.

*Tatjana:* That's me. But I am curious to find out whether *if* a god exists, then I am a fictional character.

God isn't perfectly rational and omniscient if He doesn't exist! But, at the moment, I'm only trying to convince you that theism entails the claim that we're fictional characters. So, if only for the time being, you should grant me the assumption that God exists. And, if He exists, it seems right to say that He's perfectly rational and that He's all-knowing. Any being that didn't have those properties could hardly claim to be the God of the classical monotheistic religions. Premise 1, I think, is safe.

Things already start to get shaky with premise 2. Here are some reasons for thinking that it must be true. Wouldn't it be irrational for a being to do something for no reason?

Perhaps not. Aristotle, and the Muslim philosopher Abu Hamid al-Ghazali, as well as the French philosopher Jean Buridan, all came up with examples in which a rational agent would be forced to do something without having a sufficiently good reason for doing what they do. This sort of example is sometimes described in terms of "Buridan's ass". The idea is to imagine a thirsty donkey standing exactly in between two equally fresh and lovely buckets of water. There's no reason for the donkey to choose bucket A over bucket B. And there's no reason for the donkey to choose bucket B over bucket A. They're equally close. They're equally good. They're equally full. So, whichever bucket the donkey chooses, the donkey will be making a choice that has no sufficiently good reason to determine that choice. And yet, if the donkey does nothing – perhaps because it thinks itself to be a super-rational donkey – it will die of thirst. And that's not good. So, surely the right thing to do, in a situation like that, is to act without having any particular reason for choosing the precise action you choose. You have to drink from either A or B, but there's no reason to prefer one over the other. In such situations, rationality seems to require that you make an arbitrary choice.

Okay, so perhaps a perfectly rational being can act for no good reason. But then again, surely it only acts for no good reason when it has a good reason to act for no good reason! When there is a good reason to act arbitrarily, then the action isn't really otiose. So premise 2 is still in good standing. Sometimes arbitrary actions can be rational, but otiose actions can't be!

Perhaps premise 2 confuses what would be rational for humans to do with what would be rational for God. Presented with two sequences of actions, both of which seem to promise the same results over all, and require the same effort – other than the fact that one sequence is longer and one sequence is shorter – a human agent would always be more rational to choose the shorter sequence because humans have limited resources (we've only got so much time here on earth) – and thus the longer sequence will have a higher cost. But God wouldn't have this problem, since – presumably – He's not limited in time or energy. Consequently, it's not clear that decision theory, as applied to God, would rule out His choosing a course of action with otiose steps in it. Taking detours would be no skin off God's teeth (not least because He has no skin, or teeth). So maybe otiose actions are ruled out for rational human beings, but not for a rational God.

With Goldschmidt, I'm not particularly worried by this concern. To us, it seems obvious that, whatever decision theory teaches us, it should be a basic principle of rationality not to act without good reason – unless you have good reason to act for no good reason. This rules out otiosity.

If you remain unconvinced, don't start this argument from God's perfect rationality. Just edit lines 1 and 2 to speak, not of God's rationality, but of His perfection. Perfection, you might think, always pursues the most beautiful course of action of those available, given one's ends (and all other things being equal). You might just adopt the following aesthetic principle: otiose actions are never the most beautiful way of achieving one's ends. So perfection doesn't allow for the pursuit of otiose actions, even if rationality does (though we doubt, in fact, that rationality does). So far, I think, the argument is standing up well, in the face of scrutiny. The real problems begin when we turn to premise 3.

One way of summarizing this wacky argument goes like this: if God exists, and if we could be fictional beings, then we are fictional beings. Clearly, the part of this argument that the theist would be best off attacking is the assumption that it's even possible for us to be fictional beings. That is to say: you should attack premise 3. You should say that it isn't even possible that you are a fictional being.

Admittedly, David Lewis – given his understanding of how possibility works – cannot deny the possibility that you're a fictional being (since there are surely some possible authors who dream up a YOU-text as a fiction) but note: we don't have to accept Lewis's somewhat eccentric understanding of how possibility works. So we have no reason to feel committed to accept premise 3. Sure, if you accept premise 3 without an argument, it would make my life easier. But I think it natural to resist premise 3, if you're not a Lewisian. So, I feel compelled to say more.

You might think that one of the things that's essential to your very being is that you are a concrete person who has phenomenal consciousness (phenomenal consciousness is the property of being aware of phenomenal sensations. Phenomenal sensations are states of being that have a subjective flavour – what you might call a *what-it-is-like-ness*, which philosophers call a phenomenology). If it's true that you are essentially a being that has phenomenal consciousness, then either (1) you exist, and have phenomenal consciousness, or (2) you don't have phenomenal consciousness, because you don't exist. Those are the only two options, if the possession of phenomenal consciousness really is *essential* to who and what you are. You wouldn't be able to exist without it.

Since you clearly do exist, and if the possession of phenomenal consciousness really is essential to who and what you are, then you must have phenomenal consciousness. Fictional characters, by contrast, don't have phenomenal consciousness (or, if they do, they don't really have it, or they only hold it without having it).

*Tatjana:* They really do if they are non-actual.

*Sam:* Right. Readers of earlier chapters should know all sorts of theories by now according to which fictional characters are, or are in some sense, phenomenally conscious. But I can feel the intuitive pull of those theories that say, "yeah, but come on, fictional characters aren't really conscious like you or me, are they?!" So, I'll say more to try to sell premise 3 to our more resistant readers.

So there is no possibility, whatsoever, if the possession of phenomenal consciousness is essential to who and what you are, of your being a fictional character. This just means that premise 3 is false!

But hold your horses, because this is where things get both interesting and a little tricky. You think that you're special in that you essentially possess phenomenal consciousness. But surely Hamlet also thinks that he essentially possesses phenomenal consciousness. And surely he's right. After all, he's a human being and – according to you, human beings essentially possess phenomenal consciousness. But now, you're going to say that I'm playing games with you. You *really* have phenomenal consciousness as part of your essence whereas Hamlet only *fictionally* has phenomenal consciousness as part of his essence. But if this is your argument, aren't you begging the question, and simply assuming that, unlike Hamlet, you're not a fictional character in any story?

Jaakko Hintikka (1962) argues that Hamlet can't really make the famous argument that Descartes made, to convince himself that he's a real person; a thinking being that certainly exists. Descartes's argument can be summed up, famously, in five English words, "I think, therefore I am." If I didn't exist, then how could I be thinking? Furthermore, if I wasn't the sort of being that's capable of thinking – something mindlike and conscious – then how could I be thinking about what and whether I am? Hamlet can't do that. Not really. We can. So we're not fictional. He is.

But again, that seems like it's begging the question. Saul Kripke (2013, p. 58) was convinced that Hamlet *can* make Descartes's argument. If Shakespeare had imagined Hamlet making the argument, then Hamlet would have made the argument in his story, and relative to what's true and false in his story, Hamlet's argument would have been sound.

To understand what's going on here, you have to recognize that the theist – if my argument is sound – has to think of reality as divided across two levels or perspectives. God, on this picture, exists outside of any story. He is the non-fictional foundation of the universe. From His perspective, you and I are just fictional characters – whatever exactly it means to be a fictional character (for more on that issue, see Chapter 3).

*Tatjana:* I'm somewhat confused. Does this mean we are at this point just accepting the assumption that we are fictional?

*Sam:* Yes. I'm asking you to accept for the sake of argument, my conclusion, that we're fictions in the mind of God. And then, under the scope of that assumption, I'm hoping to show you how you really would (in a very thick sense) *still be conscious*. Then, once I've convinced you of that, you can throw away the assumption, and my hope is that, at the very least, you'll have come to see that premise 3 is true. Then, if I can convince you that premise 4 is true, in addition to premises 1 and 2, then I'm hoping you'll be forced to re-accept my conclusion – this time, not for the sake of argument, but as the conclusion of an argument that follows from 4 premises.

We're not actual human beings of flesh and blood. Not from God's perspective. We're just fictional beings. We don't possess phenomenal consciousness. Not from God's perspective. We don't have it essentially. We don't have it accidentally. We don't have it at all.

Compare: from our perspective (which we share with Shakespeare), Hamlet is just a fictional character, rather than a human being of flesh and blood. Hamlet doesn't possess phenomenal consciousness – not when we assess the claim from the perspective of Shakespeare. Likewise, for the theist – if the argument is sound – human beings don't possess phenomenal consciousness when we assess the claim from the perspective of God. In addition to God's fundamental perspective, there's a second level of reality. The second level determines what is true and false from *within* the story; the story in which we live.

*Tatjana:* What does is mean that there is a second level of reality when it comes to fiction? If something is second level real, I assume, it's still real.

*Sam:* Well, sadly, this actually gets very complicated very quickly. Most philosophers think that reality or being or existence doesn't come in degrees. But I think there's a basic theistic intuition according to which, if God exists, then He is more real than anything else, because He is the foundation of reality. He is the being that confers being to all other things. The idea that we can talk about degrees of reality is a thesis that is known as ontological pluralism, that currently does have something of a new lease of life among some philosophers (see McDaniel, 2017). So, yes, in order to help you see how premise 3 could be true, I'm asking you to imagine two levels of reality. Each one is real. The ground floor, where God lives is more real. The second floor, where we live is less real. But still real. What is true relative to one of these levels of reality needn't be true relative to the other.

Now, of course, it's true relative to the story in which we live that we are human beings of flesh and blood and that we essentially possess phenomenal consciousness. In fact, it's true, relative to the story, that you're not merely a fictional character. Nevertheless, we might be in one of those strange stories where the characters discover, in the story itself, that they are characters in a story – just as Kilgore Trout discovers, in Kurt Vonnegut's *Breakfast of Champions*, that he is a fictional character devised by Kurt Vonnegut. Even in that story, it's true that Kilgore Trout is a human being, relative to his own story. All that he's really discovered is that there is some level of reality – not a mere possibility – but a level of reality that is somehow more fundamental than the level on which he lives out his life, and from *that* perspective, he's fictional.

*Tatjana:* But don't we treat stories in which fictional characters realize that they are fictional, as *impossible* stories?

It's one thing to imagine that we are building a colony on a faraway planet – science fiction, but nothing particularly strange here. It's quite another thing, it seems to me, to imagine that we discover that we are fictional characters – it's rather mind-boggling. This, to me, suggests some metaphysical impossibility.

*Sam:* I can see why you might think that this strangeness suggests impossibility. But I think that the suggestion is false, and that it doesn't survive scrutiny. In another work (Lebens, 2017), I made a first stab at trying to unpack the logic of stories like *Breakfast of Champions*, and I was able to show that it didn't involve any contradictions. According to the story, Trout lives in a world where reality has multiple levels. In his story, he is a human relative to one level of reality, and fictional relative to another level. This story doesn't entail any contradictions. So, however weird it is, I don't see any conclusive reason to think it's describing a metaphysical impossibility.

That much is true, even in his fiction, because he lives in a fiction in which he comes to realize that there's an author, who has a transcendent perspective: a perspective that lies beyond the story itself.

How can we be sure that something similar isn't true of us? And, if we can't be sure, then premise 3 seems to be onto something. It really is possible – for all that we know – and if only from some fundamental perspective, beyond our own story – that we are fictional. So, you might think it very silly to suppose that we're fictional, but I've tried to show you how things would have to be for us to be both fictional and phenomenally conscious. We could do it by living in a world with multiple levels of reality. We could then be fictional relative to one level, and non-fictional relative to another, without contradiction. And even if you think this is crazy, the fact that (I hope) you can understand how it would work, should give you reason to accept premise 3 of the argument.

If you've come along with me this far, then the last chance to scupper my argument is to attack premise 4. Now, here's the question we have to assess if we want to scrutinize premise 4. Does God add any value to reality by going to the trouble of making it exist outside of any fiction? If you say that He does, then you have to reject premise 4. But, if you can demonstrate that God would add no value to creation by making it exist outside of any fiction, then you've proven premise 4 to be true.

On first reflection, it seems obvious, doesn't it, that God adds value to our world by making it real, rather than merely fictional? And thus, on first reflection, it seems pretty obvious that premise 4 is false. But what happens on second reflection?

To whom is value added by God's making reality exist as more than a mere fiction? It doesn't seem that He adds any value for us because, relative to the layer of reality upon which we live, we aren't fictional.

*Tatjana:* I find this talk about two layers of reality problematic. We don't think of layers of reality when we philosophically talk about fiction.

*Sam:* That's right. We don't generally tend to talk as if Hamlet lives on a different "layer of reality" to us. But I think many theists would want to say that God is *more real than us*, and so (if they're right) we do – unlike fictional characters – live on a different level of reality to our maker. And thus, I'm using the philosophy of fiction, when thinking about "truth-relative to a story", but when I smuggle in this sort of talk about layers of reality, I'm moving from the philosophy of fiction into the doctrine I mentioned in response to your previous comment – the doctrine of ontological pluralism.

If premise 3 really is true, then our lives, as lived from the inside, would seem to be no different to us, even if – from God's perspective – we were no more than mere fictions. So, it's not clear that God would be adding value to our lives by making us – from his perspective – non-fictional.

So, it seems that, for premise 4 to be false, God must be adding value to *His* life by making us non-fictional. But that would be a very controversial thing for a theist to concede. Most theists will want to claim that God is perfect and that He needs nothing outside of himself, and that no value can be added to his life, because his life lacks nothing to begin with. Accordingly, premise 4 is on pretty strong ground. It's hard to see how God could be adding value to the life of any being by making our reality non-fictional from His perspective.

If all four premises are true, then it seems to follow, without further ado, that you're a fictional character – at least when viewed from God's metaphysically fundamental perspective. Admittedly, relative to the story in which we live, we're *not* fictional. That should come as a relief! But, given that – according to the theist – God has revealed himself to his creation, we're like characters in a story who have been able to figure out that there exists a more metaphysically fundamental perspective on reality than our own; and that, from that perspective, we are merely fictional, even if – from our own perspective – we're non-fictional.

*Tatjana:* But if we are fictional characters, we must be abstract or non-actual. In both cases, it's unclear how God can reveal to us. How can anyone reveal themselves to something abstract? And how can an actual being reveal itself to a non-actual if we assume island possible worlds? To say that one or the other or both is possible because it's God would seen rather ad hoc to me.

*Sam:* The moves are a little bit subtle here so I have to be careful to express myself with maximal clarity in response to your question. Yes, if we're fictional, then we're either abstract or non-actual. I agree. But I only think that we're fictional *relative to God, outside of the story that He's telling*. From that perspective, of course, God can't reveal Himself to us, or have a conversation with us, because you can't have a conversation with something abstract or non-actual. But, God *also* inserts Himself into the story as a character. Relative to the story, in which we live, we are not abstract or non-actual. We are actual and concrete. We are the sort of things that God can talk to and converse with. And thus, *in the story*, it can be true that God reveals Himself to us, even if *outside of the story* it makes no sense to talk that way. Compare: Vonnegut reveals himself to Trout, but only in the story; not outside of the story.

So, there you have it. That's my argument from theism. There's lots more to discuss here, about what this argument does to our freedom of will, and what religious significance these conclusions must carry. I have addressed a lot of these issues elsewhere (Lebens 2020). But what I want to focus on, in the remainder of this chapter, is how the atheist might be doomed to a similar conclusion!

## The Simulation Argument

Before I give you my non-theistic argument for our being fictional, we have to take a detour through a very popular little argument put forward by Nick Bostrom (2003). It's called the simulation argument. Bostrom argues that one of the following claims must be true:

1 Almost all civilizations at our current level of development go extinct before reaching technological maturity.
2 There is a strong convergence among technologically mature civilizations such that almost all of them lose interest in creating something that Bostrom calls "ancestor simulations".
3 Almost all people with our sorts of experiences live in computer simulations.

Some of the terminology here needs explanation. For our purposes, a "technologically mature" civilization is one that develops sufficient computer power to run arbitrarily many "ancestor simulations" without making a discernible difference to the left-over computer power available for other projects.

An "ancestor simulation" is a computer simulation of a physical universe to a degree of definition that, to a human observer located somehow within the simulation, would be indiscernible from the real world; like in the *Matrix* movies.

*Tatjana:* Why is it called "ancestor simulation"?
*Sam:* Bostrom imagines that, in the future, if we had sufficient computer power then, instead of writing about our ancestors in history books, we would be tempted to simulate history in simulators, to see exactly how things played out, and how they might have played out had things been only slightly different, etc.

Moreover, an ancestor simulation would include simulated people. We can (following Brian Weatherson, 2003, and in deference to the well-known computer game) call the simulated people *sims*. The sims of an ancestor-simulation are much more sophisticated than the simulated people that populate the primitive computer games of *our* civilization. Indeed, in the computer code for each sim (in a standard ancestor-simulation), "all of the computational processes of a human brain are structurally replicated in suitably fine-grained detail such as on the level of individual synapses" (Bostrom, 2003, p. 244).

Can you imagine the computer power needed to run such a simulation? Every single simulated person is programmed to think with simulated systems that are precisely as complex as a human brain! What makes these simulations "ancestor" simulations is that they simulate a time before civilization reached technological maturity.

*Tatjana:* So a technologically mature civilization is a civilization that can run innumerably many simulations of the real world before it was technologically mature?
*Sam:* Yes. Precisely.

One of the assumptions that Bostrom relies upon is an assumption that he calls *substrate independence*. The basic intuition here is that "mental states can supervene on any of a broad class of physical substrates" (Bostrom, 2003, p. 244). What does that mean? Well, it's true that our own mental states seem to supervene (i.e. rely) upon "carbon-based biological neural networks inside a cranium" (ibid.); but there's no reason to think that there couldn't be other sorts of physical systems upon which mental states could supervene. There's no reason to think that brains made out of silicon, rather than carbon, wouldn't be able to think. This is what Bostrom means, when he refers to his assumption of *substrate independence*.

Perhaps there really are silicon-based lifeforms somewhere in the universe, with silicon brains, structurally like our carbon brains. Nothing but a prejudice in favour of carbon would lead one to think that these beings couldn't be conscious. On the assumption of substrate independence, if the sims replicated the computational processes of a human brain to the level of individual synapses, there would be no good reason to deny that they were conscious. Indeed, if we do accept substrate independence, then we should assume that sims in an ancestor-simulation really would be conscious beings. They probably wouldn't think that they were sims. But they would be!

Given the assumption of substrate independence, and given some empirical observations about computer science, and very little more, it becomes hard to deny Bostrom's conclusion. Either (1) vanishingly few civilizations get to a point of technological maturity, or (2) vanishingly few people in technologically mature civilizations decide to run ancestor simulations; or, if more than a vanishingly few civilizations *do* get to such a stage, and more than a vanishingly few people in those civilizations run their own, and possibly multiple, ancestor simulations, it follows that (3) of all of the "people" who have experiences like ours, the vast majority will be sims.

Are we sims? It's hard to tell. Even if Bostrom's argument is sound, it could be that (1) or (2) is true, and (3) is false. Bostrom himself gives it about a 20% probability that we're sims (Bostrom, 2008). It's a fascinating argument and it has spawned many responses, rebuttals, and counter-rebuttals. But my purpose isn't to engage with that literature, so much as to show you why some people have thought it possible that we are sims. It is on the basis of this possibility that I argue that we are very likely fictional characters. So, at least for what remains of this chapter, I'll ask you to assume – if only for the sake of argument – that Bostrom's argument is sound.

## From Sims to Fictions

The first observation to make is that Bostrom's argument can be strengthened. We can get to his conclusion without assuming substrate independence. If sims were not conscious, then nothing could lead us to believe that *we* are sims. One thing we know about ourselves is that we are conscious. Accordingly, the assumption of substrate independence, which allows for the possibility that sims are conscious, is carrying a lot of weight. Can we do without it?

Well, let's imagine an opponent of substrate independence. She might doggedly assert any of the following claims:

(a) Only biological organisms can be conscious.
(b) Consciousness is a gift granted by God, as and when He deems fit.

(c) Consciousness is a *sui generis* property (i.e. a completely unique property, unlike any other) that doesn't automatically supervene upon any single set of processes or functions. Accordingly, just because you've got something that functions like a brain, there's no guarantee that there's consciousness there.

The truth of any one of these claims would be enough to block Bostrom's argument. Sims are not biological organisms, so, on the assumption of (a), they cannot be conscious. Short of a reason to think that God would be interested in the lives of sims, we have no reason to think that sims are conscious on the assumption of (b). Finally, on the assumption of (c), the fact that the code of each sim replicates all of the computational structure of a human *brain* is insufficient grounds for concluding that they are conscious beings.

In short, opponents of substrate independence will deny that sims are conscious. They will claim that consciousness only emerges in the presence of some special condition that doesn't automatically extend from humans to sims. Let us call that special condition, whatever it might be, the X factor. The absence of the X factor is what would block the natural conclusion that sims are conscious.

Now I ask: is Hamlet a conscious being? Well, that depends. Does he possess the X factor? Well, of course he does, in the story. If, in the story, Hamlet wasn't a conscious being, then it would be a very different, and much less emotionally engaging play. As we know from Chapter 5, when we discuss a fiction, we have to be careful to distinguish what's true relative to a fiction and what's true outside of that fiction. Relative to the *Hamlet* fiction, it's true that Hamlet has the X factor. Outside of that fiction, it's obviously false. Hamlet isn't a person. Hamlet is fictional.

A similar thought should extend to simulations. When I play on a flight-simulator, I enter a game of make-believe, according to which certain falsehoods are true. Outside of the make-believe, I'm sitting relatively still in my living-room chair. But *relative* to the make-believe, or in other words, relative to the *simulation*, I'm banking left before I begin the final descent to land at Heathrow Airport.

Even if you deny substrate independence, you have no reason to think that *in the fiction*, Hamlet lacks the X factor. And even though you deny that sims have the X factor, you have no reason to deny that *in the fiction of the simulation*, sims have the X factor.

*Tatjana:* What do you mean?

*Sam:* Basically, what I'm trying to say here is that simulations just are a species of fiction, or – at the very least – they always come pared with a fiction, which we could call the fiction of the simulation.

In other words, a simulation is a form of fiction. Just as a fiction establishes its own discourse relative to which certain falsehoods are true; a simulation will establish its own discourse, relative to which certain falsehoods are true.

Relative to the fiction, the following is true: "Hamlet doesn't know that there's a metaphysical vantage point from which it's true to say that, beyond his story, he's merely fictional, and that he only fictionally has the X factor." By contrast, and relative to a different fiction, the following is true: "Kilgore Trout didn't know that there's a metaphysical vantage point from which it's true to say that, beyond his story, he's merely fictional, and that he only fictionally has the X factor, until Kurt Vonnegut told him so, in the story, at the end of *Breakfast of Champions*."

But if all of this is true, then you too have no reason to deny that many of the things that you take to be true are only actually true relative to the story of the simulation in which, unbeknownst to you, you live. You have no reason to deny that there exists a metaphysical vantage point, beyond your own, from which it's true to say that you're just a sim. Sims are not sims in their simulated world. They are people. Sims may not have the X factor from *our* vantage point, but relative to their simulation, it could still be true that they *have* the X factor; just as you do relative to the reality in which you live.

Perhaps you'll object and say that I have drawn too tight an analogy between fiction and simulation. In a fiction, fictional characters like Sherlock Holmes are meant to be conscious beings. This is generally true even in fictions that don't explicitly spell out, in the text, that its characters are conscious. So, if Sherlock Holmes says that he's a conscious being, this would be true in the fiction. By contrast, you might think that nothing can be true in a simulation unless that truth is explicitly modelled in the computer code that underwrites the simulation. But then, why should we think that there would be variables in the code of an ancestor-simulation designed to trace the X factor, whatever that might be?

*Tatjana:* I don't quite get this step.

*Sam:* Fair enough. I'll try to be more clear. A story written in English doesn't have to describe every detail that it wants you to make-believe – for instance, the text of *Anna Karenina* doesn't explicitly describe the fact that Anna Karenina is a human being rather than a talking chimpanzee. The story invites you to pretend that it's true. You might think that simulations, unlike stories, have to be explicit.

A story written in computer code (that is to say, a simulation), you might think, can only invite us to pretend that things are true if they are explicitly described (or "coded for") in the software language of the simulation. Coders have to be more explicit than authors!

This is what I mean when I say, in the next paragraph, "even though fictions can contain truths that aren't explicitly stated in the text, you might think it a stretch to say, of a simulation, that aspects of reality not modelled using variables in its computer code are simulated too". Ultimately, I'm going to deny this claim, but some people might think that it's true, so I have to address it.

If we deny the assumption of substrate independence, then only in the presence of such variables would we have any reason to think it true in the simulation that its sims are conscious.

The worry is compounded if we recognize that what makes fiction interesting might well differ from what would make an ancestor simulation interesting. Entertainment is among the primary motivations for the production of fiction. Ancestor simulations, we might think, are not mainly produced for fun but rather to produce new information (about the past, or about how things might have been in the past, if only things had gone slightly differently etc.). To this end, it's not necessary that all aspects of reality are fully simulated. Most simulations abstract from certain aspects of whatever it is that they simulate. And even though fictions can contain truths that aren't explicitly stated in the text, you might think it a stretch to say, of a simulation, that aspects of reality not modelled using variables in its computer code are simulated too.

There are two ways to respond to these concerns. The first is to say that, since entertainment may well be among the aims of those who produce ancestor simulations, we have no reason to think that they won't explicitly model the X factor in their code, especially if our future ancestors discover what the X factor actually is! The second response is more strident. Just as a fiction can contain fictional-truths that aren't explicitly stated in the text, there's no good reason to think that a simulation can't contain simulated-truths that aren't explicitly coded.

More generally, the idea is that every simulation generates, or perhaps is, its own fiction. When I'm flying a plane in a primitive simulator, there might be nothing in the code that explicitly models the fact that the temperature at my current altitude is very low. That doesn't stop it from being fictionally true in the simulation-generated fiction, that it's cold outside of my plane. So, even if ancestor simulations don't explicitly code for the X factor, to the extent that it simulates the actions of conscious beings, and to the extent that it doesn't explicitly state otherwise, an ancestor simulation will generate a fiction in which it will be true to say, of any given sim, that it is conscious (in the fiction) and, if we're rejecting substrate independence, that it therefore possesses the X factor (in the fiction).

This simulation argument requires no assumption of substrate independence. You could be a sim, at least relative to a layer of reality more fundamental than your own, even if substrate independence is false. This argument is stronger than Bostrom's original.

## You Are Probably Fictional

The idea that you're fictional seems like such a wacky hypothesis; so wacky that, even if it's theoretically possible, we feel licensed to ignore its possibility in our day-to-day life. Yes, you could be dreaming right now. Yes, you could be a brain in a vat. Yes, all of your beliefs could be manipulated by some evil demon that controls your thoughts. All of these absurd hypotheses are possible. But, for one reason or another, we feel it's legitimate, most of the time, to ignore these possibilities. But sometimes, even the absurd *should* be taken seriously. As Bostrom puts the point:

> [I]f you enter a funny mirror hall, and you know that it often appears to people in this hall as if they have three hands, then the fact that you seem to perceive yourself as having three hands should not make you believe that your body has sprouted a new limb. Instead, you should believe that you are experiencing an illusion.
>
> (Bostrom, 2005, p. 94)

Bostrom's fundamental point is that, if the future is likely to pan out a certain way, such that ancestor simulations will be ubiquitous, then we are currently in "a special circumstance in which illusions are ubiquitous" (ibid.). The idea that we are sims might seem absurd, but what we know about computer science, and its likely trajectory, means that we might be in a sort of a mirror hall, that justifies our reassessing the evidence. It justifies our taking seriously the claim that we really might be sims. I'm going to argue that if there's a serious possibility (however slim) that we are sims, then it's *highly likely* that we're fictional (whether or not we live in a simulation, or in some *other* sort of a story). And however absurd the claim, if we should take it seriously that we might be sims, then we should take it even more seriously that we might be fictional, because – as we'll see – we very likely are!

The argument runs as follows (and don't worry if the language seems technical, because I'll try my best to unpack it afterwards). The argument is probably the most technical argument in the book. I came up with it and even I'm not sure I understand it! So, there's no shame in trying to read it through multiple times to see if you can see how the parts of the argument are supposed to be related to one another. The next step will be to assess each premise, figure out what it means, and see whether you have reason to think that they're true. Through that stage, I'll do my best to make the case for each and every premise:

1 There is a non-negligible likelihood that you are a sim.
2 If there is a non-negligible likelihood that you are a sim, then there is a non-negligible likelihood that you are living in a simulation.

3 If there is a non-negligible likelihood that you are living in a simulation, then there is a non-negligible likelihood that you are living in a fictional story.
4 If you might be living in a fictional story, then the set of fictional stories in which you might be living is much larger than the set of simulations in which you might be living.

*Tatjana:* Why? You probably explain it later.
*Sam:* Yes. A lot hinges on this premise. So far I haven't given you any reason to believe it. I will have to do that later!

5 If the set of fictional stories in which you might be living is much larger than the set of simulations in which you might be living, then it is very much more likely that you are living in a fictional story than that you are living in a simulation.
6 If the likelihood of $p$ is non-negligible, and if $q$ is very much more likely than $p$, then $q$ is likely true.

---

7 If the likelihood that you're living in a simulation is non-negligible, and if it's very much more likely that you're living in a fictional story than it is likely that you're living in a simulation, then it's likely that you're living in a fictional story. (This follows from point 6. Take your time to figure out if you can see how.)
8 There is a non-negligible likelihood that you are living in a simulation. (This follows pretty straightforwardly from points 1 and 2.)
9 There is a non-negligible likelihood that you are living in a fictional story. (This follows pretty straightforwardly from points 8 and 3.)
10 The set of fictional stories in which you might be living is much larger than the set of simulations in which you might be living. (This follows pretty straightforwardly from points 9 and 4.)
11 It is very much more likely that you are living in a fictional story than that you are living in a simulation. (Follows from points 10 and 5. This one might be harder to see. Again, there's no shame in taking your time to figure out whether you think 11 really does follow from points 5 and 10.)
12 There is a non-negligible likelihood that you are living in a simulation, and it's very much more likely that you're living in a fictional story than it is likely that you're living in a simulation. (This one is also a little tricky to see, I think. I claim that it follows from points 8 and 11.)
13 It's likely that you're living in a fictional story. (This follows from points 7 and 12.)

Once you've got your head around the structure of the argument, we can move on.

The argument has six premises (above the line), which generate seven conclusions (below the line), the final of which is that you're likely living in a fictional story. Unlike my first argument, God doesn't feature in this one. So, where does it go wrong? If the argument falls down, it must be because at least one of the premises is false.

Premise 1 follows from the simulation argument. If the simulation argument is sound, then there's at least a chance that we're sims. What I mean by a non-negligible possibility is twofold: I mean that the possibility isn't tiny (indeed, Bostrom puts it at 20%), and I also mean that it isn't the sort of possibility that we're licensed (because of its absurdity) to ignore. Remember Bostrom's mirror hall. If one day ancestor-simulations will be common, we can't afford to ignore the possibility that we might be sims. This is not a negligible possibility.

Premise 2 follows from the definition of a sim. If you're a sim, then you live in a simulation. That's what sims do!

Premise 3 follows from the central insight of the previous section; the section in which I tried to free the simulation argument from the assumption of substrate independence. The insight of that section, if indeed it's true, is that simulations are, or give rise to their own, fictional stories.

Premise 4 and 5, taken together, say that the set of candidate stories in which we might living is much larger than the set of candidate simulations in which we might be living; and, since there are so many more stories in which you might be living than there are simulations in which you might be living, it's more likely that you're in a story that *isn't* a simulation than it is likely that you're in story that *is* a simulation. Why think that these claims are true?

Simulations are limited by the capabilities of computers. Even if we're only thinking about *possible* simulations, their scope will be limited by the capabilities of *possible* computers. Indeed, that's why Bostrom went to some length, as he first presented his argument, to demonstrate the possibility that there will one day be computers powerful enough to run ancestor-simulations (Bostrom, 2003). Stories, by contrast, have no such limitations. Stories (as we saw in Chapter 2) can be viewed simply as sets of sentences or propositions or the like.

Just as the realm of possible melodies is much broader than the realm of melodies that could be played by human beings on physically possible instruments, so too, the realm of stories in which we might be living is much broader than the realm of such stories that some possible computer could one day run as a simulation.

Indeed, for all of the simulations that, for all you can know, you're living within, it's pretty easy to demonstrate that there are infinitely more stories that it's equally possible, for all you know, that you're living within. Take any simulation that, for all you know, you're living within and then, at some point in the narrative of that simulation – a point that makes no difference to the story of any of our particular lives – add one detail that no computer could ever compute.

*Tatjana:* What kind of detail would that be?
*Sam:* Ah, I'm not sure. Perhaps some mathematical fact that can only be processed once you've finished enumerating π, which is a task that can never actually be completed by any computer of finite power (and no computer in our physical universe, it has been demonstrated, could ever have infinite power. Bostrom (2003) accepts this constraint and explains some of the computer science and physics behind it).

That will give you a new "non-simulation story" in which you could be living. Now add two details that no computer could ever compute. Now we've got *two* non-simulation stories in which you could be living. Now add three details that no computer could ever compute. And so on to infinity.

Here emerges a mathematical problem that's too difficult for me to solve. We have two sets which are both infinitely large – the set of simulations in which we might be living and the set of stories in which we might be living. We know that every simulation is a story, and we know that not every story is a simulation. That means that every simulation is a member of the set of stories, even though not every story is a member of the set of simulations. Even so, the two sets might be the exactly the same size. Indeed, every even number is a natural number, and not every natural number is an even number (because some of them are odd). In other words, the natural numbers comprise a set that contains within it all of the even numbers, and yet, it's actually easy to demonstrate that the set of even numbers is exactly the same size as the set of natural numbers. They're the same size because you can pair them all off, as I do below, assigning in a systematic fashion one natural number for each even number, and we'll never run out of either type of number.

| | | | | | | | | | | | | | | |
|---|---|---|---|---|---|---|---|---|---|---|---|---|---|---|
| Naturals | 1 | 2 | 3 | 4 | 5 | 6 | 7 | 8 | 9 | 10 | 11 | 12 | 13 | ... |
| Evens | 2 | 4 | 6 | 8 | 10 | 12 | 14 | 16 | 18 | 20 | 22 | 24 | 26 | ... |

So, how can I claim that the set of stories is larger than the set of simulations? That would be like claiming that the set of natural numbers is larger than the set of even numbers. But those two sets are demonstrably the same size, even if one contains the other.

And yet, it's clear that there must be some notion of size, under which it's true to say that the set of natural numbers is larger than the set of even numbers – even if the difference in size can't be cashed out in terms of the two sets having a different cardinality (a cardinality is an answer to the question, *how many members does this set have*). The two sets have the same cardinality. Fine. But surely there's a sense, perhaps some different definition of size, in which the set of natural numbers is larger than the set of even numbers, since every even number is contained in the set of natural numbers, and not every natural number is a member of the set of even numbers.

One way to describe this is to say that the set of natural numbers is more densely packed than the set of even numbers, even if they have the same cardinality. The same should be said about the relationship between the set of stories and the set of simulations. This area of mathematics, which formulates different ways of measuring the relative size of sets, is called *measure theory*. It's far too hard for me!

Accordingly, I'll leave it to the mathematicians to iron out the formalism – and to express exactly how much larger the one set is than the other, and by exactly what measure, and how to express all of this in numbers. In the meantime, what seems overwhelmingly plausible is that the set of stories is much larger than the set of simulations in some sense that matters for this argument. This gives us both premise 4 (that the one set is much larger than the other) and premise 5 (that the sense in which the set of stories is larger than the set of simulations entails that, for any simulation in which we might be living, it is much more likely that we're living in a story).

Premise 6 is a truism. If one thing, call it *q*, is much more likely than some other thing, call it *p*, and if *p* is already of non-negligible likelihood, then *q* really should be taken pretty seriously.

In short, the argument is valid, and the premises seem to be true. And thus, we should conclude: it's likely that you're living in a fictional story. This argument probably goes wrong somewhere. Most philosophical arguments do. But it might be fun, and even enlightening, to figure out where the argument goes wrong, and why. Doing so might reveal to us something about who and what we are, or what fiction is, and why it might matter to us. And if the conclusion is true, then we have to figure out to what extent it should matter to us, and why. Either way, I hope it's a fun argument with which to end an introduction to the philosophy of fiction.

## Works Cited

Bostrom, N. (2003) Are We Living in a Computer Simulation? *The Philosophical Quarterly*, 53(211): 243–255.

Bostrom, N. (2005) The Simulation Argument: Reply to Weatherson. *The Philosophical Quarterly*, 55(218): 90–97.

Bostrom, N. (2008) The Simulation Argument FAQ. www.simulation-argument.com/faq

Goldschmidt, T., & Lebens, S. (2020) Divine Contractions: Theism gives birth to idealism. *Religious Studies*, 56(4): 509–524.

Hintikka, J. (1962) *Cogito, Ergo Sum*: Inference or Performance? *The Philosophical Review*, 71: 3–32.

Kripke, S. (2013) *Reference and Existence*. Oxford: Oxford University Press.

Lebens, S. (2017) Hassidic Idealism: Kurt Vonnegut and the Creator of the Universe. In T. Goldschmidt & K. L. Pearce (eds), *Idealism: New Essays in Metaphysics*. Oxford: Oxford University Press, pp. 158–177.

Lebens, S. (2020) *The Principles of Judaism*. Oxford: Oxford University Press.
Lewis, D. (1978) Truth in Fiction. *American Philosophical Quarterly*, 15(1): 37–46.
Lewis, D. (1986) *On the Plurality of Worlds*. Oxford: Blackwell.
McDaniel, K. (2017) *The Fragmentation of Being*. Oxford: Oxford University Press.
Weatherson, B. (2003) Are You a Sim? *The Philosophical Quarterly*, 53(212): 425–431.

## Further Reading

Chalmers, D. (2022) *Reality+: Virtual Worlds and the Problems of Philosophy*. London: Penguin Books.
www.simulation-argument.com *is a great resource for people interested in the simulation argument.*

# Index

Entries in *italics* denote figures.